Your Home Program
Home Ownership Made Easy

Copyright 2013

All Rights Reserved

Credit Coach Inc.

For More Information www.YourHomeProgram.com

Except in the United States of America, this book is sold subject to the condition that it shall not, by way of trade or otherwise, be lent, resold, hired out, or otherwise circulated without the publisher's prior in any form of binding or cover other than that in which it is published and without a similar condition including this condition being imposed on the subsequent purchaser.

The scanning, uploading, and distribution of this book via any other means without the permission of the publisher is illegal and punishable by law. Please purchase only authorized electronic editions and do not participate in or encourage electronic piracy or copyrightable materials. Your support of the author's rights is appreciated.

DEDICATION

For those with a dream of owning a home.
You are moments away from discovering how to get there.

CONTENTS

1	Buying a Home with Bad Credit	2
2	The Credit Problem	7
3	The Credit Solution	14
4	How Bad is too Bad	26
5	Income and Home Ownership	30
6	Expenses and Home Ownership	35
7	Debt and Savings (Net Worth)	48
8	Your Credit Situation	61
9	Alternative Paths to Home Ownership – Part 1: Government Assisted Options	69
10	Alternative Paths to Home Ownership – Part 2: Buying Foreclosed Real Estate	75

11	Alternative Paths to Home Ownership – Part 3: An Introduction to Rent to Own Programs	79
12	Rent to Own: How it works	85
13	Rent to Own: What to Look Out For	92
14	Rent to Own: Finding a Home	97
15	Rent to Own: Contracts and Parts of the Deal	101
16	Rent to Own: The 12 Steps for Success Using Rent to Own	105
17	Improving Your Income – Getting a Raise	117
18	Making Extra Money – Part 1 (Offline Money Making)	126
19	Making Extra Money – Part 2 (Online Money Making)	135
20	More Income Increasing Strategies	146

21	You Expenses, and How to Take <u>Control</u> of them – Part 1	149
22	Your Expenses, and How to Take <u>Control</u> of them – Part 2	156
23	Your Expenses, and How to Take <u>Control</u> of them – Part 3	163
24	Your Expenses, and How to Take <u>Control</u> of them – Part 4	171
25	Dealing with Debt and Net Worth	175
26	Tax-Related Problems	184
27	What If I need to file for Bankruptcy?	191
28	Checkpoint: Is your financial picture changing?	197
29	Credit Repair: the Credit Dispute Process	203
*	Resource Directory: Video List	214

1 BUYING A HOME WITH BAD CREDIT

Introduction

Buying a home can be a wonderful and exciting experience. It can also be stressful, especially when a person feels caged by bad credit, which locks them away from owning a home.

With bad credit, purchasing a home can be difficult. There may be more steps involved, and more hoops to jump through. This can be quite discouraging for a person who has already taken a beating from the credit system. If you've ever had credit problems, you ***know*** how bad it can be. This just adds to the stress of a process that is, for many, already stressful enough. You want the perfect home but you fear your credit may get in the way. Many of us have been there.

How Bad Credit Can Affect Your Home Purchase

Paying More

The most obvious place that bad credit will hurt your efforts to purchase a home is in the cost of the loan itself. In other words, you'll pay more in **INTEREST** when you have bad credit.

How much more will you pay?

Take a look at this:

Let's say, for the sake of our example, that two people want to buy a home.

We'll call one John, and the other Sue.

Sue has great credit with a credit score of 740, a healthy savings account, and a steady job. Homes in her area start at or about the $200,000 range.

John, who lives in the same area as Sue, doesn't have great credit. He lost his job a while back, and his credit took a big hit as a result. While he has a good job and a steady income now, he doesn't have much in the way of savings and his credit score is only 580.

John and Sue each apply for a loan with the same lender. For a $200,000 loan, both John and Sue get approved. Everything's great, right?

Not quite.

Sue's loan offer looks like this:

Home Price	$200,000
Loan Term	30 Years
Interest Rate (APR)	4.3%

Down Payment	20%
Monthly Payment	$791.79
Total Interest To Be Paid	$125,044.40

On the other hand, John's loan offer looks like this:

Home Price	$200,000
Loan Term	30 Years
Interest Rate (APR)	6.7%
Down Payment	20%
Monthly Payment	$1032.44
Total Interest To Be Paid	$211,678.40

Who will pay more for their loan? How much more?

Most of us would expect that with bad credit, John would pay more. But "how much more" can be quite shocking.

Given this scenario, John would pay almost **$100,000 MORE** than the amount that Sue would pay for the same house. Not only that, John's payments would be almost $250 per month higher.

Keep in mind, this simple example doesn't consider all the possibilities. Some lenders require larger down payments when a person has poor credit. This could put many people out of the running altogether. However, there are special programs which allow very little or even zero money down. We'll talk about those later.

But once again, even if the interest rate were the only difference, the person with bad credit could very possibly end up paying **twice** what the person with good credit does for the same loan.

Are there ways around this? You bet there are.

Don't worry, we'll get there.

For now it's important to understand the true impact of bad credit on a home loan.

Looking again at the above example, we can see that John will be paying $241 per month more than Sue,

Video Resource
Video Name: Bad Credit, but looking to Buy a Home: Options
www.YourHomeProgram.com/BookResource

every month, for 30 years.

If John makes $50,000 per year, this means that John will be paying almost 6% of his annual income every year for his more expensive loan.

If John and Sue's income were exactly the same, having a better loan on her home would put Sue ahead by the same 6%.

Now let's talk about the *lifetime cost of the loan*.

Comparing the "total interest paid" for each loan, John will pay a total of $86,634.00 more than Sue for the same loan.

What could that $86,634.00 buy?

- ✓ One college education, maybe two
- ✓ Several cars
- ✓ 20+ years' worth of family vacations
- ✓ A fancy car, and a garage to keep it in

You probably get the point.

On the flip side, if Sue took her $241 savings and invested it, managing to earn just 5% interest, in 30 years she would have over $200,000!

Considering all of this, you can probably see that the cost of bad credit over the course of a 30 year mortgage can be substantial. Bad credit hurts!

Fewer Options

One of the less obvious effects of bad credit on the home buying process is what it does to a person's *options*.

With good credit, you have choices.

With bad credit, your only choice is often to reluctantly accept what's offered to you.

The person with bad credit may not be able to afford the loan offered to them by a lender. A lender may require a larger down payment for a person with bad credit, putting the loan out of reach. The difference in monthly payment may also make the loan less affordable and more difficult to pay on time.

The person with bad credit may find themselves frustrated by the lack of help and options available for people who have had some bumps in the road.

Fortunately, help is on the way.

Options For People With Bad Credit

> *"I always say don't make plans, make options."*
> *~Jennifer Aniston*

Fortunately, there <u>**are**</u> better and smarter options available for people with bad credit.

There are three categories of bad credit that we're talking about:

1. People with very bad credit who simply cannot qualify for a home loan.
2. People with moderately bad credit, who can qualify with certain sub-prime lenders for less-than-desirable loans.
3. People with "so-so" credit who can qualify for loans but will have to pay more in interest and fees.

The good news is that regardless of which of these three categories you fit into, you probably have more options than you think.

And we're going to talk about exactly what options you have, as you continue with this program.

The key point to understand right now is: You <u>**do**</u> have options!

Your specific options will depend on the amount of time you have and your exact financial situation. These are aspects we'll cover in detail as the program progresses.

Don't Just Look at What's On Paper

If you have bad credit and you look at your situation on paper (similar to the way we did with John and Sue earlier), you may think you're in trouble. You may think that there is no way you'll ever be able to afford your dream home.

Don't be discouraged! There's a lot more to it than that!

Your home buying options are more than what your credit score and a reluctant lender will show you. Regardless of any credit situation, with the strategies that we'll cover in this program, it is possible that a whole new world of home buying options will be opened up to you.

When you have more options, it puts you in the driver seat. <u>YOU</u> become the one with the choices. <u>YOU</u> are in control.

Above all else, this program aims to create as many empowering options as possible for people who might have otherwise had none. In order to do that, we have to go past the comparisons on paper. We have to go past what you think your credit can get you, and what you think the limitations of your income are.

This is a process. And this program will help you step by step.

The Tools To Overcome

> "Although the world is full of suffering, it is also full of the overcoming of it."
>
> ~Helen Keller

There is no doubt that bad credit can be extremely costly, painful and difficult in many ways.

The key to any difficulty, however, is not how costly it is or how bad it makes you feel, but rather how you are able to overcome it. The difficulties of life do not have to define us. In fact, they can shape us in a positive way when we work to overcome them.

Your credit and financial situation can go from being a story you're embarrassed about, to a triumphant tale of how you overcame adversity.

Through the following chapters this program, you will have a chance to write and share your own success story. That is *precisely* what this program is all about.

Getting there is just a matter of having the **proper tools**, and understanding the best way to use them. We will cover all that starting in the next chapter as we dive further into your financial future, and the exciting home ownership possibilities that are awaiting you.

You *can* come out on top. This program will show you how.

2 THE CREDIT PROBLEM

A Numbers Game

Whether you like it or not, in the credit world **you are a number**. You **are** a number and you **have** a number. The number you "are" is usually your Social Security Number. The number you "have" is your credit score. You have other numbers that matter as well, such as bank account numbers and balances, credit card numbers and balances, and more.

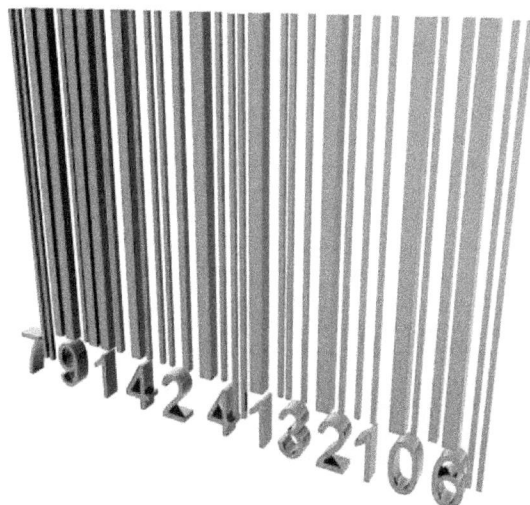

(Image Source: www.sxc.hu)

All of these numbers create a picture of "who you are" that banks use to make credit decisions. Now don't get me wrong, they don't create a **TRUE** picture of who you are. I am **NOT** saying that any of this actually gives an accurate picture of you as an individual.

To sum it up: from a banks' perspective, from a credit card companies' perspective, and from a mortgage lenders' perspective, all they are **REALLY** going by are the numbers.

The Upside To Being A Number

Believe it or not, being a number in a computer system has an upside.

Before computers, and before all of us became a digital representation in the form of numbers and bytes and bits, there were real people making real credit decisions based on real experiences and reputations.

The problem was those real people, making those real credit decisions, also had real flaws.

This meant that their decisions could be (and were) affected by things like personal preferences and prejudices. A person's ability to get a loan wasn't only about their past or present financial performance. It was about the preferences and prejudices of the decision maker. Loan decisions could be quite subjective, to the point of letting things like *race* and *social status* dictate who received the best treatment.

The plus side to being a number, then, is that in the vast majority of cases today you are no longer judged by a lender based on your looks, your race, the clothes you wear, or the family you grew up in.

In a world where decisions are based almost 100% on the numbers, the chances of being turned down for a loan because of your race, your religion, or some other unjust reason are very slim.

The numbers put us all on, what *should*, be a level playing field. Unfortunately it doesn't always work that way.

The Downside To Being A Number

```
1   21 322 12  0 2 1    95151  151 231  2121   1 2 1 2 4  9 84      212 9
654  555 6 6545045852   8    19872315  29751548  51654879      4 54
5465158222  21  989  787   52 4 22126213    1218484   00 4 548 4
00002154    45454 1    11111111  555  222 121  55 151 8847 4  1951
6574  978   132 465    456 4 49819  847    798 894   654  6 4   654
45454  190  48001       262155       700   72   42   21 84  6351 0  1
515654 4 65454 4   454549  54 9 5 44  51 8  98484 54 94 654    212 954
2  1  11  54  954  95  4  54954  4  5494954  4  45494  4  444  66  88  22  18
984815951011559   954594954011247  1213565448     15687841546
21654    6521   12  5 4 654549    65454984  65454  789  54549454
219845651  06515640  7 54106510  012340  0459510   0189751  0 6541
859454  605406540  654104  45498724  42465797    215  51200  15951005
```

When everyone is a number, it eliminates the potential *benefits* that may come from personal relationships and "real contact" between real human beings. Whether lenders will admit to it or not, the fancy computer programs that analyze your financial activity and rate you with a number (your credit score) say **NOTHING** about your personal character.

When your numbers don't tell a good story, being lost in the crowd may not be the best thing. People who have had credit problems often have stories to tell. There is often a legitimate reason for how they got there:

- ✓ Job loss
- ✓ Identity theft
- ✓ Illness
- ✓ Serious Injury

The problem with being a number is that the **true** story, no matter how meaningful, doesn't get told.

The guy, whose credit was wrecked because he couldn't work for 6 months while struggling to overcome a serious illness, gets lumped together with the irresponsible college student who didn't know enough about credit to be using it.

Don't get me wrong, both of these stories are legitimate. But most of us can probably agree that knowing these stories would tell us something more about each person's true credit worthiness than a simple number could ever possibly tell.

Sure, the numbers themselves can paint a picture. Sometimes that picture is accurate. A 580 credit score is a good sign that something has gone wrong. But the picture painted with numbers can't possibly tell the whole story.

What I'm saying here is, if a picture is worth a thousand words, a picture painted with numbers must be worth about … fifty words. And that is one major downside to being a number.

Numbers Don't Lie

You've probably heard the saying "numbers don't lie." This is true. Numbers don't lie because they don't actually say anything, <u>EVER</u>.

Yes, you heard it here first. Numbers don't lie because they don't actually ***speak***.

But the fact that numbers don't lie does *not* mean that numbers are always right. Numbers can be ***dead wrong***. (Just ask any math teacher.)

So another downside to being a number comes to life when a person (who is a number) reviews their credit score (another number) with eager anticipation (numbers are exciting, after all) only to find out that by some horrible twist of fate that their number has turned out *WRONG*.

It's a 21st century identity crisis of the worst kind. A person checks their credit report and finds that something has gone horribly wrong, and that they have been branded with a number that has nothing to do with them or anything they have ever done.

But a number that's wrong should be easy to fix... *right?*

Not quite.

Stacking The Deck

(Image Source: www.sxc.hu)

Fixing a wrong number in the credit world has turned out to be a fairly complicated matter.

Anyone who has ever had credit problems knows that fixing them can be quite difficult, and whether your story is a legitimate one or not, no matter what your story is, you still have to wade through convoluted and confusing paradoxes if you are ever going to have a hope of fixing your credit.

"But what makes it so complicated? I read online that fixing my credit would be easy!"

When I talk to someone new to credit repair, a common theme in the conversation is something along the lines of "I had no idea that it was such a mess!"

If all you do is listen to the official opinions, you may (quite understandably) be oblivious to the mess.

The story told by the credit bureaus, the FTC, the Better Business Bureau, and similar sources goes something like this:

Anyone can fix errors on their credit report if they can just write a few letters.

It would be great if that were the end of the story. But it's not.

The problem becomes apparent when people start taking that advice. Let's look at an example:

Once, there was a man named Robert who had great credit.

One day while Robert was reviewing his credit reports—admiring his great credit—he was shocked to find a fraudulent (and derogatory) account. Robert did some research online and learned that what he needed to do in order to correct the problem was to **write the bureaus** and **ask for removal** of the fraudulent account.

So Robert sent a letter to each of the three credit bureaus saying something like this:

> *"Dear credit bureau,*
>
> *Recently I found an incorrect entry on my credit report. The account number is 123-456-XYZ. This account is NOT MINE. Please remove this account from my credit report.*
>
> *Thank You!*
>
> *~Robert"*

With the problem taken care of, Robert relaxed. He was happy to have found some information that helped him to correct the situation quickly, before it became a problem.

But that wasn't the end of the story for Robert.

Three weeks later Robert got his first response from a credit bureau in the mail.

The letter stated, in essence, that the credit bureau had asked the creditor in question about the account, and the creditor said that the account did indeed belong to Robert (even though he KNEW it did not.)

The account was "verified," and would therefore stay on his credit report.

Robert wondered to himself how this could have happened. The information he read online made it sound like it would be *easy* to correct his credit report.

Suddenly the situation didn't feel like an "easy" one.

In reality Robert was a man with great credit, but his *numbers* were now **wrong**. They didn't reflect the reality that Robert knew to be true.

The horrible feeling that you get when you've been falsely accused of a crime quickly swept over Robert like a cold, dream-shattering ocean wave.

Things were starting to get complicated...

Stories like this happen every single day.

Whether we like it or not, the credit system is geared in such a way that when you have a problem to fix, there is a good chance you're going to have trouble fixing it.

The Players

To understand why Robert and so many others have hit so many road blocks when trying to fix their credit, we need to take a closer look at the major players in the credit game.

The credit system is made up of 3 major players:

1. The Credit Bureaus
2. The Creditors
3. The Collection Agencies

Video Resource
Video Name: Credit Bureaus, All you Need to Know
www.YourHomeProgram.com/BookResource

The key to understanding how and why the cards are stacked against you, when you need to fix your bad credit, is knowing how each of the above 3 players *benefits* from your bad credit.

Video Resource
Video Name: Credit Bureaus, Creditors, and Collection Agencies
www.YourHomeProgram.com/BookResource

The **credit bureaus**, for example, benefit from bad credit because they are in the business of selling DATA to CREDITORS. Creditors are their customers, and creditors buy DATA from them. The most profitable customers for creditors are ones with bad credit (because they must pay more for loans), and the credit bureaus want to give their customers the kind of data that they want. "Bad credit" data is therefore the most profitable data for the bureaus to sell, and the most profitable data for the creditors to market to. The credit bureaus have a vested interest in your bad credit.

The **creditors** want plenty of bad credit data to market to because having bad credit means people will be forced to pay more for loans. Remember the example we covered previously where we showed that bad credit could result in a person paying TWICE the amount of money for the same house and the same basic loan? Well, creditors like that. It's what they want. That bad credit mortgage will give them twice the profits of the one for the "good credit" consumer.

Collection Agencies use negative credit reporting (i.e. "bad credit") as a tool to coerce consumers into paying debts that they (allegedly) owe. When a consumer with bad credit gets a barely affordable sub-prime loan from a creditor and subsequently defaults on that loan, guess who gets the business? A collection agency! Collectors, like creditors and credit bureaus, benefit greatly from consumers with bad credit.

Playing Against Consumers

The biggest forces in the credit world are united in their stance on bad credit:

"It takes 7 years for it to go away. Time heals all wounds (and credit reports.)"

This isn't necessarily the complete truth, by the way. But it doesn't matter because they are also united in their stance against consumers.

I know this industry well, and can tell you from experience that the cards are stacked against you. The companies that manipulate the deck are all playing a game with your finances, and they want you to lose.

If this weren't the case, then it would be easy to fix credit report errors. If creditors consistently reported accurate and complete data, credit reports would be consistently more accurate. If the credit bureaus didn't profit so hugely from bad credit, they would probably design their systems in such a way as to better prevent the many errors and omissions that leave innocent consumers with "bad credit."

IF. IF. IF.

Yes, I know I said "IF" three times.

This is because it is ONLY an IF. The reality is that credit repair is made difficult by the game that creditors, credit bureaus, and collectors play:

- Creditors break the law frequently.
- Collectors break the law frequently.
- Credit Bureaus break the law frequently.

These companies break the law **frequently** by failing to handle your credit in the proper manner. **If** they never broke the law, we may not have these problems. But we *do* have these problems. This is, in part, because breaking the law has been made much more profitable than following it.

And this game is played, of course, to the determent of YOU, the consumer.

Low numbers mean high profits. The more low numbers there are, the more high profits there will be.

The system loves low numbers. The Consumer needs high numbers. (I imagine you can see the conflict of interest here.)

Costs And Consequences

If you are reading this, I probably don't have to tell you about the costs and consequences of the game that the credit bureaus, creditors, and collectors play – there are many detrimental stories, perhaps even yours.

With bad credit, buying a home could cost you twice as much. Buying a car will cost more. You'll pay more for insurance. You'll pay more for **anything** that you purchase with credit.

Bad credit could even cost you a job or a promotion.

The credit problem is a serious problem, indeed. *Especially* for those looking to buy a home.

That's why next chapter we are going to talk about the **Credit Solution**.

3 THE CREDIT SOLUTION

We've already talked about the credit problem and how it can affect your efforts to buy a home. We've also talked about how the system is geared to hold you down when you have bad credit.

Video Resource
Video Name: Being a Number (credit score): Pros and Cons
www.YourHomeProgram.com/BookResource

What can be done about it, then?

I'm about to show you.

Credit Repair

Credit repair is made difficult by the fact that the cards are stacked against the consumer. It's made *difficult*, but **not impossible**.

Even in this climate there are ways to improve your credit.

I've already mentioned credit repair a time or two in this program. Before we go much further I need to define exactly what I mean by the term "credit repair" so that we're on the same page.

For the purposes of our discussion and this program, here's the definition of credit repair:

credit repair (n) - *The process of raising your credit score or otherwise shaping your credit profile so that it looks more attractive to lenders.*

That's it. That's what I mean when I say "credit repair".

The main stream view of credit repair says that credit repair is nothing more than the process of "removing negative items" from your credit report. One problem with this view is that it can be somewhat self-contradictory: removing negative items doesn't *ALWAYS* necessarily improve a person's credit. Believe it or not, some people have removed certain negative items which have resulted in a subsequent credit score **drop**. We'll talk more about that later, when I tell you about the types of negative items that you'll be better off leaving alone.

Another way my view of credit repair differs from most is that most people leave out a lot of important options that are available for those wanting to raise their credit score. It isn't just about removing negative items... there is more you can do.

This chapter we're going to go a little more in depth into the topic of credit repair, and how it can affect your ability to buy a home. Throughout the program we'll continue to touch on these topics and build on the foundation that we're laying today.

Doing credit repair yourself can be a lot of work and can take a lot of persistence. For those who need credit repair but would prefer the help of an expert, there are options for that too.

Miranda's Story

Miranda was a single Mom whose credit had taken a big hit during her divorce. She was living in an apartment with her three kids, doing what she could to make ends meet.

Miranda needed more space to raise her children, but home rentals in her area were not affordable. After talking to a friend who was a real estate agent about home prices and monthly payment amounts, Miranda learned that if she could qualify, buying a home would result in a much lower monthly payment than renting one.

But there was a problem. It was the *credit problem*. Miranda had a credit score of 560.

Miranda's real estate friend told her that if she could get her credit score up to around 620, there was a good chance she could get approved for a loan at somewhere around 7%.

On a $100,000 home loan, a 7% APR would make Miranda's numbers look like this:

Video Resource
Video Name: What is Credit Repair?
www.YourHomeProgram.com/BookResource

Loan Amount	$100,000
Loan Term	30 Years
Interest Rate (APR)	7%
Down Payment	0%
Monthly Payment	$665.30
Total Interest To Be Paid	$139,508.00

The total payment amount after PMI (Private Mortgage Insurance, required on loans with little or no down), insurance, and tax on this loan would be around $820. This is right around what Miranda would have to pay to rent a comparable house in her area.

Miranda decided to work on improving her credit score, and check again in a few months. She enlisted the help of a local credit repair expert and followed the instructions given for the process of improving her credit score.

Some negative items were removed from her credit report, others were corrected, and some weren't changed at all. Miranda also applied for a couple of new credit lines and started making payments on small balances in order to build more positive credit history. In a few of months, Miranda checked her credit and found her credit score had gone up over 100 points.

Her credit score was now 680.

She went to her real estate friend again with her new and improved credit score, and together they looked into her options for home loans.

Miranda filled out some paperwork and went through the process to get pre-approved for a loan. Within days, she was pre-approved for a loan of $100,000 at 5.8% interest. Let's see how this affected her numbers:

Loan Amount	$100,000
Loan Term	30 Years
Interest Rate (APR)	5.6%
Down Payment	0%
Monthly Payment	$574.08
Total Interest To Be Paid	$106,668.80

With taxes and PMI included, Miranda's total monthly payment would be around $730. That's well below what she would pay to rent a comparable house in her area.

Miranda realized that she was on to something good here, but she wasn't quite done yet. With a little more work, Miranda thought she could do even better. She went back to working on her credit.

After a few more months, Miranda had raised her credit score to just over 700. She went back to her real estate friend and once again went through the process of being pre-approved.

Once again, Miranda was pre-approved for a $100,000 loan, but this time with an interest rate of 5.0%.

Here's how the new interest rate changed her numbers for the $100,000 home loan:

Loan Amount	$100,000
Loan Term	30 Years
Interest Rate (APR)	5.0%
Down Payment	0%
Monthly Payment	$536.82
Total Interest To Be Paid	$93,255.20

Video Resource
Video Name: Credit Repair Process
www.YourHomeProgram.com/BookResource

This would put her total monthly payment including PMI, insurance, and taxes at around $690.

This is substantially less than what she would pay to rent a home in her area. At this stage, Miranda did what most of us would do in her situation: *she started looking for a house!*

New Possibilities

If you take nothing else away from this chapter, take this:

Credit repair opens up new possibilities!

Credit repair is one tool in a tool belt designed to give you as many options as possible on the road to home ownership.

The key to Miranda's story, and perhaps to your story too, is to understand that "bad credit" isn't a death sentence. It is an **obstacle in the road**, not the *end of the road*.

Credit repair is *the solution* to the bad credit problem. Are there other strategies for buying a home with bad credit? Yes! But regardless of what strategies you eventually decide to use, credit repair is something you're going to need to do.

Does this mean you'll have to work on your credit for a year or two before you can get into a home?

Not necessarily. In fact, there are options that can get you into a home rather quickly if you play your cards right. (More on that later!)

Credit repair makes home ownership possible for many people who might have otherwise thought it was out of the question.

- Can you buy a home within a year or two of bankruptcy? Yes. (Don't worry, I'll show you how.)
- Can you buy a home with less-than-stellar credit? Yes. (Again, I'll show you how.)
- Can you start the process of buying a home before you've started to fix your credit? Yes. (And I'll show you how to do that too!)

Credit repair coupled with the strategies that I'll show you in this program will open up a whole new world of home ownership possibilities that you probably didn't even know existed.

Keeping the goal of home ownership in mind, let's take a closer look at the credit repair process and how it works.

An Overview of The Credit Repair Process

As you probably know, nobody has just one credit report. You actually have several. The ones we're going to be focusing on for the purpose of our credit repair discussion are the credit reports generated by the three major credit bureaus. The "big 3" credit bureaus are Equifax, Experian, and TransUnion. When we say "credit bureaus" in this program, these are the credit bureaus we are referring to.

The credit repair process, for the purpose of working towards home ownership, can be broken up into 4 main parts:

1. CREDIT DISPUTES: Removing and correcting incorrect credit reporting from your credit reports.
2. BUILDING CREDIT HISTORY: Adding positive credit history to your credit report.
3. CREDIT PROFILE MANAGEMENT: Adjusting your credit profile in other ways for the best possible chances of success.
4. RESOLVING OUTSTANDING ISSUES: Resolving any outstanding bills or debts that could end up on your credit report if you don't do something about them.

Let's talk about each of these parts in a little more detail.

Credit Disputes

A credit dispute is a letter sent to a credit bureau, creditor, or collector for the purpose of fixing your credit. A credit dispute may include documentation and evidence to support a claim. Credit disputes also need to have identifying information included to verify the identity of the person sending it.

The elements of a credit dispute generally include:

- ✓ Letter format with a greeting and salutation, either hand written or (for best results) using different fonts and colors.
- ✓ A description (including account number or other details) of what is being disputed.
- ✓ A description of WHY the item is being disputed. (i.e. the amount is wrong, the date is wrong, the account doesn't belong to you.)
- ✓ A description of what action you want taken. What do you want them to do with your dispute? (Remove the item, correct the item?)

- ✓ Identifying information that is sufficient to confirm your identity. For the credit bureaus this may mean a recent utility bill or other proof of your current address.
- ✓ Any documentation to support your claims, such as copies of bank statements or police reports, etc.

This might seem like a lot at first but it all fits nicely into the flow of a well-crafted credit dispute.

Here's an example:

{NOTE THE LETTER FORMAT}

Credit Bureau Name
Credit Bureau Address
City State Zip

Your Name
Address
City State Zip
Your Phone

Date

Re: Account [account number/name]

Dear [Credit Bureau], {GREETING}

I am writing today to dispute the following item on my credit report:

[account number / name]   {WHAT IS BEING DISPUTED}

This account is fraudulent due to the fact that I was recently a victim of identity theft. I did not open this account.   {WHY THE ITEM IS BEING DISPUTED}

Please remove this account from my credit report immediately.   {THE ACTION YOU WANT TAKEN}

Sincerely, {SALUTATION}

[signature]

[Your Name]   {IDENTIFYING INFORMATION}
[Date of Birth]
[Social Security Number]

P.S. Please see the attached ID theft affidavit and police report {DOCUMENTATION OF CLAIMS} with regards to the identity theft. I have also included a copy of a recent utility bill and a copy of my driver's license {PROOF OF CURRENT ADDRESS/IDENTITY} for identification purposes.

Note that this credit dispute isn't lengthy. There are no long legal arguments. There isn't any fluff.

Most credit disputes can be as simple as this one. Sure, there are times when more complicated approaches are needed, but letters, like the one above, are really what's at the heart of the entire process of credit disputing.

When sending credit disputes, you won't always be dealing with the credit bureaus.

Your Home Program
Our Advisors Are Available To Answer Your Questions
Call **1-800-245-7349** for Home Ownership Made Easy!

You can also send credit disputes to collectors and creditors.

The rules are a little different depending on who you are sending a dispute to, but the basic process remains the same.

Now you may be wondering about a discussion we had earlier. Remember the story we told earlier where a valid credit dispute was sent to a credit bureau and the credit bureau responded saying that the item had been verified?

What happens if you send off the above letter and the credit bureau says the information is accurate (or "verified"), and that it's going to stay on your credit report?

Is that the end of the road?

Not even close. It's just the beginning of the battle.

When a dispute gets verified or the bureau, creditor, or collector otherwise fails to follow through with the requested action, that is when you move to what I call "Round 2 Disputes".

A lot of people get tripped up here so let me explain.

IF the credit bureaus, creditors, and bill collectors always followed the law to the letter, a dispute like the one above which is legitimate and truthful would be enough.

But that is not the way things are.

Instead, the bureaus, collectors, and creditors frequently break the law. Disputes get ignored. Consumers get abused. Disputes for items that should very clearly be removed come back as "verified".

This creates an atmosphere in which the only way to <u>really</u> get something done using credit disputes boils down to a single word:

PERSISTENCE.

If you're going to see results from the credit dispute process, you have to be persistent. You can't just take "no" for an answer, and walk away with your tail between your legs. You've got to stay and fight, and be a big enough pain in the rear so that it is no longer profitable to ignore you.

Don't worry, there are tactics and follow up methods you can use that are very effective and have helped thousands of people accomplish their credit repair goals.

But this fight is precisely why many people choose to let a professional help with their credit repair efforts... because true credit repair professionals already have the systems in place to deal with *many* rounds of disputing if necessary.

Whether you choose to do it yourself or use a professional, you're going to have to deal with this credit dispute process on some level. Later in the program we'll dive a little deeper into the topic of credit disputes for those who need it.

Building Credit History

One aspect of credit repair that is often neglected is that of building a positive credit history.

Consider the following hypothetical scenario:

> *A 30 year old woman has a few derogatory accounts on her credit report. She wants to get approved for a loan so she sets out to "repair" her credit.*
>
> *She manages, through the process of credit disputing, to get every single derogatory account removed from her credit report.*
>
> *She is sure, with all those negative items removed, that she will be approved for the loan now. She goes to the bank and applies for the loan.*
>
> *A few weeks later she gets a letter in the mail saying that her loan application has been* <u>DENIED</u> *due to INSUFFICIENT CREDIT HISTORY!*

This is a simplified scenario that is completely hypothetical, but I imagine you get the point.

Removing negative items without adding new positive accounts to offset them won't get you very far. Adding positive accounts with positive credit history has the effect of showing an amount of renewed responsibility on your part and can actually help to offset the negative scoring effects of some of the "problem entries" on your credit report.

With this approach, it actually is not necessary to remove every single negative item.

In fact, in many cases it is not *advisable* to do so.

Using this and similar strategies in the process of credit repair, many people have found that they can have a fairly healthy credit score even with things like late pays, charge offs, and bankruptcies on their credit report.

Credit Profile Management

Credit profile management involves dealing with more than just negative items on your credit report. There are several things that can affect your credit score that are NOT tied to data that your creditors report to the credit bureaus.

Two examples are:

- Inquiries, and

Video Resource
Video Name: Credit Utilization and Home Ownership
www.YourHomeProgram.com/BookResource

- Credit Utilization

Let's talk about Inquiries first. An inquiry is a record that the credit bureau keeps of when someone (anyone) asks to see your credit report.

There are two types of inquiries... "hard" inquiries and "soft" inquiries. Hard inquiries affect your credit, while soft inquiries don't. If you have a lot of inquiries on your credit report this can negatively affect your score. As of right now, only the inquiries in the last year or so will matter. If you have problems with a large amount of inquiries, there are things that you can do to remedy the situation. We'll talk more about that later in the program.

Credit utilization refers to how much of your total available credit you are using. You can calculate your credit utilization by totaling up the balances of your credit cards, and comparing that to the totals of all your credit limits on the same cards. If your credit card balances totaled $18,000, and your total credit limits totaled $21,000, then your credit utilization would be...

$18,000 / $21,000 = **86%**

In this case you would be using 86% of your total available credit.

Having a credit utilization number that is too high is a bad thing. Having a number that's too low is bad, too. Most experts say that the best credit utilization to have is somewhere between 40% and 60%.

Credit utilization accounts for a good chunk of your credit score, so improving these numbers definitely yield credit score benefits.

The most common credit utilization problem is using *too much* of the available credit, or having **HIGH CREDIT UTILIZATION**. There two main strategies to fix this:

1. Pay off a large portion of your credit card debt
2. Add a new positive account with a healthy credit line to change your utilization

Option #2 is the most realistic for the majority of people in this situation. Here's how it works:

> *Let's say you're using 86% of your available credit as in our example above. You have $21,000 of total available credit and you are using $18,000 of it. You have HIGH CREDIT UTILIZATION. One way to fix this would be to pay off a portion of the $18,000. This option is out of the question since you don't have an extra $8,000 in your pocket to pay off debt with. Your only other option is to add a new credit line. You apply for a special subprime credit line (a merchandise card) with a nice, high credit limit. Overnight you add $10,000 to your "total available credit". Your credit utilization has changed to $18,000 / $31,000 = 58%. Your credit utilization is now 58%, which is much more acceptable than the 86% you had before. As a result of this change, your credit score goes up!*

That's the essence of the preferred approach to addressing credit utilization problems. It is preferred

Your Home Program
Our Advisors Are Available To Answer Your Questions
Call **1-800-245-7349** for Home Ownership Made Easy!

because it has the added benefit of giving you the opportunity to add new positive credit history to your report, which is an important step (as we discussed earlier).

If you have high credit utilization and need to do something about it, there are options out there that can help.

Resolving Outstanding Issues

This is an often overlooked aspect of credit repair that is **very** important when home ownership is the ultimate goal.

This step could be thought of as a sort of *preemptive* credit repair.

Imagine the following scenario:

> *You have been working to repair your credit so that you can be approved for a loan. You finally make some progress and are ready to submit your loan application, when you get a nasty surprise: a new collection account has just popped up on your credit report! After some investigation, you find out that the collection account is for an old phone bill that you meant to pay but obviously forgot.*

The "resolving outstanding issues" step is all about avoiding this type of scenario.

There are numerous issues that may not be credit problems today, but they will be **tomorrow** if you don't do something about them. Since home ownership is a **long term** goal, you can't afford to ignore these looming problems.

Here are some examples of common issues that can come back to bite you in the credit report:

- Old phone bills or utility debts

- Unpaid rent
- Unused bank accounts that have been sitting empty for years
- Unpredictable or insufficient income
- Any bills that are in dispute but not yet on your credit reports
- Forgotten or otherwise unattended credit lines

These are just examples, but hopefully you get the idea.

If there is **anything** at all that could end up as a negative entry on your credit report if left untreated, then *now* is the time to do something about it!

Credit Repair And Buying A Home

When you apply for certain loans, the process if fairly simple and the lines are pretty clear.

Home loans can be a little more complicated, though.

Home loans are one type of loan where the lender will often want to take a closer look at your situation when making the decision. Things like proof of income may be required. You may get questions about particular items on your credit report. Any unpaid collections or charge offs that remain on your credit report will have to be paid.

The amount of debt you have will matter. The amount of available credit you have will matter, too.

You don't need to have perfect credit to buy a home, but you will want everything going for you that you can possibly get in order to be approved for the best interest rates.

When home ownership is the goal, credit repair is really about shaping the credit report so that, as much as possible, you will fit what the lender is looking for. This won't necessarily mean removing or hiding every negative thing about your credit. Some negative items won't really hurt your score or your chances of buying a home. An older paid charge off, for example, may not actually hurt your *score* at all, and can show the lender that you've had a bump in the road that you have properly handled and taken care of. That doesn't show anything but a high level of responsibility.

Keep this in mind when you are working on the credit aspect of the path to home ownership. Your credit report does **NOT** have to be perfect. The point is to get your SCORE up and to shape things in such a way as to have the best chances of getting the best rates possible.

Credit Repair Is One Trick

It's also important to remember that credit repair is just one trick the bag for you to use on your path to home ownership. We're going to talk about more tips and strategies that you can use throughout this program that will help you reach the goal of home ownership. Credit repair is part of the puzzle. It's one thing that you should do... but not the *only* thing.

The Limits of Credit Repair

Bad credit isn't a death sentence. In most cases, something can be done to fix it.

There are some things, though, that **can't** be done.

Not every negative item can necessarily be removed from your credit report. Not every negative item *needs* to be, either. Later in the program I'll give you some specific examples of items that can usually stay on your report with minimal scoring effects.

One thing that we should make clear about credit repair and buying a home:

You can't use any tricks that are designed to hide your negative credit history or give the impression that you have a different financial status than what you actually do. The kind of tricks I'm talking about are things like creating a "new credit profile" or using what some call "credit privacy numbers". These "tricks" are not only unethical, they are ***illegal*** and can lead to a lot more harm than good. You are much better off working within the limits of legitimate (and legal) credit repair methods than risking everything for any "instant fix" that is simply too good to be true.

> *"But what if I have a bankruptcy on my credit report? How bad is <u>too</u> bad?"*

That's exactly what we're going to talk about next chapter when we start into the steps necessary for buying a home after bankruptcy, and other important secrets to buying a home with bad credit that you won't want to miss

4 HOW BAD IS TOO BAD

If you have some big dings on your credit, you may be wondering exactly how bad your credit has to be before you should consider yourself a "lost cause".

The truth is that there are no lost causes in the credit world. Something can *always* be done, given that you have the will and the determination required to make it happen.

This chapter we're going to focus on what some consider to be the "worst of the worst" when it comes to credit report offenses. We're going to talk about **bankruptcy**.

I believe I've already made it clear that bad credit isn't a death sentence. Bankruptcy isn't a death sentence either. Contrary to what some people may believe, you <u>CAN</u> buy a home with a bankruptcy on your credit report. In many cases a person may be able to do so in as little as two short years after their bankruptcy.

How that's possible will take some explanation, which I'll try to provide as we continue with our discussion, starting with...

The 4 Steps Required To Buy A Home After Bankruptcy

> **SIDE NOTE:** I should probably make note that the much of the following will apply whether you're dealing with a bankruptcy or some other big credit issue... so if you don't have a bankruptcy on your credit report, keep that fact in mind throughout the discussion, and think about how the same information might apply to your particular situation—as much of it will.

One of the main keys to successfully reaching your goal of home ownership after bankruptcy or any other major credit hiccup is that you should have a clear ***intention***, and act in accordance with that intention.

Set the purpose before you. Write the goal on the mirror, on sticky notes, and anywhere else you can think of. Then, be very intentional in your efforts to work towards that goal. This subtle strategy can make a world of difference. Many people fail to get anywhere in life simply because they are floundering about without any clear goals or intentions. You need to decide *not* to be one of those people.

With your intention clear in your mind, you can now start work on the 4 steps that are <u>required</u> in order to buy a home after bankruptcy:

Step 1: Start working from day one to improve your finances.

Step 2: Start saving for a down payment immediately.

Step 3: Evaluate whether a rent to own strategy will help you, and if so, take action.

Step 4: Work to improve your credit score using the Post-Bankruptcy Credit Score Improvement Plan

That's really all there is to it. Did you expect it to be more complicated? It isn't. While not exactly complicated, the steps I've just showed you are *deceptively* simple. As we get further into the program we will dive more into various details that will help you work through each of these steps.

Our first course of action will be to evaluate your financial situation so that you can begin to work on improving it. (In order to know where you're going, you really need to understand where you currently stand.) Once we dive into the steps necessary to improve your financial situation, you will start to get a picture of how you can save and build towards a healthy down payment. We'll also cover the "rent to own" option in detail.

The fourth step is the one that we'll focus on today, which means it is time to learn about...

The Post-Bankruptcy Credit Score Improvement Plan

Background

Before we get started into the details of the Post-Bankruptcy Credit Score Improvement Plan, I need to give a little background on the subject.

You may not have realized it, but in the credit scoring system you are graded on a ***curve***.

This means that you are "judged" (for lack of a better word) based not only on your own credit performance, but on your performance *in comparison with* other consumers in your category.

This "curve" is accomplished through the use of what are known as "Scorecards". A scorecard is essentially

Video Resource
Video Name: Bad Credit, but looking to Buy a Home: Options
www.YourHomeProgram.com/BookResource

the category that defines how your credit score will be calculated.

The two most popular credit scores both use scorecards, and both have what we call a "Bankruptcy Scorecard".

If you have a bankruptcy on your credit report, then you are scored according to the bankruptcy scorecard. This means that your credit performance will be calculated in comparison with other people who have bankruptcies on their credit reports.

What Scorecards Really Mean

What the bankruptcy scorecard means is that it's not your credit performance alone that matters (i.e. the fact that you have a bankruptcy on your credit report), but rather your credit performance in light of your scorecard (i.e. how you perform in comparison with other people who have bankruptcies).

Imagine the following scenario:

> *John and Sue both filed for bankruptcy.*
>
> *After the bankruptcy, Sue started rebuilding her credit, correcting incorrect entries on her credit report, and started*

new positive credit accounts. She was very careful not to miss a single late payment.

John, on the other hand, opened a couple of new credit accounts and within the first few months already had a couple of late payments again.

After about 12 months, Sue's credit score is at about 680, and John's is in the low 500s.

Think about this scenario for a moment. For Sue, it's clear that she's making changes, and improving things. Her score goes up dramatically as a result. For John, however, a late payment within just a few months of bankruptcy is a big red flag. John's score drops accordingly. The situation could be summed up like this:

*They **both** apparently had some financial problems and filed for bankruptcy. Sue **learned her lesson** and made the necessary changes to not let it happen again. **John didn't.***

Video Resource
Video Name: Is Bankruptcy a Credit Score killer?
www.YourHomeProgram.com/BookResource

What this means to you is that after your bankruptcy, you need to start working right away to demonstrate that you are responsible and that you are getting back on your feet.

If you keep your credit clean after a bankruptcy and take a couple of basic steps, your post-bankruptcy credit profile will be much, much better.

So What's The Plan?

The post-bankruptcy credit score improvement plan has 3 simple steps. Here they are:

STEP 1: Keep your credit <u>CLEAN</u>.

In order to appear as though you've learned your lesson (like Sue, above); you need to keep your credit perfectly clean. This means <u>no</u> <u>new</u> <u>derogatory</u> <u>items</u> can be reported on your credit. This is an absolute must.

STEP 2: Make sure the items on your credit report are being reported correctly as "included in bankruptcy".

One of the biggest things that hurt your score when you have a bankruptcy on your credit is items that were included in the bankruptcy that don't get listed as such on your credit report.

When you have incorrectly listed items on your credit report that aren't being reported as "included in bankruptcy", it makes it looks as though you are like John, and that you have a bankruptcy **<u>AND</u>** have already started getting negative marks on your credit again.

You need to avoid that misconception by using credit dispute tactics to correct the incorrectly listed items on your credit report. We'll talk more about credit dispute tactics later.

STEP 3: Build new credit history by adding new, positive credit accounts.

When you're on the bankruptcy scorecard, having new positive credit on your credit report can have a ***very positive*** impact. New credit accounts will help you start building a positive payment history again, and can have a dramatic effect on your credit score.

Using this and the previous two steps of the post-bankruptcy credit score improvement plan, many consumers have found themselves with credit scores as high as 700 within a year or two of their bankruptcy.

How Bad Is It?

As I hope you've learned from what we've talked about this chapter, there are many cases in which your credit may not be as bad as you think.

You may *feel* hopeless... I understand that feeling.

The reality is that there <u>is</u> hope, and your situation may not be as bad as you think.

The next module of the program is all about deciphering your financial situation, and determining exactly where you stand in terms of income, expenses, debt, and credit.

I'll walk you through the process of fully assessing your entire financial situation, including your credit. We'll talk about how to <u>REALLY</u> read your credit report, and cover the little quirks and tricks to watch out for that many people miss.

Video Resource
Video Name: How does Bankruptcy affect your Credit?
www.YourHomeProgram.com/BookResource

5 INCOME AND HOME OWNERSHIP

How much income do you need to own a home? How much house can you afford with the income you have?

I'll answer these questions and more this chapter as we get into the details of your income as it relates to *home ownership*.

What Kind of Income Do I Need?

One of the most important aspects of your income for home buying purposes is stability. You need to be able to demonstrate that your income is **stable**.

If you're self-employed, you'll probably have to provide bank statements and other documentation to show that your income has been stable over a certain period of time.

If you're employed, the longer you have been so, the better. Many lenders will want you to have been in the same job (or at least working in the same field) for 2 years or more.

Stability is important both for the purposes of being approved for a loan, and for managing the expense of maintaining your home and paying your monthly house payments. If you do not have a stable and predictable income, it will be difficult to gauge what you can and can't afford to pay for a home.

An unstable or unpredictable income can get you in trouble down the road, so it's important to have a *stable* source of income.

How Much Income Do I Need?

How much income you need will actually depend on the cost of the house you are going to buy, the interest rate you get approved for, and what your expenses look like.

Generally speaking, in order to be approved your total payment including taxes and insurance cannot be more than 29% to 33%[1] of your monthly gross income. The percentage that applies depends on what kind of loan it is, but let's take 33% as an example:

If your gross monthly income is $3,500, your total monthly payment with insurance and taxes cannot be more than $1,085 ($3,500 x .33).

This doesn't mean you should shoot for a payment that is right at that limit. It's just the maximum payment you can have with your current income.

Based on the above percentages, a simple way to get a rough estimate of what income you need for a particular house payment is to take the house payment and multiply it by 3. So a house payment of $1,200 is going to require a MINIMUM of somewhere around $3600 in gross monthly income.

There's more to the story though. This calculation doesn't take expenses into consideration. When we talk about expenses next chapter, we'll talk about how expenses play a role in the calculations for affordability

---

[1] Note: Information subject to change, for latest FHA info check the FHA website.

and loan approval.

For now, the thing to know about income is that for loan approval purposes, you're going to need a monthly gross income that is at LEAST 3 times the amount that the total house payment (including taxes and insurance) will be.

With that in mind, here's a table that shows a *rough* estimate of the amount of income needed for the given home loan scenario. Keep in mind that the following table does NOT take your expenses into consideration. (We'll talk about the role expenses play next chapter.)

ESTIMATES OF INCOME REQUIREMENTS FOR 30 YEAR MORTGAGE			
Loan Amount	Interest Rate	Monthly Payment (Including Estimated Taxes, Insurance, etc.)	Required Minimum Monthly Gross Income
$200,000	7%	$1,838.00	$5,514.00
$200,000	6%	$1,707.00	$5,121.00
$200,000	5%	$1,581.00	$4,743.00
$200,000	4%	$1,463.00	$4,389.00
$150,000	7%	$1,379.00	$4,137.00
$150,000	6%	$1,280.00	$3,840.00
$150,000	5%	$1,186.00	$3,558.00
$150,000	4%	$1,097.00	$3,291.00
$125,000	7%	$1,149.00	$3,447.00
$125,000	6%	$1,067.00	$3,201.00
$125,000	5%	$988.00	$2,964.00
$125,000	4%	$914.00	$2,742.00
$75,000	7%	$700.00	$2,100.00
$75,000	6%	$640.00	$1,920.00
$75,000	5%	$593.00	$1,779.00
$75,000	4%	$548.00	$1,644.00

How Much House Do I Need?

Many people buy a lot more house than they really need. One key to keeping your home affordable is to figure out how much house you need in order to be happy and comfortable in your home.

Sometimes when people find out they have been pre-approved for a certain amount, they look for houses in that range. Don't do that.

Instead, decide how much house you need, and find out what *that* kind of house will cost you. If you get pre-approved for a higher amount, stick with what you know you need.

How much house you need will depend on several factors. How many people are in your family? How much stuff do you have? Do you need a special place for "alone time", and does the house have enough available space to provide that? As you can see, the decision is a very personal one. No expert can tell you exactly how much house you need. You have to decide on your own, based on your family's needs, your personal preferences, and your lifestyle.

How Much House Can I REALLY Afford?

What a lot of people don't realize is that whether or not you can afford a given house depends on a lot more than just the loan and payment amounts.

Here are some questions to ask yourself when considering the cost of living in a particular house.

Does the house need repairs? Is it a fixer-upper? If so, you need to include the cost of repairs in your estimates. Can you afford to live in the house AND fix it up?

How expensive will the house be to heat and cool? Houses with vaulted ceilings, for example, are more expensive to heat and cool. What are the average utility bills of the house? The larger the house is, the more expensive the utilities are going to be. This is a factor you should take into consideration.

Is there a housing association? Housing associations can add dramatically to the cost of living in a house. What are the association fees? Are there any fines or fees if you break an association rule? Are the association rules ones you can live with? These are all things that deserve attention if you're considering moving into an area where there is a housing association.

How many light bulbs are in the home? This probably sounds like a silly question, but it serves an important purpose. There are certain things with every home that you are going to have to pay to replace periodically. The bigger the home is, the more those things are going to cost. Light bulbs are just one example, and for our purposes light bulbs can be representative of this general category of expenses. If you are currently living in an apartment, you may have anywhere from 10 to 15 light bulbs to replace. Moving into a home, that number could double, triple, or even quadruple, depending on the size of the home. It's wise to keep these types of expenses in mind as you consider the potential cost of living in a home. They can add up quickly.

The point of these questions is this:

There are expenses that you will have when you own a home that you do not have when you are renting either a home or an apartment. You need to look at your housing choices closely so that you can get a good idea of what these extra expenses will be, and how they will affect your ability to afford the home.

Two Key Questions About Income

This discussion about income boils down to two key questions. The questions are:

1. How much do you make?

and...

2. How much do you *keep?*

These questions are at the root of what your lender is going to be analyzing when they look at your income and expense figures.

Let's look a little closer at these questions now.

How Much Do You Make?

How much money you make is probably a figure you are very aware of. Some people aren't as aware as they should be, though. Let's calculate your income now so that you have it for reference as you proceed with this program.

If you don't know your monthly gross income, you can calculate it by taking your hourly wage and multiplying that times 2,080 (the number of hours you will work in a year working 40 hours a week), and divide the resulting number by 12 (the number of months in a year). If you know your weekly gross income amount, you can also take that number and multiply it by 52, and divide the result by 12 to get your average monthly gross income.

Using Hourly Wage:

AVG. MONTHLY GROSS INCOME = HOURLY WAGE x 2080 / 12

Using Weekly Gross Pay From Paystub:

AVG. MONTHLY GROSS INCOME = WEEKLY GROSS INCOME x 52 / 12.

Take the resulting number, and any additional income you may have, and plug it into the following table.

SOURCE	MONTHLY AMOUNT	NOTES
Your Regular Income		Your monthly gross income.
Spouses Regular Income		Your spouse's monthly gross income.
Extra Income		Any extra income you receive consistently that isn't included in your monthly gross income from employment or business.
TOTAL MONTHLY GROSS INCOME:		Add up the middle column and put the result in this box. This is roughly the amount that your lender will look at when considering your income for the purpose of your home loan.

How Much Money Do You Keep?

This is a question that surprisingly few people know the answer to. It may pay to consider this question early in the game because it <u>**IS**</u> a factor that your lender will look at when you apply for a home loan.

How much of the money that you make every month do you actually keep? Are your monthly expenses excessive? Do you have large payments to other debts that are eating up your monthly cash flow?

These are all things that we'll get into next chapter when we talk about the role that your expenses play in your quest for home ownership.

6 EXPENSES AND HOME OWNERSHIP

When we calculated income last chapter, we calculated your MONTHLY GROSS INCOME. We didn't take out income taxes and other taxes, health insurance costs, or any other expenses. Expenses are important though, and can not only affect your ability to be *approved* for a loan, but they can also affect your ability to *afford* the loan that you get approved for. (Just because you can get approved for a loan, doesn't mean you can afford it!)

This week we're going to talk about what your expenses are and how they can affect your path to home ownership.

The Five Categories of Expenses

For the purposes of this program we're going to break up your expenses into five categories. The reason for this approach is simple: not all expenses are created equal. Some expenses are ones that you pay whether you like it or not. Income taxes are a good example. Stop paying income taxes, and you'll buy yourself a stay in an apartment with bars. Taxes are also usually taken out of your paycheck, so you never actually see the money. Many people's health insurance costs are also paid this way.

For these and other reasons, we have broken up expenses into several categories. Here they are:

Required And Unseen Expenses - Taxes and health insurance would fall into this category for most people. Since our previous income calculations were for monthly GROSS income, you'll need to include these expenses in your expense calculations in order to get an accurate number. To get a figure for this category of expenses, most people will be able to look at their pay stubs.

Required Bills - For most people, bills like electricity, gas, water, and trash are required and non-negotiable. These are bills that most of us have that we have to just "live with". Sometimes we can do things to lower them (which we'll talk about later), but this category of expenses is one that we all generally have to pay, and have little control over. Many expenses in this category can have negative consequences if not paid. Alimony and child support payments could be included in this category.

Negotiable Bills - These are bills that can to at least some extent be reduced or eliminated. Some examples are phone bills, long distance bills, cell phone bills, cable bills, internet bills, subscriptions to newspapers and magazines, and memberships such as gym memberships or YMCA memberships. This is one category of expenses in which people can often afford to cut back. Debt payments such as credit card and car payments fall into this category.

Regular Required Expenses - These are expenses that all of us have that don't come in the form of bills. Some examples are things like groceries, school enrollment, and various other necessities. Some of these expenses can't be reduced, and others can. Many times they will vary according to location, family size, lifestyle, and other factors.

Extra Expenses - These are the expenses we all love and hate. They're the expenses that give us pleasure (snacks and drinks, dining out, entertainment), but often come back to bite us in the end. This is THE category of expenses that is most often found to be "out of control". Part of the problem with these extra expenses is that people don't *track* them well enough to know what they are spending. Keeping a spending diary for a week or two can give you the necessary insight you need to understand what you're REALLY spending in the "extra expenses" category. Obviously, this is a category of expenses where many people can afford to cut back. It also happens to be one of the most difficult areas to cut back because of the discipline required.

Totaling Your Expenses

Let's walk through the process of calculating and totaling up your expenses using the above 5 categories.

Estimating Your "Required and Unseen" Expenses

To estimate your average monthly income tax withholding, FICA tax, and health insurance costs, the easiest thing to do is to look at a pay stub.

Do you get paid every week? Then you'll take the total of any health insurance premium withheld and any taxes withheld, and multiply that by 52, and divide the result by 12. This will give you a fair estimation for your monthly "Required And Unseen" expenses.

WEEKLY PAY STUB EXPENSE CALCULATIONS						
TAXES	+ INSURANCE	+ OTHER	= WEEKLY	TIMES 52	DIV. BY 12	= MONTHLY
				x 52	/ 12	

If you get paid every 2 weeks, then take the same information and multiply the number by 26, and then divide that number by 12.

EVERY-TWO-WEEK PAY STUB EXPENSE CALCULATIONS						
TAXES	+ INSURANCE	+ OTHER	= BIWEEKLY	TIMES 26	DIV. BY 12	= MONTHLY
				x 26	/ 12	

If you get paid twice a month (on the 1st and 16th, for example), then take the total of your taxes and insurance and multiply it by 2 to get your estimated monthly "Required and Unseen" expenses.

TWICE A MONTH PAY STUB EXPENSE CALCULATIONS					
TAXES	+ INSURANCE	+ OTHER	=SEMIMONTHLY	TIMES 2	= MONTHLY
				x 2	

There may be circumstances under which the above calculations won't be enough. I can't cover every special circumstance here, so if you know there are other Required And Unseen expenses that you pay, never see, and have little or no choice in, then be sure to include those in your total.

Adding Up Your Required Bills

Some bills can't be avoided. It doesn't mean we don't still have choices (which we'll get to later in the program), but even though in cases you can *reduce* them, there are some bills that you're just going to have to live with.

Bills that would fall under this category are electric bills, gas bills, water and sewer bills, and trash bills. If you're currently living in an apartment, you may not have to pay for your water, sewer, and trash. You need to keep this in mind and find out what these expenses will be when you move into a home.

In some parts of the country, the cost of **heating** and **cooling** a home (using gas and electricity) can vary greatly throughout the year. It is not uncommon for homes in colder areas to have heating bills in the hundreds of dollars. Keep these sorts of variations in mind when you are estimating these expenses. Also keep in mind that they will typically go up substantially when moving from an apartment to a house.

I recommend averaging your bills to get an estimated monthly figure, and to make sure your account for the variations that occur throughout the year.

The following worksheet will help you do this.

Required Bills Worksheet

INSTRUCTIONS: Fill out the amounts for 12 months' worth of bills in each category. If you don't have record of the exact amounts, then estimate with your best guess. Add up each row and put the total in the column at the far right to get each month's total "Required Bills" figure. Then add up the amounts in the last column (the "SUBTOTALS" column), and divide the resulting number by 12 to get your average monthly amount for Required Bills.

MONTH	Water/ Sewer	Trash	Electric	Gas	Auto Insurance	Other 1	Other 2	SUB TOTALS
January								
February								
March								
April								
May								
June								
July								
August								
September								
October								
November								
December								
							ANNUAL TOTAL	
						MONTHLY AVERAGE *(ANNUAL TOTAL / 12)*		

Adding Up Your Negotiable Bills

This is one area that you'll want to pay particularly close attention to. This is the category of bills that is *expendable*. In other words, there are bills that you pay for services that you **don't** absolutely NEED, or that you can possibly reduce or otherwise change services or options to make the most of your money.

Common bills in this category include Cable TV, Cell Phones, Phone And Long Distance Bills (including "extras" like call waiting and voicemail), Newspaper and Magazine Subscriptions, Gym memberships, and more.

We would also include most categories of debt in "negotiable" bills because in many cases changes can be made to payment terms or even loan amounts if you're willing to work at it. Using debt negotiation or debt settlement techniques, or other strategies to manage debt, it's possible that you can make drastic changes in the area of your debt and debt payments if you put some effort into it.

Use the following form to add up your bills in this category.

NEGOTIABLE BILLS	
Monthly Bill Type	Current Monthly Amount
Cable TV	
Phone Bill	
Long Distance	
Cell Phone(s)	
Newspapers	
Magazines	
Gym and YMCA Membership(s)	
Credit Card Payments (total):	
Car Payments (total):	
Other Loan Payments (total)	
Other:	
Other:	
TOTAL ▶	

Your Home Program
Our Advisors Are Available To Answer Your Questions
Call **1-800-245-7349** for Home Ownership Made Easy!

Is a car payment really negotiable? What about a student loan payment? Yes and no. You can't usually call your bank and tell them you want to lower your car payments and get very far doing it. However, something **CAN** be done about your car payment. You're not stuck with it. Same with student loans. There are always options for the brave and creative among us. More on that later!

Adding Up Your Regular Required Expenses

There are some expenses that you don't receive bills for that are more or less required. These include things like groceries, school enrollment fees, and may include the costs of child care (such as a regular babysitter or daycare) if you didn't include those in the "Required Bills" worksheet above.

The easiest way to add up your regular required expenses may be to take a bank statement for a given month, and add up the expenses that fit this category, including grocery store trips and payments to babysitters or daycare.

You can use the following form for your calculations. List the appropriate expenses in the available blanks with the monthly amount for each, and total them at the bottom.

REGULAR REQUIRED EXPENSES	
Expense Type/Name	Monthly Amount
Groceries	
Gas for car	
Oil Changes/Car Maintenance	
Child Care	
TOTAL ▶	

Tracking And Estimating Your Extra Expenses

If you've made it this far, I commend you. I know it can be tough facing all these numbers.

You'll probably be pleased to know that we're almost done with all this number stuff, but first we need to get through one more category of expenses: EXTRA EXPENSES!

This is probably your favorite type of expense, because this is where you have all your fun. It is also the most difficult category of expenses to track, and often the most difficult for people to cut back on.

Figuring how much "extra" you really spend requires some special steps. Here they are:

STEP 1: Create a spending diary using a small spiral notebook. Write down the date you start, and then start recording expense entries, with at least the item description (general description is fine) and the amount.

STEP 2: Record all of your extra expenses for two or three weeks. Record any "spending money" expenses, any entertainment, movies, dining out, coffee on the way to work, etc. Include any extra spending that you do on credit cards, with cash, or with checks or a debit card.

STEP 3: Total up your extra expenses after you have kept the spending diary for at least 2 or 3 weeks, and divide the total by the number of weeks you kept the spending log. So if you keep a spending log for 3 weeks and you spent a total of $300, you would do this: $300 / 3 = $100 per week. This gives you an estimate of your average weekly "extra" spending.

Total of Expenses From Spending Diary:	/	Number of weeks the spending log was kept	=	Spending Per Week
	/			
				▲▲ Use this number for s STEP 4.

STEP 4: Take the number from step 3, multiply it by 52, and divide the result by 12. This is your average monthly extra expenses.

MONTHLY EXTRA SPENDING ESTIMATE				
SPENDING PER WEEK	TIMES 52	DIV. BY 12	=	MONTHLY
	x 52	/ 12		

Bringing It All Together

Now that we've made it through all that expense tracking, it's time to combine all the numbers in one place and find out how much your expenses REALLY are each month.

Take the numbers from each of the categories covered above, and plug them into the following table.

MONTHLY EXPENSE TOTALS	
EXPENSE CATEGORY	AMOUNT
Required And Unseen Expenses	
Required Bills	
Negotiable Bills	
Regular Required Expenses	
Extra Expenses	
TOTAL MONTHLY EXPENSES:	

The total here should be a fair estimate for your total regular monthly expenses that you pay to anyone and everyone in any given month.

Now, as an added bonus, you can take your total monthly expenses and subtract it from your monthly gross income that we calculated previously to find out how much money you have left after ALL of your spending each month.

-	=
GROSS MONTHLY INCOME	TOTAL MONTHLY EXPENSES	YOUR CASHFLOW

If the number above "YOUR CASHFLOW" is positive, then it means you're spending <u>less</u> than you make every month. That's a good thing.

If the number above "YOUR CASHFLOW" is *negative*, then it means you're spending <u>MORE</u> than you make every month... and that's something you're going to need to fix right away!

If the number is a positive but small number, don't worry. I'll cover a lot of tools and tactics later in the program for improving your income and expense scenario.

What The Lender Looks At

Remember when we talked about how much income would be required to buy a home? We discussed the requirements of some lenders that your house payment not exceed 29% to 33% of your gross monthly income. The percentages we covered are referred to as *front end debt-to-income ratios*.

There are also "back end" ratios that lenders look at, for which the percentage range is somewhere in the vicinity of 42% to 45%.

The back end ratio calculation takes the following expenses into consideration:

- Your total future house payment
- Your credit card payments
- Auto loan payments
- Any other recurring debt payments

Notice that this includes other **debt payments**, which above we categorized under "negotiable" expenses. Later in the program we'll talk about various ways you can improve this back end ratio including, but not limited to, by way of reducing your payments and balances on debts.

How Back End and Front End Ratios Work Together

Let's look at example using both front end and back end debt-to-income ratios.

For the purposes of this example, imagine that your monthly gross income is $4,000 per month. Your **maximum** payment amount using the front end debt-to-income ratio of 33% is $1320.

Let's say you want to buy a home that is $125,000, and your payments are going to be approximately $1,149. Can you afford the home? **You are within the limits for the front end ratio, so let's look at the back end:**

You have $200 worth of minimum credit card payments every month, $300 worth of student loan payments every month, and a $200 car payment.

$1,149 + $200 + $300 + $200 = $1,849

Your total payments for the back-end ratio calculation are $1849.00. Can you afford the house?

The back end debt-to-income ratio requirement is **43%.**

Video Resource
Video Name: Income versus Debt: Front-end to Back-end Ratio
www.YourHomeProgram.com/BookResource

$1,849 / $4,000 = 46.2%

In this case, you would NOT be able to purchase the home because your debt payments are *too high*.

What can you do if you find yourself in this situation?

It is not uncommon for home buyers with bad credit to find themselves in a situation such as this one. Can anything be done about it?

YES!

Remember that your bad credit is <u>NOT</u> a death sentence. It isn't a "can't buy a home" sentence either.

Problems with bad credit, excessive debt, and income can all be addressed in such a way as to eventually land you in the home of your dreams. You just have to stick with it.

As the program progresses we're going to talk in detail about how you can improve your income, expenses, and credit. This will put you in the driver seat and give you the tools and the ***power*** you need to overcome the problems you are facing in these areas.

For the above scenario, the logical course of action would probably be to shop around for a better loan and work on your credit to get approved for better rates, and to, at the same time, work on tackling your debt to improve that side of the equation. Again, we'll get more into all that later.

For now, the key thing to understand is that it is possible for a person to have **enough income** to get approved for a loan, but for their **expenses** to ultimately cost them the deal.

Other Factors

There are other monthly expenses that a lender may look at, and there is a long list of other considerations that go into the home loan approval process. For our purposes in this discussion of expenses, the main point to walk away with is that lenders <u>**DO**</u> consider more than just your income. If your expenses are out of control, it's going to be a problem.

What You Should Look At

One thing to remember in the course of home shopping is that even if a lender says you can afford something, it doesn't mean you can afford it.

You need to look at your big picture. You need to look at not just what your finances look like "on paper", but what you know they are like in reality. Are you always struggling to get from one paycheck to the next? If so, that's not something that you can expect to magically improve when you buy a home.

For that reason and others, you need to look deep into your own situation and decide what you really can and can't afford, and *then* see how that compares to the lender's numbers.

It's a smart move to think about things like what your spending habits are now, and how they will change when you move into a house. What surprises are going to come up? Will your regular expenses change, and if so how?

These are good questions to consider, and they are an important part of the process of *planning* for your future in home ownership.

Planning For Home Ownership

There are a variety of things you should consider related to expenses when you are planning for home ownership. I'll cover the main ones right now.

Geographical Variations In Utility Cost

If you're moving to a new area, or even to a different part of the same city, one thing you will need to look into is what the utility costs are like where you are moving.

Costs for water, sewer, trash, electricity, and gas can vary depending on your location.

Water and sewer rates in some cities vary by location. Trash rates can also vary by location.

The cost of electricity and natural gas can vary by region, and the climate in different parts of the country can play a big role in determining what you will pay to heat and cool your home.

Think about where you live now, and compare it to where you'll be when you move into a home.

Your utility rates will generally go up in a home compared to an apartment. If you're renting a home of the same size that you will someday buy, your utilities may stay more or less level, and could even improve if the home you are buying has been made to be more efficient (which is more likely to be the case than it would be for a rental home.)

Geography affects utilities. Even things like trees, fences, and the direction certain windows are facing can play a part in what you'll pay for heating and cooling.

These are good things to think about when you're planning for home ownership.

How Home Ownership Changes Your Regular Expenses

Bigger homes cost more to maintain and to use. We gave some insight into this earlier when we asked the question "How many light bulbs are in the home?"

Moving from a 10 light bulb apartment to a 50 light bulb home is going to cost more money. Your ***regular expenses*** are going to go up.

Regular maintenance can also add up in a home. Maybe you'll need to get the gutters cleaned periodically. Maybe the home will have a water filtration system that you have to purchase supplies for. These are **regular expenses** that might not be "regular" in your current situation.

Whether it's pest control, lawn maintenance, annual weatherization, or something else, there is a good chance that there are going to be regular expenses associated with living in your own home that you don't have now.

At the very least, you should spend some time thinking ahead to these potential expenses, and consider them when deciding what you can and can't afford.

How Home Ownership Changes Your "Extra" Expenses

Do you like to decorate? If so, the cost of your interior decorating hobby is going to increase when you buy a home. There will be more pictures to hang on the walls, more decorative fixtures to buy, and endless lists of things that you will want to change and update as you live life in your new home.

This is normal. It's human nature. And in today's world, it costs money.

Owning a home will change the way you spend money. Your extra expenses will change, and in certain categories, are certain to grow.

Many people spend more on entertainment and entertaining after they buy a home. Social get-togethers and cookouts become more common. Basketball goals and volleyball nets get put up. Pool tables and air hockey games get bought.

Even if you don't like to decorate or entertain, home ownership can still increase your extra expenses.

After just a week or two of living in your newly purchased home, something is going to happen. You'll be sitting there enjoying all the wonderful hominess and something will happen.

You'll be staring at an empty wall (after all, you don't like to decorate), and suddenly it will occur to you:

If I move that wall over just a foot, I could have room for...........

And so it begins. Here's a secret about owning a home that you may not know:

Your home has the capability to suddenly become not just a home, but a ***hobby***.

A lot of people who own homes find that they end up spending more money on "extra" things for their homes for no other reason than because they ***want to***. Making your home "yours" with minor remodels, decorating, some paint here and there, is all part of the fun of home ownership.

What's the moral of the story?

Owning a home can change your extra expenses in unexpected ways. It's best if you can be prepared for that ahead of time!

Changes In Commute Costs

Unless you purchase a home that's the exact same distance from your work, your commute costs will probably change.

In a perfect world, they'd go down. You can't always get a place closer to your work though.

So your commute costs could go *up*.

When looking for a home, be sure to consider the location in relation to your work, the grocery store, schools, and any other places you will frequently visit.

These things may seem minor, but thinking about them ahead of time can pay off in the long run.

Changing Your Spending (And Your Life)

I have some good news for you.

No matter what the state of your income and expenses may be, there is *always* room for improvement.

If you feel that your expenses are well under control, or if you don't, you can still benefit from making some minor (and even major) changes to the way you do things in order to improve your quality of life.

Consider this:

Every single monthly expense dollar that you can save is another dollar in your pocket.

If you can combine a number of strategies and end up saving yourself $500 per month, then guess what? You just gave yourself a $500 per month RAISE!

This is a powerful idea that a lot of people have trouble realizing the full potential of.

What if you took each of the 5 categories of expenses, and found a way to save just $100 per month in each? *You'd have your $500 per month raise in a hurry!*

What if you went through the 5 categories of expenses, and found ways to save $200 in just 3 of the 5 categories? *That's a $600 per month raise!*

When you employ strategies to get (and keep) your spending under control, you instantly make yourself wealthier than you were before.

Later in the program we're going to talk in detail about how you can do seemingly magical things with your expenses by using various strategies across each of the 5 categories of expenses. A treasure chest of ways to potentially save hundreds or even thousands of dollars is right around the corner.

Before we can cover that, we need to look at another important aspect of evaluating your finances: your net worth! Next chapter we'll talk about everything you need to know about debt, savings, and home ownership. Think a down payment is hopeless? Think again! I'll tell you how to find the "hope" you're looking for next chapter!

7 DEBT AND SAVINGS (NET WORTH)

The amount of savings and the amount of debt you have *both* matter when you are buying a home. In today's market, problems in either area can hurt your chances for loan approval.

Too much debt is a bad thing.

Too little savings is a bad thing.

If you have one or both, it's time to start thinking about a fix.

The Difficulty of Saving (The Save And Spend Cycle)

When you're on a tight budget, saving money can seem difficult. Many people find themselves in a pattern that I call "save and spend".

They struggle to save a little money. They probably put it in a savings account. Something comes up, and suddenly they have to spend the money they just saved. Discouraged, they put off saving for a while. Eventually they decide to save again, and once again struggle to put aside a little money into a savings account. Once again, something comes up...

Some people stay in this pattern for a very long time. It's extremely difficult to save money when you have to struggle just to get a little money set aside, and then seemingly around every corner another emergency comes up that you have to use your savings for.

If this pattern sounds familiar to you, don't despair. I've got good news. There **IS** a way out of it, and I'm going to reveal it to you this chapter. But first let's talk about...

The Debt Fund Cycle

Some people don't have any savings at all. There is no emergency fund or money set aside for this or that. Many of these people use their credit cards as a type of "emergency fund".

If you are using your credit cards as an emergency fund, you might find yourself on something similar to the "save and spend" cycle.

You have a chunk of debt you want to pay off. You manage to squeeze extra tight and put a little extra money towards your debt for a couple of months. Then, something comes up. Suddenly you have to dip back into your emergency fund (i.e. your credit card) to take care of an emergency room visit or other unpleasant surprise. You're back where you started. Discouraged, you pay your minimum payments for a while. Eventually you decide to try to pay down your credit card balance again. You manage to squeeze a little extra into a couple of month's payments to make some progress. Then, something comes up.

Cycles like these can be stressful and discouraging. It can feel like there is no hope of ever getting free of the burden of your debt.

There is hope, though. If you are a person who is in a cycle like one of the ones I've talked about here, or you've otherwise fallen into the debt trap, then keep reading. Help is on the way.

The Debt Trap

For people in situations like those mentioned above, debt can grow extremely easily, and at the same time can be insanely difficult to pay down.

It is not uncommon for people to feel *helpless* and *trapped*. The good news is that there is a way out. You don't have to stay in your debtor's prison. You <u>CAN</u> break free.

How?

I'm not an expert on prisons, mind you, but one thing I have heard time and time again:

People can get released early for "good behavior"!

Now I'm going to guess that you're only imprisoned by debt, and not by bars... but the thing you should take from this is that the very first thing that needs to change for you to break free from the prison of your debt is ***your behavior.*** Changing <u>**YOU**</u> may be the key to your freedom.

If you somehow manage to get out of debt *without* changing your behavior, guess what will happen?

You'll be back in the **debt prison** before you can say "credit card!"

You might think you're immune, but it happens all the time. The only way to get out of debt and stay out of debt is to change the way you think, the way you live, and the way you ***spend***.

Cash Flow, Savings, And Debt

We've already talked about income and expenses. We discussed how lenders look at your income and expenses, and covered the five categories of expenses that we'll continue to use at times throughout this program.

If you'll recall, in the expenses segment we added up your expenses and compared them to your income to get your ***cash flow***. Your cash flow is simply a description of the money you have coming in and going out. More specifically, it is best viewed as a measure of **what's left** after all of your expenses have been subtracted from your income each month.

If you have a lot of money left, you have what's called a ***strong positive cash flow***. If you have very little, you may still have a positive cash flow, but a rather weak one.

If you get a negative number when you subtract your expenses from your income, it means you have ***negative cash flow***. Negative cash flow is a problem that won't go away on its own. You have to do something to fix it, and the sooner the better.

"Why are we talking about cash flow now? I thought this chapter was all about savings and debt?"

Earlier we talked about the save and spend cycle and the debt fund cycle. These two cycles describe a process that <u>MANY</u> people who are on tight budgets and struggling with debt or lack of savings go through *several times a year*.

> **And the reason we're talking about cash flow right now is because, believe it or not, a healthy positive cash flow is an important key to breaking these cycles.**

The more positive cash flow you have, the more money you will have to dig out of debt or put towards savings. **Obviously, you will probably need to do both if you want to buy a home in today's market.**

So your cash flow, or your income and expenses, need to be addressed in a big way. Luckily we're going to devote quite a bit of time to learning how to drastically improve your income and expenses later in the program. For now, just understand that **cash flow** is part of the key.

The next thing you need to have is a budget. By "budget", I don't mean a bunch of limits on what you can spend. I mean you need to have a PLAN that describes what you are going to spend.

Video Resource
Video Name: Cash Flow, Savings and Debt
www.YourHomeProgram.com/BookResource

I mean it. Don't set limits on your spending. Just PLAN for the spending that you already do.

This alone can help you break out of the save and spend or debt fund cycles. Here's how...

Let's say you're in the middle of your usual save and spend cycle. You have positive cash flow with about an extra $200 leftover each month. You manage to set some of that aside for a couple of months so that you have $400 in savings. You're making progress.

Then something comes up.

An unexpected vet bill wipes out $300 of your $400 in savings. You feel defeated. You have the (by now familiar) feeling that you are *never* going to be able to accumulate any reasonable amount of savings.

End of story?

Not this time.

You realize that these things regularly come up. So you do the unthinkable. You plan for them! You add a $300 annual unexpected vet bill into your expenses. That's about $25 per month. This means you add $25 per month to your regular monthly expenses for the "unexpected" vet bill. If you're good at managing your checking account and looking ahead, you can even plan for the entire $300 at this time next year.

That's one $300 surprise that you've now planned for.

When the next one happens, plan for that too.

When you take this approach, two things will happen:

1. You will realize that you don't have as much money as you thought. When you start planning for every single expense, even surprises, your positive cash flow might tighten up a little. You may even find that you actually are going backwards and have negative cash flow when you calculate in your *unexpected expenses*. If that's the case, don't worry. We'll show you how to do great things for your cash flow when we talk about improving your income and expenses later in the program.
2. You will be taken by surprise less and less. Eventually, you'll have almost every unexpected hiccup planned for. No, you won't be able to predict the future, but for every hiccup that comes along, you'll probably have an emergency expense already built into the budget to cover it.

After operating in this fashion for a while, eventually your unexpected expenses will no longer be unexpected. They will *be under control!*

THEN you can once again work to put away money for savings, or to pay towards debt... and guess what? You'll actually start to make **progress**. You'll start to *actually save* money!

Savings Momentum

There comes a point when saving money that it almost magically becomes easier to save.

I like to refer to this as a "momentum" effect: the more you save, the more easily you can save even more!

What really happens when you gain this savings momentum?

Part of what happens is that you break out of the "save and spend" cycle. You reach a point where you've planned for most unexpected expenses, and even those for which you do have to dip into savings don't make a big impact on your savings account because you've already built a healthy balance.

The other part may be mostly psychological. When you have $1,000 in savings, having to take $200 out for an unexpected expense doesn't feel as much like defeat. Adding more money to that $1,000—even small amounts—somehow feels better than adding money to a very low or zero balance did. The more savings you have, the more momentum you gain.

Increasing Your Options

As you start to increase your level of savings, you start to increase your *options*—not just with home buying, but in other parts of life too.

The more savings you have, the more options you have.

When you have enough savings, it can give you better options in a number of scenarios:

- ✓ When you have an unexpected expense come up, you have *options* for how to deal with it.
- ✓ When you want to buy a car, you may have the *option* of paying cash for it.
- ✓ When a lender offers you a loan with a low down payment, you have the *option* of paying more and saving big in the long run.

Saving money increases your options. If you haven't already, it's time to start saving!

Your Current Debt And Savings (Your Net Worth)

We have taken the time to evaluate your income and expenses already. Now it's time to look at what most call your "net worth". For the purposes of this program, your net worth is your total savings, cash, checking, and retirement account balances minus your total debt.

The real goal of our net worth calculations is to work towards finding money for your down payment. Because of this, I personally believe you should leave out retirement and any other asset that you wouldn't want to let go of. As a general rule, only include positive assets in your net worth calculations *if* you are willing to let go of them to accomplish your goal of home ownership.

Now let's calculate your net worth. You can use the following worksheet for your calculations.

Assets		Debts	
Savings Account Balances (total)		Credit Card Debt (total)	
Checking Account Balances (total)		Medical Debt	
Retirement Account Balances (total)		Tax Debt	
Cash On Hand		Auto Loan Balances (total)	
Investment Account Balances (total)		Other Debts (total)	
Other			
TOTAL:		TOTAL:	

Now take the totals of each column, and subtract the "debts" total from the "assets" total. This is your net worth.

TOTAL ASSETS	- TOTAL DEBTS	= NET WORTH

If the number under "NET WORTH" is positive, then you may be in pretty good shape. If the number under "NET WORTH" is negative, then don't despair. You aren't alone.

The good news is that while lenders do like to see healthy account balances and positive net worth, having some debt and/or lower or negative net worth won't necessarily keep you out of the running for a home.

If you have excessive debt, it's something you'll need to get under control. There are strategies and tactics you can use to tackle your debt that will increase your chances of success. We'll talk about that in a moment, but first let's keep on the subject of savings for a moment longer and talk about down payments.

Down Payments - Why You Need One, and How to Get It

The standard down payment requirement is usually 20%. Some loans may allow as little as 3.5%, and there may even be special programs that require no money down.

For the sake of planning, it's best to plan on needing money for a down payment. Not only will the bank warm up to you easier if you can offer a down payment, but it will help YOU in the long run too.

Let me explain how.

Imagine the following loan scenario, and imagine paying *zero down*. Because of the zero down payment you will be required to pay PMI (Private Mortgage Insurance), which will increase your monthly payment. Here's what your loan will look like:

Home Price	$200,000
Loan Term	30 Years
Interest Rate (APR)	6%
Down Payment	0%
Monthly Payment (Incl. PMI)	$1,309.10
Total Interest To Be Paid	$231,676.00

Note that this monthly payment includes *over $100* of PMI.

Now let's look at the same scenario, but with a 20% down payment. There is no longer PMI, and look at the bottom line, the "Total Interest To Be Paid".

Home Price	$200,000
Loan Term	30 Years
Interest Rate (APR)	6%
Down Payment	20%
Monthly Payment (NO PMI!)	$959.28
Total Interest To Be Paid	$185,340.80

The monthly payment on this loan is over $300 per month LESS making it much more affordable. And look at the difference in interest to be paid. By putting up 20% for a down payment, you could **save over $45,000 in interest** over the life of the loan! You will get back more than what you paid down in interest saved, AND save over $300 on your monthly payment.

That's a substantial savings, and just one of the reasons you should start saving *now* for a down payment.

The Cost of A Down Payment

When your credit is less than stellar, the bank may require a larger down payment than they otherwise would. A lender that might offer someone with good credit 10% down may require 20% down from a person with bad credit.

With this in mind, you should plan for having a good sized chunk of money for a down payment.

How much money do you need?

That's going to depend on a lot of things, including but not limited to the housing market in your area, the size and cost of home you need, and the exact percentage that the lender requires of you.

If you plan on 20%, you can make your calculations from there based on your local markets.

A 20% down payment on a $100,000 loan is **$20,000.**

A 20% down payment on a $200,000 loan is **$40,000.**

A 20% down payment on a $300,000 loan is **$60,000.**

You may look at those numbers and think that it will be next to impossible to save enough for a down payment. Don't worry, there may be cheaper options—and even if there aren't, you can probably come up with more money for a down payment than you think.

One smart move is to work on your credit for a year or two before buying. While you're waiting, you can save for a down payment, AND improve your credit score. By the time you get your credit cleaned up, you may be able to get approved for a loan with only a 10% down payment, or even less.

Later in the program we'll talk about how you can make *real* progress towards home ownership **before** you fix your credit and have your down payment money.

For now, let's focus on how you can tackle the seemingly impossible task of coming up with the funds for a down payment.

The Down Payment Push

Regardless of the size of your home loan, the down payment is probably going to *feel* like lot of money to have to come up with. It may feel like a lot, but it is **not** impossible.

Let's talk about what can be done about down payments. The following plan can be referred to as the *down payment push*. It's a focused effort. It's a financial sprint to the finish line.

Here's how the plan works:

1. **Research** housing options in your area, and get a feel for what the cost will be like when you decide to buy.
2. Use **every method possible** to pack away money for a down payment over the course of a year.
3. At the end of the year, **evaluate** where you are in relation to your goal. If you need to adjust your plans, do so. If you're reached your goal, then set the money aside for the time when you're ready to buy.

The reason we limit it to a year is simple:

- ✓ It gives you an "end in sight" to the hard work of saving for a down payment.
- ✓ It forces you to *sprint* rather than try to make a marathon out of it. You have to work *fast*.

There are a lot of methods for coming up with down payment funds that you can use for the down payment push. Here is a list, in no particular order.

- **Automatic Savings Payments** - Sometimes the best type of savings plan is one that you don't have to think about. This can be a great help, *especially* after you have broken the save and spend cycle that we talked about above. Many people will find if they can just take $25 out of each paycheck, they can save up $500 or $1,000 in a year without "feeling" it much at all.
- **Part Time Job** - Getting a temporary or part time job can be a really great way to make extra money to go towards a down payment. Remember, you're only committing to a year of *focused effort*. A part time job or other seasonal or temporary income opportunity is a great way to add a boost to your down payment push. An extra $600 per month from a part time job will give many people between $6,000 and $7,000 after income taxes.
- **Take on Odd Jobs** - If you're handy or skilled in carpentry or can bag leaves and run a lawnmower, taking on various odd jobs throughout the year can be a great way to make a few extra bucks. What are your skills? Can you find a way to put them to use in this manner? If so, it could add $1,000 or $2,000 to your down payment *easily*.
- **Tax Refunds** - Do you get a tax refund every year? If so, save it! A lot of people spend their tax refunds before they ever get them. Don't do that. Instead, don't plan on having it to spend at all, and save it instead. Many people get tax refunds in the thousands. This could easily add $3,000 or more to your down payment.

- **Sell Your Stuff!** - Many of us have all sorts of stuff around that we don't use or need. If that's you, then sell your stuff! This could mean anything from selling miscellaneous items on eBay or Craigslist (and making up to $1,000 doing it) to selling bigger ticket items such as boats and cars. Selling your stuff could yield anywhere from $1,000 to $10,000 to go towards your down payment.
- **Get A Roommate** - If you currently rent, then consider getting a roommate to split the rent with. If your rent is currently $800 per month and your roommate pays half, in just one year you could have $4,800 in savings! Just make sure you SAVE that rent money instead of spending it. (Treat it like you would your rent; just put it in a savings account instead.)
- **Spend Less** - Later in this program, we'll go into detail with methods and tactics for getting your spending under control. *What are the possibilities?* What if you could save $100 per month in each of the 5 categories of expenses? In one year you'd have $6,000 extra for your down payment. (We'll spend several chapters on the subject of expenses later in the program.)
- **Utilize Family Gifts And Friendly Loans** - If your parents have the means to help, they can gift you up to $24,000 that you won't have to pay income tax on under current tax law (note: always check with a qualified tax advisor to see what the current laws are and how they apply to your situation.) If you're married, you could get up to $48,000 gifted to you. Even a fraction of that would be helpful! Loans from friends and family can also be an option, but remember that you need to pay them back, so don't get in over your head (and don't jeopardize family relationships or friendships for the sake of your down payment!)
- **Dip Into Retirement Funds** - This isn't always a wise thing to do, but in some markets it can make sense. To be safe, always talk to a qualified financial planner before taking steps that could negatively affect your long-term financial well-being. If the market is right and you have funds available in retirement accounts, it may (in a few cases) be worth it to dip into your retirement funds for a portion of your down payment. This could yield $5,000 or $10,000 for the right person in the right financial situation and market.

Are you doing any math here? Looking down this list of ideas, it should be easy to see how a person who implements every single one of them that they can possibly implement could end up with $20,000, $30,000, or even $40,000 (or more) for a down payment in just one short year.

And this is what the down payment push is all about. Take one year, and go crazy. Do <u>EVERYTHING</u> you possibly can to squeeze every last dime into a fund for your down payment. Commit to one year, and commit to <u>STOPPING</u> after that year is over. When you've reached the end of the year, you can look at what you've saved, and evaluate whether you need any more or not.

Using this method of focused effort, many people who see a down payment as a hopeless endeavor today can end up with the money they need for a 20% down payment in just one short year.

Dealing With Debt

Most of this chapter we've spent talking about how you can save more. There's another side to your net worth calculations that you can also improve on: your *debt*. If you have excessive debt, it can certainly be a problem and an obstacle in the path to home ownership. Lenders want to see that you have your finances under control. In this section and later in the program, we'll talk about what that means for your debt.

Are you buried in debt? Don't worry; there are things that can be done. Let's start by talking about...

The Types of Debt You Have

There are two main types of debt: *secured* and *unsecured* debt.

A secured debt is a debt secured by collateral of some kind. Home loans and auto loans are good examples of secured debts.

An unsecured debt is a debt for which there is no collateral, such as a most credit cards or a personal loan from the bank. Student loans and medical bills would also fall into this category.

Under each type of debt we could add two sub-types. These are types of loans that can occur for either unsecured *or* secured debt.

Installment Loans - These are loans that have a set number of payments that are scheduled in advance. A mortgage and an auto loan (secured debts) are examples of installment loans. Many debt consolidation loans (unsecured debts) are also installment loans.

Revolving Accounts/Credit Lines - These are loans that have no fixed term, and often a variable interest rate, that you have to pay a minimum payment on the account. The loan is not for a fixed amount, but usually has a limit to the amount you can borrow (i.e. a credit limit). You can add to the balance of the loan while paying on it, and carry a balance month to month. Credit cards would fall under this category, as would HELOCs.

The key difference to remember between revolving and installment loans is that installment loans always

have a fixed term. They have an *end in sight*.

Revolving accounts on the other hand, some would argue, are designed to keep consumers in debt *for life*.

Types of Debt And Your Credit Score

For the purposes of your credit score, it's important to understand how debts affect scoring.

Your credit score is affected by the *variety* of debts you have, the *amount* of debt you have, and the amount of "available credit" you have on open ended (revolving) credit lines.

The factor that has the strongest effect on your score is your current balances on revolving accounts compared to the total credit lines of those accounts. This is referred to as your "credit utilization" or "debt to credit ratio", and it accounts for a relatively large portion of your credit score.

The most common problem with credit utilization is using too much of your available credit. This is a problem that can usually be easily addressed by adding additional credit lines to your credit report in order to change your debt to credit ratio. If you have bad credit, you may be wondering how you can "easily" add additional credit lines to your credit report. This is typically done using merchandise or other sub-prime credit lines such as sub-prime Visas or MasterCards. Secured credit cards can also help somewhat, though the credit lines are usually smaller.

The range and types of debts you have also has an effect on your score, but to a lesser degree than your debt to credit ratio.

Lenders And Debt

For purposes of buying a home, too much debt can be a problem.

We've already talked about debt to income ratio and how it can affect your ability to get approved for a home loan. The requirements for debt to income ratios vary, but it is pretty safe to say that if you have excessive debt and high payments, you might have trouble getting approved.

In today's atmosphere of tightened requirements, things like the number of accounts, the amounts of credit lines and types of accounts may also be more closely scrutinized.

Buried In Debt?

Having large amounts of debt is a common problem. Many people have student loans in the range of $20,000 to $40,000. Credit card balances of $8,000 and more are extremely common. Medical debt is also very common. Auto loans are too, as relatively few people pay cash for their automobiles.

Add all this up and it can start to look like a large and impassable mountain of debt.

A home loan will add to your debt. If you're already buried in debt, this could be a problem. Many people find themselves buried seemingly beyond hope, even without a home loan.

If you have excessive debt, it is something you're going to have to deal with sooner or later. Some people will *have to* reduce their debt (i.e. their debt to income ratio) in order to get approved for a home loan. Others will simply want to make sure their debt situation is under better control before taking on a mortgage. Regardless of which camp you're in, let's talk a little about what can be done about the impassable mountain of debt.

Digging Out

If you are buried in debt or just want to get out of debt, there are several options available. I'll give a brief overview of each here. We'll go into much more detail later in the program.

Debt Consolidation - A debt consolidation loan trades one type of debt for another. The key difference is that with a debt consolidation loan, there is a clear end in sight. A consolidation loan usually takes unsecured and revolving debts such as credit card accounts or personal credit lines, and puts those debts into a single installment loan with a fixed payment and (hopefully) reasonable interest rate. Many people can save money on interest by using debt consolidation, simply because they will have a much lower interest rate on the debt consolidation loan than they do on their credit cards.

Debt Management/Credit Counseling - Credit counseling is kind of a poor man's debt negotiation program. The basic idea is that you trade your many monthly payments for a single manageable payment paid to the credit counseling service, which in turn uses pre-arranged agreements with creditors to get interest lowered or removed on your accounts. Credit counseling services can save money, but for many people they can get better results by calling their creditors directly and negotiating workouts for themselves.

Debt Elimination - Debt elimination is the process of using any variety of methods in order to pay off your debts faster. Debt elimination can include any combination of other methods, including those listed here such as debt consolidation or debt settlement. This is probably the most common approach that people use for tackling their debt.

Debt Settlement - Debt settlement is the process of negotiating settlements with your creditors in order to pay off your debts for a percentage of what is actually owed. You can do this yourself, or you can use a debt settlement company. There are pros and cons to each approach. Debt settlement hurts your credit, which may create more hurdles for you if you want to buy a home. As we've already talked about earlier in the program, bad credit isn't "final" and you *can* recover from it, so for those who are truly buried in debt (especially those for whom bankruptcy is an option on the table), debt settlement may be something to consider.

Bankruptcy - If all else fails and you're being sued and pursued by creditors and collection agencies, protecting yourself by filing for bankruptcy may be the best (if not only) option you have. If you're reading this, there's a good chance you're not in this boat. Maybe you've already been down this path... and if so, that's okay. Bankruptcy is something that you can recover from.

If you take nothing else from reading about these options, take this: you have *choices* when it comes to dealing with your debt. If you're in trouble, there's probably a way out. Yes, excessive debt can certainly create a delay on the road to home ownership, but it doesn't mean you're out of the running.

For the purpose of being approved for a home loan, having your finances and payments in a manageable state and being able to demonstrate that you can handle the debt you have is more important than being "debt free".

Your Home Program
Our Advisors Are Available To Answer Your Questions
Call **1-800-245-7349** for Home Ownership Made Easy!

Other Debt Problems

One way in which debt problems can definitely hinder your quest for home ownership is from the credit issues that can arise out of having excessive debt, or in other words, *more debt than you can handle.*

Things like late payments, charge offs, collection accounts, judgments, and tax liens are all the results of debt that somehow got out of hand.

If you have problems like these, you'll be glad to know that **I'm going to give you the tools you need to**

deal with them as this program progresses. The process of fixing these problems is called "credit repair", but before we can get into that, we need to have a good and realistic picture of exactly what your credit situation is.

Next chapter, we'll take a closer look at your credit and the credit problems you have when we do a full and complete assessment of your credit situation.

8 YOUR CREDIT SITUATION

This chapter we're going to do an in depth assessment of your credit situation. I'll walk you through the process of getting and reading your credit reports, and point out some quirks and tricks that you'll want to watch out for. Let's get started with the first step required for this chapter...

Getting Your Credit Reports And Scores

The two main places to get your credit reports AND scores are:

www.myfico.com and www. truecredit.com

You can also get your credit reports (without scores) once a year for free through the official "annual credit report" service by visiting:

www.annualcreditreport.com

You can either get online access to your credit reports or have paper reports mailed to you. For our purposes it doesn't matter which you choose to do.

You'll need to get your credit reports from each of the three major credit bureaus (Equifax, Experian, and TransUnion).

Understanding Your Credit Score

To best gauge your current credit status, it's best if you order your credit scores with your reports. This will require a small expense but it will be helpful to know what your score currently is, especially if you have plans to improve it. (How else would you measure your success in your credit repair efforts?)

Since you'll probably be ordering your credit scores (if you don't already have them), let's talk a little about what makes up your credit score.

There are two main types of consumer credit scores: the FICO score and the VANTAGE score. Here are the main points about these two credit score types that you should know:

- You can get your **FICO** scores from www.myfico.com and your **VANTAGE** scores from www.truecredit.com
- The FICO score is the score currently used by most Mortgage lenders. If you want to use the score that your mortgage lender will probably use, then get your FICO score.
- Generally speaking, if your FICO score is low, your VANTAGE score will also be low, if your FICO score is high, your VANTAGE score will also be high. If you manage to raise a low FICO score, it probably means your VANTAGE score will go up by a comparable amount.
- The FICO and VANTAGE score use different scoring ranges. The FICO score range is 300 to 850, and the VANTAGE score range is 501-990.

According to www.myfico.com, the makeup of a FICO score goes something like this:

- ➢ 35% Payment History
- ➢ 30% Credit Utilization (Debt to Credit Ratio)

- 15% Length of Credit History
- 10% Types of Credit Used
- 10% Credit Inquiries/Recent Credit Search

Do you see the 30% for "credit utilization"? This is precisely why problems with your debt to credit ratio (such as too much debt) can have a negative impact on your credit score. Also notice that 35% of the credit score is for "payment history". Late pays, charge offs, and similar negative items that may appear on your credit report would fall under that category.

According to VantageScore.com, the makeup of the VANTAGE score goes something like this:

- 28% Payment History
- 23% Credit Utilization (Debt to Credit Ratio)
- 9% Amounts of Recently Reported Balances
- 8% Length of Credit History / Types of Credit Used
- 30% Recent Credit
- 1% Available Credit

This breakdown, as you can see, is a little different than the FICO version but similar enough that there aren't going to be huge differences in scoring between the two, other than the obvious difference with regards to the scoring ranges used.

The big thing to take away from both of these scoring breakdowns is that your credit score is about a lot more than your "credit history". It's about more than paying on time or paying late, or having a charge off or a collection account.

Reading Your Credit Reports - The Basics

With the above in mind, it's time to look at the process and method of reading and understanding your credit reports.

Your credit report may contain several types of information. Let's look at the types of information typically included on credit reports:

- **Personal Information** - This includes you name and any alternate spellings or aliases, current and past addresses, phone numbers, and more.
- **Trade Lines** - This will include information on any current and past loans. It will include auto loans, credit cards, medical credit lines, merchandise cards, and any other credit line or debt that reports to the credit bureaus. The listing for each account should include things like an accurate account status, type, and credit limit.
- **Payment History** - Your payment history on accounts reflecting whether you paid on time, or were 60 or 90 days late, etc.
- **Authorized User Accounts** - Accounts for which you are an authorized user but not the account owner may also be listed.
- **Public Records** - Information about bankruptcies, foreclosures, judgments, and more will show up on your credit reports.

- **Collection Accounts** - Information reported by collection agencies can show up on your credit reports too. These accounts are notorious for having inaccuracies that hurt your credit score.
- **Inquiries** - An inquiry is a record of when someone requested your credit report. Inquiries will be listed on your credit report, and whether or not they are "hard" or "soft" inquiries will be indicated in some fashion. Inquiries only stay on your credit report for 2 years.
- **Consumer Statements** - Any "consumer statements" that you have requested to have added to your credit report should also be listed.

Each of your credit reports will have information in these categories on it, though not all of your credit reports will necessarily have the *same* information.

The information on your credit reports can vary between bureaus for several reasons.

First, the reports are from three different credit bureaus with different databases and data collection and retrieval methods. You can expect slight (unimportant) differences for that reason alone.

Other reasons for differences may include things like actual **errors** in the reporting of one bureau or another, and creditors that only report to one or two bureaus versus all three (so that the corresponding account doesn't show up on all three reports).

If you notice big differences from one credit bureau to another, you should pay close attention, because sometimes this can lead to the discovery of costly errors on your credit reports.

How To <u>REALLY</u> Read Your Credit Reports

Reading your credit reports might seem simple enough. There's a little more to it though, and we're going to talk about that now.

Debt To Credit Ratio

One thing to look at when you read your credit reports is your debt to credit ratio.

To calculate your own debt to credit ratio (for each credit report), you do the following:

1. Add up all of your credit limits listed for your open accounts.
2. Add up the balances for any accounts with outstanding balances.
3. Divide the balance total by the credit limit total to get your debt to credit ratio (otherwise known as "credit utilization").

There are a couple of points here that people often miss. The first is that you need to make sure your credit limits that are listed actually match the credit limits on your cards. Inaccurate credit limits can **<u>HURT</u>** your credit score, and some credit card companies have been known to take advantage of this fact. Double check your credit limits to make sure they are correct.

You should also check your balances to make sure the balances being reported are accurate and up to date.

Who Am I? Where Do I Live?

Your personal information is another key area to review. If you have incorrect, old, and outdated personal information being listed on your credit report, then this information should be corrected or removed.

Information that falls into this category includes things like old addresses, old phone numbers, and old or misspelled names and aliases.

The tricky thing about old and incorrect information is that it may be tying you to an old derogatory credit account and you don't even know it! Because of this, removing and correcting this information can sometimes result in a negative account going away without any further interaction needed.

What's Negative?

Another tricky aspect to reading credit reports is understanding which "negative" items really matter. The reality of credit scoring is that the major credit scoring models (FICO and VANTAGE) put ***more weight*** on the information from the **last couple of years**. This means that the more recent a negative item is, the more it will hurt your credit score.

The not-so-obvious side effect to this is that there can be older negative items on your credit report that may not be hurting your credit score much at all.

A paid charge off that is 5 years old probably has very little impact on your credit score, for example. If you have accounts like this, they should be low priority on your credit repair hit list.

Believe it or not, sometimes removing older negative accounts can actually cause your credit score to ***drop***.

People's scores have also dropped when removing a ***bankruptcy*** from their credit report. Yes, you read that right! This is one reason why under certain circumstances it's advisable to have expert help when reviewing your credit reports!

Your Home Program
Our Advisors Are Available To Answer Your Questions
Call **1-800-245-7349** for Home Ownership Made Easy!

Targeting Negative Items

When you are reviewing the items on your credit report, there is one main thing you should be looking for:

<u>INCORRECT</u> REPORTING.

In other words, you're looking for errors of any kind on your report. For each negative item on your report, the dates, the balances, status, and other account details should be correct.

If not, this is "incorrect reporting", and should be the subject of your credit disputes (which we'll cover later in the program!)

The best way to look for incorrect reporting is to take the following two steps:

1. Review each credit report individually. Look for any information that is inaccurate, INCOMPLETE, or that may be unverifiable (as many old accounts are). Look for incorrect or

missing information, or any questionable information that you feel may not accurately reflect reality and should therefore be verified.
2. Compare your three credit reports, and look for inconsistencies between the three. This can be a big help with spotting all kinds of potential problems.

Which Ones Matter?

Going through the process of reviewing your credit reports, you'll probably come up with a list of negative items that you're concerned about.

Which ones matter for the purpose getting into a home?

First and foremost, the ***most damaging*** negative items are the ones that hurt the worst. This usually means the newer accounts, and the unpaid accounts. 90 day late pays and charge offs are more damaging than 60 day late pays. An unpaid collection is probably more damaging than a paid one.

Obviously, getting your score up is the number one priority, so targeting negative items that hurt your score the most makes sense. Sometimes it's difficult to determine exactly what those are, which again, is where expert help can come in handy.

Another consideration when applying for a home loan is that in many cases a lender may require outstanding derogatory accounts to be PAID before you can be approved for a loan.

Video Resource
Video Name: Repossessions and Home Ownership
www.YourHomeProgram.com/BookResource

This means any unpaid charge offs or collections appearing on your report that don't get removed in the credit repair process will probably have to be settled or paid in full.

An important note along the lines of "what matters" is this:

If you have a foreclosure, a short sale, a repossession, or some other credit blemish (such as a bankruptcy) that you are afraid might keep you out of the running for a home, the good news is that there is ***STILL HOPE***.

Soon I'm going to teach you about some **alternative paths to home ownership** that are *almost guaranteed* to keep you in the running, no matter what kind of credit problems you have.

Cash Flow, Net Worth, And Credit

Now we're going to talk about the financial triad that is made up of your cash flow, your credit, and your net worth.

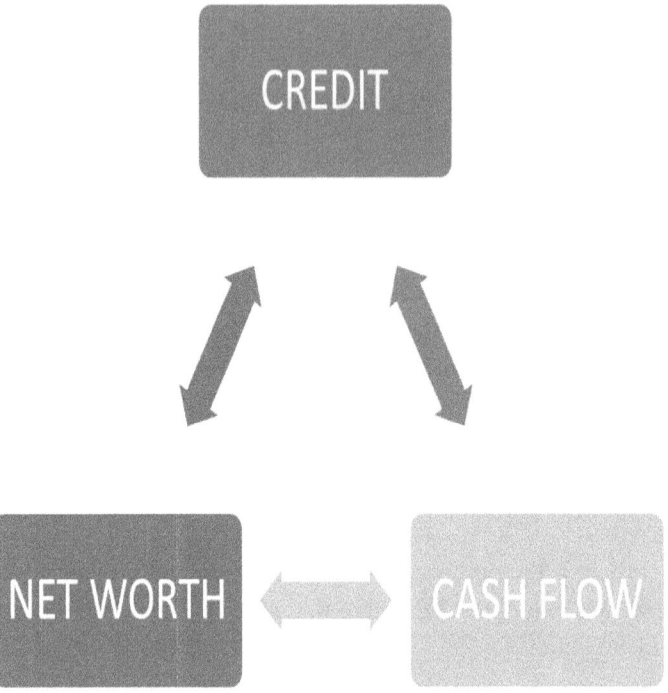

With good credit, everything becomes more affordable. You'll pay less for insurance. You'll pay lower rates on loans. Your mortgage payments and overall cost, as we've already discussed in detail, will be substantially lower with good credit.

So credit, then, affects your **_CASH FLOW_**. Bad credit means you'll be making bigger payments on loans and even rent or insurance policies, and that means _less available cash flow_.

The lower your cash flow, the more difficult it becomes to save money, and the more difficult that it becomes to pay off debt. With low cash flow it also becomes much easier to go deeper into debt, because with every "oops" along the way there is a good chance you'll be dipping into your credit. So your _cash flow_ affects your **_NET WORTH_**.

Your net worth, as we've discussed, can have a negative impact on your credit all by itself. People with negative net worth and very tight cash flow are much more likely to have problems with their credit, as they are more likely to fall behind on payments and eventually have credit problems related to being buried in debt. So both _net worth_ and _cash flow_ can have an impact on your **_CREDIT_**.

If you make improvements in one of these three areas, it will become easier to manage the other two. If you can manage to make improvements across all three of these areas, you will probably be **<u>MUCH</u>** better off as a result.

Credit is part of the puzzle, but it isn't the only part.

Cash flow is part of the puzzle, but if you ignore the other two you're almost certainly going to have problems.

Net worth is part of the puzzle, but without a healthy positive cash flow, net worth is sure to suffer.

The three elements of this financial triad are tied together. They're married. There is no separating them.

If you were to only focus on your credit and ignore the other two parts of the triad, you would almost definitely find yourself in trouble again eventually. They are the three legs of a tripod, and you need to strengthen them all in order to make it work.

For the purposes of being approved for a home loan, you're best chances are going to come about by making a solid effort across all three of these areas to improve your financial situation and, in turn, your life.

Addressing all three of these pieces of the puzzle is important key to your success. (And that's just one thing we're going to teach you to do in this program!)

In a few chapters we'll get down to business with your cash flow, your net worth, and your credit, and we'll talk about what actions you can take with your income, expenses, and the credit repair process in order to successfully address all three pieces of your financial puzzle.

The Credit Meter - How Bad Is It?

What does the *official* credit meter say about your credit? What is your credit score, and what does that really tell you? What do your credit reports tell you that your credit score does not?

Let's find out.

The Official Credit Meter

The official credit meter for **FICO** scores looks something like this:

300 - 579	580 - 619	620 - 679	680 to 719	720 - 850
BAD OR VERY BAD	BELOW AVERAGE/ POOR	AVERAGE	ABOVE AVERAGE/ GOOD	VERY GOOD TO EXCELLENT

People in the below average or poor range have a slim chance of being approved for a home loan. People in the average range have a better chance, but will not get the best rates. People who are in the "above average" range will get better rates, while people in the very good to excellent range will usually qualify for the best interest rates available, assuming that the other two legs of their financial triad (i.e. cash flow and net worth) are steady and strong.

That's the official credit meter. It's what the bank looks at, and it's what most consumers look at, and the official stance that you'll hear from almost every official source is that whatever your meter says is the whole story, *period*.

It isn't the whole story, though, as we're going to discuss in a moment here. So instead of feeling branded and locked into place when you map your credit score on the above "credit meter", you should look one or two spaces to the right and try to imagine what the possibilities may be.

The Unofficial Credit Meter

There is no pretty scale for the unofficial credit meter, because the unofficial meter is about a lot more than just your credit score.

The unofficial credit meter takes the actual data from your credit report into consideration, and not only what it currently is, but what it can or will be in the future.

Let's look at an example so that you can see what I mean.

> *Imagine you have a credit score around 670. You notice that your credit report has several hard inquiries on it that are almost a year old. You also have a late payment on your credit report that you don't believe is accurate.*
>
> *Does your credit score tell the whole story? Is the "official" credit meter accurate?*
>
> *Probably not.*
>
> *With a little work, and a little patience, you can probably find yourself higher up the credit meter in a relatively short amount of time.*

The main difference between the unofficial credit meter and the official credit meter is that the unofficial credit meter takes the possibility of **change** into consideration.

It's not just a question of "where am I now", but a question of "where can I be in a few months if I take action and make changes?"

There are many things that can be done to shape your credit that will give little improvements to your credit score. Add these things up, and some people will get substantial changes of 100 points, 150 points, or more. The possibilities for improving your credit score aren't obvious until you look at your reports with an optimistic (and preferably trained) set of eyes to see what your FICO score alone couldn't possibly tell you.

Later we're going to talk about how you can find and create more options. We'll go into some more detail on ways that you can improve your credit score (not just reluctantly accept it), and we'll even talk about some tactics that make it possible for YOU to get into the home of your dreams, *even with your current bad credit*.

Next chapter we're going to start talking about something you won't want to miss. We'll cover some unique options and strategies that you may not have thought of. I call it "alternative paths to home ownership", and we're going to be talking about it starting next chapter!

9 ALTERNATIVE PATHS TO HOME OWNERSHIP, PART 1: GOVERNMENT ASSISTED OPTIONS

Introduction

Starting this chapter we're going to be talking about alternative paths to home ownership. We'll start by talking about the loan-based options that you've probably heard about, and beginning next chapter we'll move into some exciting new territory that you won't want to miss.

When it comes to government backed home loan programs, the main goal is making a loan reachable for someone for whom it may not have otherwise been reachable.

For government guaranteed loans, the government provides insurance to the lender which the lender can fall back on should the buyer default on the loan. In return, the lender generally gives up what would otherwise be their built-in insurance policy: the *down payment*.

This, in theory, makes the loan more affordable for you (or at least more immediately obtainable) because you won't have to come up with funds for a 20% down payment. There may still be a very small down payment required, or possibly none at all.

FHA Loans

FHA loans are loans from private lenders backed by the Federal Housing Administration. The requirements of any loan program whether government backed or other are subject to change, so always be sure to verify the latest requirements for yourself. The website for the federal housing administration can be found by visiting www.fha.gov. (Note, you will be redirected to HUD.gov as FHA is a part of HUD.)

For people with bad credit, an FHA loan may be a workable loan option. If you've had a bankruptcy you can be approved (as of this writing) for an FHA loan within a year or two. Things like late payments and charge offs won't rule you out, especially if you can show that your credit problems were due to an isolated event such as a job loss or medical problem. Judgments will need to be paid, and tax liens will need to be satisfied. Collection accounts may need to be paid as well.

You may have to wait several years after a foreclosure, but again if you can show that circumstances out of your control led to the foreclosure, exceptions may be made.

FHA loans, as with other home loans, will require varying amounts of paperwork to verify income, employment, and other pertinent data.

As of this writing, the down payment requirement for FHA loans is 3.5%.

The Downside To Government Backed Loans With Little Or No Money Down

The idea of paying little or no money down on a home loan might sound good. Yes, not having to come up with a down payment can certainly make a loan more immediately reachable.

But is it a good idea?

Wisdom tells us that "just because you *can* do something, doesn't mean you *should*." This wisdom will certainly apply to many who are considering loans with little or no money down.

A home loan with no down payment may seem more affordable up front, but in reality the loan is **less affordable** in the long run. You'll pay more in interest and will have to pay Private Mortgage Insurance, which means your monthly payments will be higher and less affordable.

This is an important thing to understand up front if you choose this path. Less than stellar credit combined

Video Resource
Video Name: Get more Cash for Home Ownership
www.YourHomeProgram.com/BookResource

with a low down payment can add up to a loan that you can barely afford.

The two main choices to address this issue are:

1. Find other ways to make the home more affordable. See below for some ideas along these lines.
2. Find another option altogether. We'll be talking about some exciting possibilities in the chapters to come!

In two short chapters we'll start talking about options that can help you get into a home NOW with nothing down AND work on fixing your credit at the same time, and ultimately avoid the pitfalls normally associated with bad-credit home buying. We'll also talk about buying foreclosed real estate for people with bad credit but plenty of cash, or even people with "OK" or BAD credit—and no cash at all!

For now, let's talk about how you can improve on the *affordability factor* of a home loan where you pay little or no money down.

Affordability Options

I'm going to share a few options for making a "little or no money down" home loan more affordable for the long term. These options won't necessarily be available for everyone, but should give you an idea of where to start looking if you choose to go this route either now or down the road.

Your Home Program
Our Advisors Are Available To Answer Your Questions
Call **1-800-245-7349** for Home Ownership Made Easy!

Buy Smaller And Step Up

The most obvious way to save money on a loan is to simply spend less. The strategy here is simple:

Buy a smaller house for 25% to 40% less than your "ideal" home, and once you have saved for a down payment and improved your credit, step up to a better home using your savings (and possibly even equity) as money down on the new home.

What does this accomplish? For one thing, it can make your FHA or VA loan more *affordable*.

Imagine this scenario:

A house that fits your needs and lives up to your wish list costs $200,000. You don't have $40,000 for a down payment, so you are offered a loan at 6% with down payment assistance in which the entire $200,000 is financed.

Under these circumstances, your loan might look something like this:

Home Price	$200,000
Loan Term	30 Years
Interest Rate (APR)	6%
Down Payment	0%
Monthly Payment (Incl. PMI)	$1,309.10
Total Interest To Be Paid	$231,676.00

Instead of signing up for this loan, you reason that since you can't afford the down payment, maybe you should "down size" the loan amount through other means. You find a cheaper home that isn't perfect but that you can be happy with for a few years. The home costs $150,000. With 100% financing, your loan for this home might look something like this:

Home Price	$150,000
Loan Term	30 Years
Interest Rate (APR)	6%
Down Payment	0%
Monthly Payment (Incl. PMI)	$981.83
Total Interest To Be Paid	$173,758.00

As you can see, the loan for $150,000 is certainly more affordable in terms of monthly payment and total interest paid over the course of the loan.

It pays to remember that just because you get approved for a particular loan amount, doesn't mean you should get a loan for that amount.

Simply by reducing the loan amount by 25%, you can make it "as if" you had paid a down payment on a $200,000 loan.

The big plus to this approach is that you can get into a more <u>affordable</u> loan which will enable you to better <u>save</u> for a down payment on your dream house.

Your smaller, perhaps older, and less expensive house becomes a stepping stone to the home you've always wanted.

When it comes time to step up, assuming you have been working on your credit and saving for a down payment, you'll be in much better shape and probably have several attractive loan options to choose from.

Fixer Uppers

HUD has a special program (203(k)) for financing fixer-uppers.

If you have found a "dream house to be" that needs some work to help it see its full potential, an HUD/FHA 203(k) loan may be just what the doctor (or handy man) ordered.

Usually, a bank is going to be reluctant to finance a fixer-upper home. With the HUD 203(k) program, however, it makes financing the cost of the home <u>AND</u> the cost of the necessary repairs possible.

Many times fixer-uppers can be had at a great discount, even with the costs of renovation considered. The HUD 203(k) program has the potential to turn a fixer-upper into a dream home at a reasonable cost.

Foreclosed Homes

Purchasing foreclosed homes has for years been known as a good way to get a great deal on a property. The process can be tricky to navigate, but for a person with some patience, time, and some cash available, buying a foreclosed home can be an attractive option.

We'll talk more about purchasing foreclosed homes next chapter (including how you can buy foreclosed real estate even if you don't have the money-in-hand!)

HUD Homes

A HUD home is a home that the government acquired through foreclosure on an FHA-insured mortgage.

In other words, a HUD home is one of those "government foreclosures" that you've probably seen and heard ads for. The good news is, you can safely ignore those ads.

The official site where HUD homes are listed is located at:

http://hudhomestore.com/HudHome/Index.aspx

Often times 203(k) eligible fixer-uppers can be found in the HUD home listings, along with other homes for which the prices can be quite reasonable.

HUD Good Neighbor Programs

People in law enforcement, pre-k through 12th grade teachers, firefighters, and EMTs who live or want to live in certain areas designated as "revitalization areas" may be eligible for HUD's Good Neighbor program. Through this program, a person who can commit to living in a home for 3 years can acquire a home at a 50% discount off the list price.

While this program is restricted to people in very specific situations, it could save a bundle of money if you meet the necessary criteria.

State And Local Home Buying Programs

There are various state and local programs, some of which are funded in part through the federal government, which may be available to help get you into a home at a price that won't break the bank.

The HUD website has links to information on such programs, available at:

http://www.hud.gov/buying/localbuying.cfm

An example of this type of program would be a "homebuilder" program, in which several families work together to build each-other's homes under the direction of a qualified expert. These types of programs can make home ownership more reachable for some... but availability varies by state and specific location.

Better Options?

After researching the available options, you might find yourself starting to wonder:

"Isn't there a better way?"

Yes, I believe there is.

The problem is that when you get a loan—ANY LOAN—with bad credit, you get an *expensive* loan that has a greater chance of becoming difficult to afford in the future. Skipping the down payment only makes that loan more expensive.

If you decide to rent while you fix your credit, you're essentially "throwing money away" on rent for the entire time it takes to get your credit into shape and save for a down payment. Sure, you'll get a better interest rate (assuming interest rates on home loans don't rise in that time), but you'll pay a good chunk of money right into your landlord's pocket in the meantime.

If your rent is $800 per month, you'll be spending $9600 per year on rent. If you rent for 3 years while working on your credit and saving for a down payment, you'll pour $28,800 into your landlord's pocket and have nothing to show for it.

Don't get me wrong, I'm an advocate of improving your credit before you dive into a home loan. But I believe there may be a third option—a better way—where you can *realize* your dream of homeownership <u>AND</u> work on your credit at the *same time*.

What I'm talking about is rent-to-own programs, and we're going to talk about how you can use rent-to-own programs to **change the rules** of the home ownership game *very* soon. (If you want to learn the right way to do rent-to-own, then stick around!)

10 ALTERNATIVE PATHS TO HOME OWNERSHIP, PART 2: BUYING FORECLOSED REAL ESTATE

Introduction To Buying Foreclosed Homes

We've already mentioned foreclosures when we brought up HUD homes last chapter. Buying a foreclosed home can certainly be considered an "alternative path to home ownership".

I'm going to tell you up front that running out and attempting to buy foreclosed real estate is <u>NOT</u> something that is likely to be a smart move for 99% of the people reading this. It's just too easy to mess up and get in trouble. There are much better ways to do things that are much less prone to errors and problems—paths that are a lot more "user friendly", to say the least.

That said, with all the apparent interest in foreclosed real estate (surely you've seen the ads), I thought it would be beneficial to spend a chapter covering it with you.

Cash Rich, Credit Poor

Many of the government backed loan options can be described as catering to the "cash poor, but credit acceptable" crowd. This means they are people who simply don't have the cash to put down on a loan, they may not even have cash for closing costs, but their credit is acceptable enough to get them in the door.

Buying foreclosed real estate is <u>NOT</u> for people belonging to that group.

There is another group of people who the foreclosed real estate market *might* be a better fit for. Sometimes people have credit problems, but still happen to have a lot of spare cash. One leg of the financial triad has suffered, essentially, but they've managed to keep (or get) the other two (meaning cash flow and net worth) on track.

Some people in this group are what you might describe as "cash rich, credit poor". They don't have the credit to get approved for a loan, but they have a lot of cash that they could use if they could only find the right deal.

It is ***possible*** that it can pay off for people in this position to consider their options in the area of buying foreclosed real estate. (Note, that if you're in the "credit poor, cash poor" boat, there may be one potential option tied to foreclosures that you could look into... we'll talk about that later!)

The fact that buying foreclosed real estate usually means a ***cash transaction*** puts this option out of reach for many. The fact that buying foreclosed real estate can be a complicated process that even trips up the experts makes it *questionable at best* for many others.

How Buying Foreclosed Real Estate Works

The traditional method of buying foreclosed real estate usually involves the following basic steps:

1. Get very familiar with state and local laws governing the foreclosure process.
2. Find the listings and properties, find a deal that looks good, start your research.

3. Get your paperwork and your offer in order, do a title search, do your due diligence to make sure this deal is what you think it is and doesn't have any of the (common) pitfalls that can come with buying foreclosed real estate.
4. Show up at the public auction and bid. If you win, pay 10% (or the required percentage down), and pay the rest of the money for the property within 30 days. (Make sure you get title insurance!)

From what I've said so far, you are probably thinking that it's a lot more complicated than the above 4 steps make it look.

It is.

Let's talk a little more about the process...

Where Can I Learn About The Laws Related To Foreclosures?

It is imperative that you be familiar with your state and local laws related to foreclosures. Places that can get you started are websites like hud.gov, realtytrac.com, and foreclosures.com. *(Note: The commercial sites can be a bit tricky to navigate without signing up for something, so watch out!)*

Do yourself a favor at this stage: don't try to buy foreclosed property on your own!

That might *sound* silly but it's not. Buying foreclosed property can be quite complicated, and there are too many ways to get tripped up to not consider enlisting the help of a qualified real estate professional or an attorney.

You wouldn't do your own brain surgery, *would you?*

Of course not.

Don't do this on your own, either.

Where Can I Find Foreclosure Listings?

Foreclosure listings can be found in local newspapers (those with a "public notices" section), posted at the courthouse, or online. The best websites to check for foreclosure and REO ("Real Estate Owned"—we'll talk about this in a moment) listings include:

www.homepath.com (Fannie Mae)

www.homesteps.com (Freddie Mac)

www.hudhomestore.com/HudHome/Index.aspx   (HUD Homes)

va.equator.com (VA Foreclosed Homes)

www.realtytrac.com (Also a good place to learn about the process of buying foreclosures.)

So What Does REO Mean?

REO stands for "real estate owned", and it means properties that have been acquired and are owned by the bank. REO properties count as liabilities on bank's balance sheets, so banks want to get rid of them. You can find REO listings by searching certain sites (above) on the web or contacting a real estate agent in your area.

The plus of REO listings for you is that sometimes REO deals can be had at good prices, and they don't have all the potential pitfalls associated with buying a foreclosed home at auction. They aren't necessarily always clean and clear deals either, though, so you still have to be careful. REO properties are often sold "as is", and like foreclosures, may not turn out to be the "great deals" that they appeared to be on paper (or on your computer screen).

Do I Really Have To Pay Cash?

For REO deals, the answer is usually "no" __IF__ you can qualify for financing. For reasons that we've already discussed, you may be better off fixing your credit and getting your finances in order first before you get into a mortgage. If you're buying a foreclosure at a public auction, then cash is about your only option. One approach that some have used is having a relative use available cash to purchase the property, which the "real" buyer in turn buys from the relative once the financing is in order.

There is one more alternative that we'll talk about shortly in which you can avoid the "cash" probably __AND__ possibly involve a few of the problems inherent with buying foreclosed real estate.

What Kind of Deals Are Possible?

As I've already mentioned many—and what you may perceive to be *too many*—times, buying a foreclosed property is risky as there are a number of possible pitfalls. I am saying this so much mostly because it is *true*. If you don't know what you're doing, you can end up buying your way into quite a mess.

Most people's dreams of foreclosure deals (and those magical stories that their dreams are based on) aren't exactly representative of what most foreclosure deals actually amount to. Many foreclosed properties are in serious need of some serious work (if not demolition). Many "deals" may not turn out to be deals at all.

I guess this is a good time to talk about some of the common problems associated with foreclosure deals...

Foreclosure Buying Pitfalls and Problems

If I haven't scared you away from buying foreclosed real estate yet, maybe this will. Let's look at some of the problems with purchasing foreclosed real estate.[2]

1. **It can be complicated and confusing.** The process of researching everything that needs to be researched and making offers and bids, and determining what exactly you're getting for your bid, is all quite complicated. This is why we recommend consulting with an expert if you decide to buy foreclosed real estate: because it takes an expert to understand and navigate the process!
2. **It is easy to not get what you think you're getting.** In part due to #1, it can be difficult to know whether you're actually going to end up with the great deal that you think you're getting. Some people have gone to foreclosure auctions and bought second mortgages, for example, without knowing it. Oops.
3. **Possibility of title problems and other undisclosed issues with the property.** A title search and title insurance are essential, but there may be other problems with the property that the seller

---

[2] I should note here that shopping REO properties may eliminate some of these issues (some, but not all!)

(the bank) won't exactly be forthcoming with. As an example, you may buy a home to live in only to find that you cannot occupy the home until certain repairs are made. Those repairs could be costly, and your deal may no longer be a deal!
4. **Bought and sold "as is".** You don't get the perks you might get through buying the normal way. The house may be in serious need of repair, and that's just something you have to deal with.
5. **Cash only means you're 100% invested.** Using retirement money to buy foreclosed real estate probably wouldn't be the smartest move for most people. When you finance a home, you're only into the home for the amount of down payment, upgrades/updates, and payments that you've put into it. When you pay cash, sure you might get the home at a 20% or 30% discount... but you are 100% invested. The only way to get your money back out is to use a home equity loan or sell the home. The cash only factor also means that some people simply won't be able to go this route.

A Possible Alternative For The Rest Of Us

Buying foreclosed real estate isn't for everyone, but there are some people out there who do it all the time, and do it quite well.

If you're in the "credit poor and cash poor" boat, I'm going to give you the one scenario under which buying foreclosed real estate might be a good move for you.

Let's say, for the sake of example, that you found a truly perfect foreclosed real estate deal. The house is the perfect house, in the perfect neighborhood, but: you don't have the cash, OR the credit to buy it.

The auction is held, and someone else gets the house. End of story? Maybe not.

One method that some people have used to take advantage of foreclosed real estate deals and either use financing or even a rent to own option, is to **approach the winning bidder** on the property, and offer *that* person a deal.

This isn't a sure thing, and it isn't always going to work, but with the right person in the right situation with the right deal... it *could* work.

Some people have gotten started investing in foreclosed real estate in a manner similar to this. They go to auctions not to bid, but to meet the bidders. They develop a rapport and eventually even relationships with the regulars. Then when the time is right and the deal looks good, they approach the winning bidder with an offer.

For the winning bidder, this can be a welcome opportunity to avoid some hassle they might otherwise have to endure and get a quick return on their investment. Even a rent-to-own offer might be acceptable to a winning bidder in the right circumstances.

Using this approach, a person with bad credit AND cash problems could potentially work their way into the home of their dreams at a great price, and with the best financial arrangement possible.

Important Note: Investing in real estate and buying foreclosed real estate are complicated matters. Always consult with an attorney and/or a qualified real estate professional before signing up for anything we've discussed this chapter. For more information on buying foreclosed real estate and REO properties, see hud.gov, realtytrac.com, and homepath.com.

11 ALTERNATIVE PATHS TO HOMEOWNERSHIP, PART 3: AN INTRODUCTION TO RENT TO OWN PROGRAMS

We've already talked about how buying a home with bad credit can be a problem. Often with bad credit, lenders want a bigger down payment. As we discussed previously, simply having *bad credit* can make it difficult to get your cash flow under control, which in turn makes it difficult to come up with the funds for a down payment.

In the previous two chapters we talked about a couple of fairly common "alternative paths" to home ownership that could (ideally) ease this burden.

The first option we discussed was government sponsored programs. Homeownership programs featuring government backed loans have the strength of requiring little or no money down. However, a major issue with these options is that if your credit is bad, you could very well still be ruled out, especially in an atmosphere where lending has been tightened. The "little or no money down" option also makes the resulting loan *less affordable* in the long run.

We also talked about buying foreclosed real estate. There are numerous problems with this approach, one of which is the fact that many foreclosure sales are cash transactions. The ones that will qualify for financing will probably not be the "deals" that you imagined, and you'll be back in the boat of needing a loan but having bad credit and either not qualifying at all, or not qualifying for a loan with terms you can afford.

This chapter, we're going to start our discussion about a not-so-common path to home ownership: rent to own.

When rent to own is done right, it has the capability of being the ultimate answer for the bad credit home ownership question. It is, for a person with bad credit, a far better option than either of the previous two alternative paths to home ownership that we've discussed. There is a good possibility that a person could **combine** the rent to own approach with one of the approaches from the last two chapters, which is a powerful and exciting possibility. The rent to own program is the key part of the puzzle, though. It's what has the capability to give the options we've discussed in the last two chapters the nitro-boost of home buying power that they are missing.

Video Resource
Video Name: Rent-to-Own: Lease Option
www.YourHomeProgram.com/BookResource

The Advantages Of The Rent To Own Approach

In certain markets, the rent to own approach can be <u>extremely</u> advantageous. In most markets, it can work (and work quite well) for the person with bad credit.

Imagine for a moment a scenario in which there has been a big upset in the housing market. Everybody is nervous, the government is changing the rules, and a lot of people have a lot of homes to sell that they can't seem to get rid of.

There are sellers who are struggling and ***need*** to sell. There are buyers who want to buy but don't qualify because of the tightened lending restrictions.

In a situation like this, the rent to own approach can do amazing things. It can match up a non-qualifying buyer with a desperate seller, and give them **both** what they need to solve their housing dilemmas.

Even in situations where the market isn't quite so rough, the rent to own approach can be a life saver. When you have bad credit, you're often faced with two options:

1. Buy now and pay dearly for the decision
2. Don't buy now (or at all)

Many people in the bad credit camp don't even have the first option available to them.

The rent to own approach gives them yet another option. In fact, it gives them a ***far superior option***.

Here are the main advantages of the rent to own approach:

- ✓ **Another "Now" Option** - Rent to own gives you another "now" option. You don't have to wait to get into the home of your dreams with rent to own. You can do it <u>now</u>.
- ✓ **The Perfect "And" Option** - Rent to own is perfect for people with bad credit who need to work on their credit and improve their finances. *Why?* Because they can use the rent to own approach ***and*** improve their credit and their finances, and ultimately be in the best position possible to be approved for a *quality* loan. Rent to own works perfectly in conjunction with other alternative paths to home ownership, and with credit repair and debt reduction and more. It's the perfect "and" option for people whose situation warrants a well-rounded approach. (The rent to own system that I'm presenting to you in this program is the ultimate and perfect example of this.)
- ✓ **Buying Time At The Best Possible Price** - The rent to own approach gives you the time you need to repair your credit and save for a down payment, while <u>ALSO</u> giving you the opportunity to make real progress towards home ownership. Sure, you could fix your credit and get your finances in order without using the rent to own approach, but this approach allows you to "buy" the time you need to do those things, and also get a return on your investment.
- ✓ **A Flexible Approach** - If you signed up for a sub-prime loan *today* with a large down payment and a so-so interest rate, then guess what? *You're stuck!* With a rent to own arrangement done right, you're *anything but stuck*. You have choices. You have flexibility. If you sign up for a rent to own program today and things don't go the way you planned, you aren't locked into your decision to buy.
- ✓ **Real Progress** - When you do rent to own the right way, you'll make real progress towards home ownership as you ***earn equity*** through doing things like paying your rent and making improvements to the property. I'll explain exactly how to do this later.
- ✓ **Try Before You Buy** - Renting to own is the ultimate try before you buy approach. Sometimes when a person buys a home, they find out about an unadvertised "downside" to the home after

moving in. These downsides and would-be deal breakers can be quite serious. With rent to own, you'll have the option to walk away should you encounter any nasty surprises after moving in. You can truly "try before you buy".

Problems Solved

With its many strengths and advantages, the rent to own approach solves several problems associated with other paths to home ownership. Here's a rundown:

PROBLEM - Can't get approved for a loan with bad credit.

SOLUTION - Rent to own. You can start buying **now**, *while* you work on your credit.

PROBLEM - Can only get approved for loans with high interest rates.

SOLUTION - Rent to own. You can work on your credit and go the traditional loan route after the rental period is over (when your credit is better).

PROBLEM - Can't afford the large down payment that the lender wants.

SOLUTION - Rent to own. With the rent to own approach you can get into the home **now**, and *still* have the **time** you need to save for a down payment.

PROBLEM - Can get a loan with little or no down, but the monthly payments are then barely affordable.

SOLUTION - Rent to own! Save money in the long run by renting to own, saving for a down payment, and getting a *more affordable* loan than you otherwise could have gotten.

PROBLEM - Don't have the necessary cash to buy the once-in-a-lifetime foreclosure deal.

SOLUTION - Approach the winning bidder with a win-win rent to own offer!

As you can see, the rent to own approach solves its fair share of problems.

Are there problems that "renting to own" can't solve?

Sure there are. Let's talk about those now...

Problems That Renting To Own Won't Fix

There are problems for which "rent to own" is not the solution. There are situations in which renting to own won't work.

Here are a few problems that a rent to own approach can't fix.

Apathy

If you are apathetic about your credit and financial situation, a rent to own program probably won't be much help to you. The greatest benefit of a rent to own program is that you can essentially build equity, fix your credit, save for a down payment, and live in the home that you intend to buy—and do it *all* before you ever get approved for a loan. If you don't take action on the other steps and stop when you get your foot in the door, you may not ever actually be able to take ownership of the house. What I'm saying is that the rent to own approach requires *action* and *effort* on your part. You have to work on your credit AND save for a down payment during the period in which you are renting in order for this to work. If you are apathetic, lazy, or otherwise procrastinate away your opportunity, then even the magic of the rent to own approach probably can't help you.

Lack of Responsibility

You have bad credit. That's okay, and I'm not going to hold it against you. A rent to own approach can be a real life saver for a person with bad credit who is trying to get things turned around. If, however, a person is irresponsible and careless with their credit throughout the rent-to-own process, they will probably not make any real progress towards home ownership. In order for this to work, you have to be responsible and take care of your credit and your finances. (If you're concerned, don't worry... I'm going to give you tools in this program to help you do that.)

Unrealistic Goals

If you make $40,000 a year and you want to get into a million dollar home, a rent to own program isn't going to help you. (In fact, nothing will.) That's a bit of an exaggeration of course, but the simple point of the matter is this: in order for a rent to own approach to work, you need to be able to *afford* the home in the first place. Using rent to own as a stepping stone to a loan where you'll be stretched beyond your means will end in nothing but financial ruin and broken dreams. Keep your goals realistic, and be sensible about what you can and can't afford.

Title Problems

If a property has title problems and the seller/landlord can't provide a clear title, a rent to own approach will **not** magically make the title problems go away. The thing to understand about title issues is that regardless of any rent to own agreement, title problems can cost you the deal. You can lose valuable money and time. Obviously, it's best to steer clear of properties where the seller can't provide a clear title.

The Seller's Financial Problems

If a seller is in foreclosure or upside down on the loan, the rent to own approach probably won't work with that seller or property.

Maximum Potential

When you use a rent to own approach correctly, one of the greatest benefits is that it empowers you to **maximize** the potential of your cash flow, your credit, and your net worth.

Remember the financial triad that we talked about earlier in the program?

With a rent to own program you can make the most of your financial triad, starting right where you are.

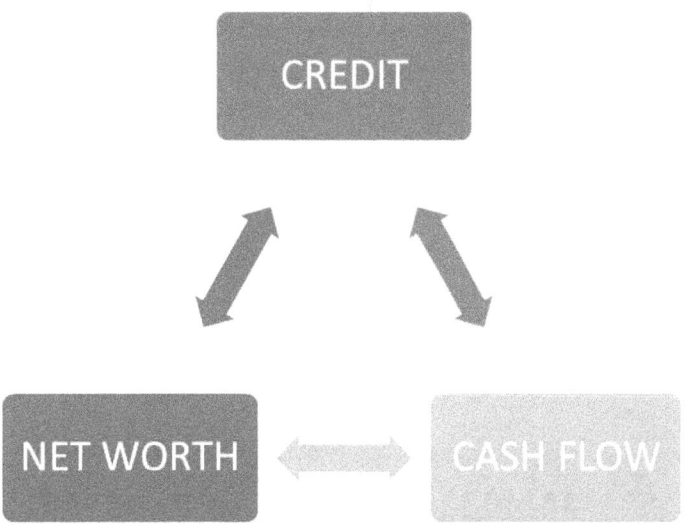

You can make the most of your **credit** by essentially bypassing the traditional credit system for a year or two, while *still having your payments count towards the purchase price of your home*. You can build equity with your perfectly bad credit, and no lender can stop you!

You can make the most of your **cash flow** by taking the time in which you are renting to improve on your financial situation. If you're tight now, but you know how you can improve your financial situation, a rent to own program can give you the time and space you need to make the necessary changes to your income and expenses. When it comes time to go through with the purchase, you'll have a healthier financial picture moving forward with the process.

You can use the rental period of a rent to own agreement as an opportunity to pay down debt and increase your savings, thus improving your **net worth**. One of the key components of a proper rent to own plan is saving a bundle of money for your down payment. You'll be much better positioned for the long run because you're 30 year fixed mortgage will be more affordable with a hefty down payment.

For those in the "cash poor, credit poor" boat who are struggling with each aspect of their financial triad, a properly structured rent to own plan can give them the most bang for their buck right now, and give them the breathing room they need to get things in order for later.

The person who can't afford the high interest loan can buy time to work on their credit and their cash flow.

The person who can't afford the big down payment will have time to save for it.

The person whose credit prevents them from qualifying for a home loan can get into a home *before* their credit is fixed, and then work on turning their credit around.

The Best Sub-Prime Option

Hopefully you can see that when done right, a rent to own program is one of the best options—if not *the* best option—for would-be home buyers struggling with bad credit.

Other sub-prime home buying paths have historically been littered with potholes and pitfalls. ARMs and other loans designed for the sub-prime market have been known to backfire in a serious way. This is, in part, due to the fact that bending and twisting up the loan terms so that a buyer can squeeze in the door only goes so far. A serious downside to ANY of these loan-based strategies is that if things take a turn for the worst, the buyer's only way out is selling the home, or (perhaps more often than not) through foreclosure or deed in lieu of foreclosure.

A rent to own program works differently though, and has very little chance of coming back to bite in the way that the other sub-prime home buying options have a tendency to do.

The program that I'll present over the next few chapters is structured in such a way as to put the bad-credit home buyer in the best possible situation, with the most options, with the best chances of success.

Starting next chapter we'll get into the details of how rent to own programs work, and how you can use them best to your advantage.

Video Resource
Video Name: Rent-to-Own: Process
www.YourHomeProgram.com/BookResource

12 RENT TO OWN: HOW IT WORKS

This chapter we're going to cover the basics of how the rent to own approach works. Let's get right to it, shall we?

The 3 Required Elements For A Rent To Own Approach To Work

In a best case scenario, a rent to own arrangement will involve the following three things:

1. A buyer who will benefit from a rent to own approach.
2. A motivated seller.
3. A property that the buyer *wants* to live in, that will serve the buyer's needs.

That might sound pretty simple, but there is more to it than meets the eye. These 3 pieces are an integral part of the rent to own puzzle, so let's talk about each in a little more detail.

The Right Buyer

A few different types of buyers can benefit from a rent to own approach. If you're reading this, there is a good chance that you are one of them.

People with bad credit and low savings/net worth are probably the top candidates for rent to own arrangements. If you can't get approved for a loan or the loans for which you can get approved have undesirable terms, the rent to own approach may be a good fit for you. Rent to own is a perfect option for the "cash poor, credit poor" crowd.

People who are on the road to recovery with their credit and ready to make some progress towards home ownership are also typical rent to own candidates. With rent to own, you can give yourself a little more time for your credit to heal, *and* start the home buying process. You just need the right seller and the right property to get started!

Sometimes a person will want to move to an area or buy a home but they are unsure of the decision in one way or another. Maybe they don't know the neighborhood. Maybe they are completely new to the city and don't know which part of town they will want to live in. In these cases, a rent to own agreement can be a great tool because it allows a person to rent but have the *option* to buy if they decide they want to stay.

For a rent to own program to work, there needs to be a buyer for whom the rent to own program makes sense. I'm guessing that in this case, that buyer is *you*.

The Right Seller

For a rent to own approach to work, there needs to be a seller who is (ideally) highly motivated or otherwise open to the rent to own option.

A lot of different types of sellers may fit into this category.

One example is a seller who has moved into another home already and hasn't been able to sell their old home. These sellers are often juggling two house payments, and after a few months that can start to get old!

Another example might be a landlord who owns rental houses who is ready to sell one or more of their rental houses. This may be a person who has been in the rental business for years, and is ready to "cash out" and retire. It may be a landlord who simply *needs the money* that selling one of their rental homes can bring in.

In reality, virtually anyone with more than one home who is trying to sell one of them could easily fit into this category: people who inherited property; people with vacation homes; recent movers—you get the idea. People in these scenarios will tend to have a sense of *urgency* about selling their home. That's basically what you're looking for.

The sellers that you should watch out for (i.e. that are *not* good for a rent to own approach) are the ones who are in financial trouble. We'll talk more about this later.

Video Resource
Video Name: Rent-to-Own: Lease Option
www.YourHomeProgram.com/BookResource

The Right Property

The best property to rent to own is the property that you *want* to live in and that you can *afford*. Essentially, you want to try to get as close as you can to your *best case scenario* home. As I said last chapter, your goals need to be realistic here. By "best case scenario" I mean the home that is *as close as you can get to your dream home considering your financial constraints and what you can reasonably expect to afford.*

The right property won't stretch you too far. It won't be "too much house".

It **will** be a property that you can see yourself living in for years. It will be a property that you can be *happy* to call <u>home</u>.

This can be tricky to find, but not impossible. I'll give you some tools and ideas to help with finding the right home in a couple of chapters.

Some people use the rent to own home as their first step, and then step up to their ideal home 5 or 10 years down the road. This is a perfectly reasonable game plan if it is an approach you're comfortable with. Going this route you can afford to be a **little** less picky about the home you choose to rent to own. *(You still need to get a home that you can live with and that you will be happy with, just in case things don't go as planned.)*

How The Rent To Own Process Works

The rent to own process requires several basic steps. We'll go over them now.

1. **Step 1 - Find the right seller and the right home.** The first phase of the rent to own process it the house hunting phase. You could also consider it "seller hunting" since you need to find the right *seller* too.
2. **Step 2 - Create and Sign The Rent To Own Paperwork.** Like with any contract or agreement, there is paperwork involved in the rent to own process. The main three parts of a rent to own agreement are the Rental Agreement, the Lease Option Agreement, and the Sales Contract. (We'll go into detail about rent to own contracts and agreements later in the program.)
3. **Step 3 - Pay Any Agreed Upon Deposits And Fees.** This usually involves a security deposit, and what is called an "option fee", which is essentially an amount of money you pay to keep the option open to *buy the home* at the price specified in the rent to own paperwork. We'll talk more about option fees and security deposits when we get into the details of rent to own contracts later.
4. **Step 4 - The Rental Period.** As part of your rent to own agreement, there is usually a *rental period* specified. This is the period of time in which you will pay rent on the house and all aspects of the rent to own agreement which apply to your paying rent on the house will be in effect. (For example, during the rental period, the portion of the rent which has been agreed upon to be applied to the purchase price of the house (called the "option credit") will be so-applied.) The rental period is also your opportunity to make the necessary changes to your financial picture, such as repairing your credit or improving your income and expense scenario. The rental period, also called the "option period", is the period of time in which you retain the **option** to buy the home according to the previously agreed upon terms.
5. **Step 5 - Purchasing The Home.** This actually takes place sometime *during* the rental period, often towards the end. This is when you exercise your option to buy the home. This is the step you will take after you get your credit and finances in order, and can get approved for suitable financing.

There are details in this process that we'll cover more fully later, but this should give you an idea of the basics. To fully understand this process and how it can benefit a person in the right situation, it will help to look at an example scenario. Let's do that now...

An Example Rent To Own Scenario

Let's take a more detailed look at a rent to own scenario to demonstrate just how valuable this tool can be.

> Jacob wanted to buy a house, but he was afraid his bad credit and limited savings might be an issue. Jacob decided to look into his options, so he went to a lender to see if he could qualify for a loan.
>
> The lender told Jacob that he <u>could</u> qualify even with his bad credit. *Good news, right?*
>
> Not quite.
>
> Because of Jacob's bad credit, he would be required to pay the full 20% down on the home. For a $150,000 home this means Jacob would have to come up with $30,000! This seemed too far out of reach for Jacob. He usually had only about $200 leftover at the end of each month, and it would take him a very long time to come up with $30,000 at that rate!
>
> Here are the loan terms that Jacob was pre-approved for:

Home Sale Price	$150,000
Loan Term	30 Years
Interest Rate (APR)	7.3%
Down Payment	20%
Monthly Payment Including Taxes	$971.44
Total Interest To Be Paid	$176,168.40

With taxes added in, the payment would have been over $150 ***more*** than the $800 that Jacob was paying for rent at the time.

Jacob knew that he had to do something different. The $30,000 down payment was well out of his reach since he had only $3,000 in savings, and the house payment would leave him with a measly $50 per month left in his budget, which *wasn't enough*.

Jacob decided to take action and make some changes. He decided to use "rent to own" to make progress on buying a home while he worked to get his finances in order.

Jacob found a real estate agent who was willing to help him seek out a home that he could rent to own. They eventually found a seller who was willing to enter into a rent-to-own agreement.

After working out the details of the deal, Jacob and the seller came up with a rent to own agreement that looked something like this:

- The sale price of the house would be set at $135,000. Jacob aimed for ***less*** than he was pre-approved for originally so that he would be sure to get a loan that he could handle.
- Jacob's rent would be set at $800.
- $300 of Jacob's monthly rent would go against the final sale price of the house.
- Jacob would rent the house for 3 years (the lease term) and have the option to buy the home at any time during those 3 years.
- Jacob would pay an "option fee" to the seller of $3,500. This is a one-time non-refundable fee that Jacob would **not** get back. Jacob would also pay a $500 deposit which he would get back after the lease term.

Jacob had to work hard to come up with an extra $1,000 to cover the option fee and deposit. He worked some extra hours, and borrowed a little money from family and friends.

Once he had the money he went through with the agreement and the signing of the paperwork.

Then, Jacob went to work!

Jacob knew that his financial triad was holding him down. He knew he needed to improve his credit and his net worth, and that improving BOTH of those would be easier if he could improve his cash flow.

Jacob worked on his expenses and income, and between making some changes on his taxes and cutting back on some expenses, Jacob was able to come up with an additional $300 per month of "extra" income.

Next Jacob went to work on his savings. Jacob took a number of steps and took on extra income generating work as part of his "down payment push" plan. Between his extra income from side jobs and the extra money he freed up in his cash flow, Jacob was able to put away $650 per month to go towards a down payment. Jacob also took on some seasonal work for a couple of summers which added another $4,000 to his down payment funds. Jacob

Jacob also went to work on his credit. After Jacob freed up some cash flow and had some extra money coming in, he was able to put aside a small amount of money each month to work on improving his credit.

After about one and a half years, Jacob had saved $15,700 to go towards a down payment, and was making good progress towards improving his credit. He decided to relax a little and not work so hard, and from then on put away $150 per month towards his down payment fund.

10 months later, Jacob checked his credit and found his score had increased substantially. He contacted a lender to see what his loan might look like, and things looked good.

Jacob decided to exercise his option to buy the home he was renting, and went through the process to secure the financing for the home.

He had a total of $17,200 to go towards a down payment, and had $8400 in "option credits" which would be taken off the price of the home.

Since Jacob's credit had improved substantially, he qualified for an FHA loan with a 3.5% down payment. Since he had more than that for the down payment, he used it, and this is what his final loan ended up looking like:

Home Sale Price	$126,600
Loan Term	30 Years
Interest Rate (APR)	5%
Down Payment	$17,200
Monthly Payment Including Taxes	$773.64
Total Interest To Be Paid	$123,807.00

Jacob's house payment ended up a little less than what he paid for rent. He got a better interest rate with his better credit, and came out much better on the loan, saving over $50,000 in interest.

Because Jacob already made several changes that improved his financial situation, he ended up much better off than he started out. He had more cash flow, better credit, and a home he could call his own.

You might be thinking at this point about the money Jacob put into the deal at the beginning. Remember that "option fee"? That probably hurt. You won't necessarily always have an option fee in a rent to own agreement, but in a scenario like the one we've described here, it really doesn't hurt or matter. Why not? Because, Jacob paid $3,500 to get into a rent to own agreement that ultimately saved him thousands. Over $8,000 of his rent money went towards the purchase price of his home, not to mention the money he saved on interest by not financing that $8,000.

He got into the home quickly, and got to live in the home he was buying while he worked on improving his credit and his finances.

That's a great place to be. If you plan carefully and play your cards right, you might end up there too.

Making The Most of The Rent To Own Process: The Rental Period

This brings up an important point that we should talk about regarding rent to own programs and how to make the most of them.

For you the buyer, getting the most out of a rent to own arrangement really boils down to one thing:

how you *use* the **rental period**.

In a rent to own arrangement, the time you are renting is the time to work your rear-end off to improve your financial triad. It's the time for the down payment push. It's the time to keep your credit squeaky clean and clean up any negative information you have. It's the time to get your expenses under control (if you haven't already) to give yourself the best possible cash flow scenario.

In order for a rent to own program to really pay off, you need to utilize the rental period to work on your credit and your finances.

Things that must happen during the rental period for a rent to own program to yield the most benefit are:

- ✓ **Your credit must improve.** You have to work on your credit and work to raise your credit score during the rental period. This can take time, so you need to have a rental period (a lease, or "option period") that is long enough for you to accomplish your credit goals.
- ✓ **You must pay on time.** You need to pay your rent and other bills no time. Depending on how your agreement is structured, failure to pay your rent on time could jeopardize the whole deal.

- ✓ **You must save for a down payment.** Don't count on zero down financing. Even if you think you'll qualify for a low down or zero down loan, do the "down payment push" and save everything you can to go towards a down payment.
- ✓ **You must improve your net worth and your cash flow.** If you struggle in either of these areas, you will be much better off in the long run if you can take the time during (or before) the rental period to make some improvements in this area.

There are other improvements that can help you during the rental period as well. If you're handy with fixing up and remodeling, you could do a few limited improvements to the home to increase your equity in the home (effective *immediately* the day you take ownership).

The point here is that during the period in which you are renting the home, you should make the most of the opportunity to improve your situation. It is a huge opportunity for those who use it correctly, and in a well-executed rent to own agreement both the buyer *and* the seller will ultimately win.

Time And Choices

Before we close this chapter, I want to say one last thing about rent to own agreements:

They are GREAT for you the buyer because they give you both **time** and **choices**.

You have time to improve your credit; time to save for a down payment; time to improve your cash flow; time to get to know the neighborhood.

In the event that something goes wrong, you have **choices**. You are NOT locked in. One thing a *properly structured* rent to own agreement does not do is "require" you to buy the home at the end of the rental period. It is your CHOICE. You have the **option** to buy.

If things don't go your way, you can gracefully bow out with minimal damage (as compared to if you had purchased the same home right away.)

This is great flexibility to have for a person with bad credit who is trying to get things turned around in an unpredictable world.

We've talked a lot about rent to own deals the last couple of chapters, and by now you probably have a good idea of what the potential advantages can mean for you. *Rent to own arrangements can have certain pitfalls, though.* Next chapter, I'll tell you about a few VERY IMPORTANT things to look out for with rent to own deals.

13 RENT TO OWN: WHAT TO LOOK OUT FOR!

For the many advantages that rent to own programs have for the right buyer, there are also a few pitfalls to look out for. This chapter we're going to talk about some potential "gotchas" that you'll want to be on the lookout for.

Not only will we talk about the potential pitfalls of renting to own, but I'll also give you some ideas for how to remedy these potential issues.

Keep in mind as we continue with this chapter's discussion that for many people in the right situation, the benefits of renting to own can far outweigh the risks, <u>as long as the deal is structured correctly</u>.

The 6 Biggest Potential Problems When Using The Rent To Own Approach

What goes wrong with rent to own arrangements? How can things get *messed up?*

There are 6 main areas in which a wrench can be thrown into the gears of a rent to own arrangement. Those main areas are:

- Seller Financial Problems
- Contractual Problems
- Property Problems
- Market Problems
- Integrity Problems
- Buyer Financial Problems

Let's look at each of these areas in detail so that you can have a full understanding of what each means. In each of the following sections, I'll describe the problem, as well as potential remedies to the problem.

1. Seller Financial Problems

If the seller is having financial problems, this could be ***bad news*** for you. The short solution to seller financial problems is to ***never*** enter a rent to own agreement with a seller who is having financial problems.

What kind of problems are we talking about here?

There are a number of seller financial problems that could result in problems for your rent to own agreement and the pending purchase of your home.

These include...

- ✓ **Credit problems** - if the seller is behind on payments on the property, the payments must be brought current or the home could be foreclosed while you're renting! If the seller isn't currently behind but falls behind later, the same thing could happen.
- ✓ **Tax problems** - if the seller has tax problems that have not been disclosed, this could jeopardize the rent to own deal down the road.
- ✓ **Loan and/or equity problems** - Several things could happen here. If a seller doesn't have enough equity in a home, it could create problems depending on the structure of the agreement. If

there is a second mortgage on the home or the seller otherwise owes more than what the home is worth, this could be a big issue for a rent to own arrangement.
- ✓ **Savings Problems** - In some rent to own arrangements, the seller literally must *give back to the renter* a portion of monies paid out in rent (i.e. the "option credit") at the time of purchase. This money can, in turn, be used by the renter towards a down payment or towards the purchase of the home. If the seller is not responsible and cannot handle saving money, they may not have the money available to give the renter when the time comes.
- ✓ **Money or house related problems resulting from life's changes** - if the seller goes through a divorce, for example, they could *lose the home* in the divorce proceedings.

What can be done to address and avoid these problems?

For starters, check your landlord's credit. That might sound strange, but I'm not kidding. Obtain (legally) and review your landlord's credit reports to make sure that there aren't any signs of financial trouble. If you find things like late payments, charge offs, collection accounts, tax liens, or similar credit problems, then beware! (You should probably move on to another seller.)

Another thing you can do is get what's called a "condition of title" report for the property. This will tell you how long the seller has owned the property. The longer they have owned the property, the better it is, as the more stable they are and the more likely they are to have plenty of equity in the property. (Note: 2nd mortgages, or loans secured by the home, will also show up on the landlord's credit report.)

For landlord savings problems, or in other words, cases where a landlord would be so irresponsible as to not be able to give you the "option credit" that they agreed to, one simple approach is the simply apply the option credit directly to the selling price of the house. This means that if you agree on a selling price of $150,000, and the option credit is $400, after paying for 2 years you could buy the house at $150,000 - $9600, or $140,400. Note: In order for this solution to work, the seller must have enough equity to support it or simply own the home outright.

If the landlord goes through a major life change that somehow affects your rent to own agreement, there might not be much you can do to remedy the situation.

The best advice for this and perhaps ALL of the seller / landlord related issues is to make sure you work with a seller/landlord whom you can trust. This might mean getting references, or sticking to sellers that your real estate agent knows well and has worked with on rent to own arrangements before.

2. Contractual Problems

One problem that can come up in rent to own to own agreements is problems related directly to the *contract*. For starters, it's important that you use a "lease option" agreement instead of a "lease purchase" agreement. The lease option agreement gives you the ***option*** to purchase at a later date. The lease purchase agreement *requires* you to. There is a big difference.

There are other issues of various kinds that can stem from lease option agreement or sales contract. We'll talk about these potential issues in more detail later in the program when we talk about the details of rent to own contracts.

The best way to avoid contractual problems is to be very detailed and thorough (enlist the help of an attorney if need be). We'll talk about this and other remedies for possible contractual issues in a couple of chapters.

3. Property Problems

A number of problems can arise that are related to the property itself. Repairs, renovations, and maintenance, for example, are at the heart of some rent to own risks.

To avoid such problems, the first step is to make sure everything is spelled out clearly in the lease option agreement. Who will fix the furnace if it breaks? Who is responsible for keeping the gutters cleaned? What repairs and renovations are you as the tenant and future buyer allowed to make?

All of this should be spelled out in the lease option agreement.

Other property-related problems could be things like surprises about structural problems or other issues that could come up during the rental period. The best insurance against these types of issues is getting a thorough home inspection *before* you sign any agreement or pay any lease option fees.

4. Market Problems

There are several problems related to the markets that can creep up in a rent to own arrangement. One example is that the purchase price could be unfair or inflated. The simple remedy to this would be to do some market research and make sure that the agreed upon purchase price is fair.

Other market related problems can occur when the markets go up or down, and the agreed upon (fixed) purchase price stays the same.

If home values in the area go down, you as the buyer could end up paying more for the home than you would for a comparable home in the same neighborhood because your agreed-upon price is now outdated.

A seller could end up taking <u>LESS</u> for the home than they would otherwise accept when rising home values in the area result in the agreed upon purchase price being lower than what it would otherwise be if it were priced according to market conditions.

Both of these potential issues are risks that the buyer and seller generally have to accept if they are to enter a rent to own agreement. (With a possible exception that we'll talk about in a couple of chapters.)

5. Integrity Problems

One potentially serious issue when using the rent to own approach is that of a dishonest seller.

A seller could take your "lease option credits" and run, in theory. This would be illegal, of course, but a dishonest seller could certainly do it, and possibly even get away with it if you don't have the funds to pursue them legally.

A seller could fail to pay the mortgage and keep accepting your rent money. This could result in the home being foreclosed and you being out of luck. (Note: one way to avoid this is to pay your rent to the mortgage company directly.)

The list of problems that *could* happen with a dishonest seller is long.

However, if you do your homework and are careful, the list of *likely* problems is non-existent.

If you are working with honest people who have a proven track record, the chances of being ripped off are slim. How can you make sure the person you are working with is honest and/or has a proven track record?

Here are some ideas...

1. Only work with people you know. This is the most restrictive option, but maybe the safest.
2. Only work with sellers with whom your real estate agent has an existing positive relationship. This is less restrictive than #1, and as long as your real estate agent is honest, is probably a safe bet.
3. Get references from the seller and check them.
4. Try to only work with sellers who have successfully completed rent to own deals before.

Acting on one or more of these ideas will greatly reduce the likelihood that you'll be caught in a situation where a seller's dishonesty wrecks the deal.

6. Buyer Financial Problems

The **most common problem** that can arise out of any rent to own agreement is when the *buyer's* financial difficulties get in the way.

This could mean several things:

- You have an unexpected job loss
- You have a major medical problem or other catastrophe
- You have a major life change that affects your financial status and/or your ability (or desire) to purchase the home
- You don't do the work necessary to get your credit and finances in order during the rental period

Of those, the biggest pitfall is probably the last one. Some things you can't plan for and you can't prevent. Job loss, medical issues... these things just happen. They are also **not very likely** to happen to most people at any given time.

The best that you can do is address the potential under the fourth bullet point, and make sure you do the work necessary to fix your credit and your finances.

To be <u>clear</u>: in order for a rent to own arrangement to work out for you as the buyer, you <u>MUST</u> work on your credit and improve your finances during the rental period.

If you don't, it's probably a great opportunity lost, and money down the tube.

There are some "buyer financial problems" that you can't do anything about. But this is one that you can. Work on your credit. Work on your finances. If an unexpected disaster strikes, you can't help it. Otherwise if you stick to the game plan you'll be living in the house that you <u>**OWN**</u> in just a couple of short years.

Be Vigilant, But Not Afraid

The key to addressing most of the issues that can come up in rent to own deals is vigilance. Do your homework, basically.

It's important to put this in perspective by saying this:

Problems can arise in the midst of **ANY** real estate deal. It doesn't matter whether you are paying cash, financing a home, or renting to own, the complexity and nature of real estate deals means that there is always going to be a potential for problems of one kind or another.

The best thing you can do is be vigilant and stay on top of the process. If you do this, your rent to own deal will likely be no more risk-ridden than any other real estate deal taking place in the same town on the same day.

Next chapter we'll talk about how you can go about finding the best rent to own opportunities with the least likelihood of having the kinds of problems that we've discussed this chapter. Stay tuned for some helpful money saving and deal saving information!

# Video Resource
Video Name: Rent-to-Own: Process
www.YourHomeProgram.com/BookResource

14 RENT TO OWN: FINDING A HOME

Later in the program we're going to talk in depth about how to find and choose a home. This chapter we're going to focus purely on the *rent to own* aspect, and talk about **how to find a <u>rent to own opportunity</u> when searching for a home**.

There are several places that you can look for rent to own opportunities, and as with any time you're searching for an "opportunity" of *any* kind, the real key is being able to determine and separate the good from the bad. I'll provide some guidance along these lines this chapter.

The 5 Best Places To find Rent To Own Opportunities

If you're looking for the best possible rent to own deal with the best possible chances of success, then you need to think seriously about <u>HOW</u> to find such a deal. It's not just going to fall into your lap.

You need a motivated seller... you need someone who is "OK" with the extra effort that a rent to own deal will entail. You also need someone who isn't going to make the deal turn sour in one of the ways we talked about last chapter. You also need to be able to find both a home and rental terms that you can afford.

There are 5 places I know of where you are the LEAST likely to get a "bad apple" rent to own deal. Here they are...

Option #1: Friends And Family

Many people overlook this obvious choice. Almost everyone knows someone who is selling a home or who is thinking about selling a home.

The likelihood of running into "seller related" trouble with someone you know is relatively low. Someone you know and care about who knows you and cares about you too will probably want to preserve your family relationship or friendship, and will therefore not be likely to pull anything underhanded in the contract phase or any other time during the rent to own process.

Of all the possibilities when dealing with friends and family, perhaps the best is when you can find a friend or family member with ***rental property*** that they wouldn't mind selling to you through a rent to own arrangement. If someone has multiple rental properties, they aren't likely to have the cash flow problems that a single "motivated seller" may have (which could result in some of those rent to own "pitfalls" we talked about!)

Option #2: Rental Ads

Imagine this scenario:

> *A person who has purchased a home gets a new job in a different city. Now they need to move. They go to the new city with their new job, and put their old home on the market.*
>
> *The eventually buy a new home in the new city, while **still** waiting for their old home to sell.*

> *Months go by, and nothing.*
>
> *They have two house payments, two mortgages, and a house that is many miles away from their current life that they are trying to keep up with.*
>
> *Having been stretched to the limit for such a long time, the person grows tired of waiting for a buyer and decides to try* **renting out the property.**

If at all possible, that is the kind of rent-to-own seller that you want to find. There are risks involved of course, but if they have good or great credit and you can insure that your payments will be applied as they should be, sellers like this can be a dream come true for someone looking for a great rent to own deal.

For the seller, you are a renter with a *vested interest* in the condition of the house. (i.e. You're going to take care of it.) They get to have the house payment **paid, and** get to **sell the house**, in one sweeping rent to own transaction.

For this reason and other reasons, the "rental" ads are a great place to find rent to own opportunities. You may find a seller who gave up and decided to rent. You may find a landlord who wants to retire and cash out of his or her rental properties.

There is a good chance that either could be found by searching the rental ads in your local newspaper and on websites like Craigslist.

Option #3: Use a Real Estate Agent

One good way to find rent to own deals is to enlist the help of a qualified real estate agent. A real estate agent can search the MLS (multiple listing service) for potential rent to own leads.

It is best if you can find a real estate agent who has experience setting up rent to own deals, as this will give you the best advantage all the way around. Their experience should help you to avoid some possible pitfalls, and they may have contacts that will be helpful in your search for the right property and the right deal.

Your real estate agent should help you look for listings that meet one or more of the following criteria:

- ✓ The home is in your price range
- ✓ The listing includes the term "rent to own" or related terms
- ✓ The home has been on the market for several months
- ✓ The home is vacant

The reason for the criteria listed here should be obvious, but we'll cover it just in case.

You need a **home in your price range** because you need to be able to afford it when you are ready to buy. (It doesn't matter if you can work out a rent agreement that you can afford if you can't afford to actually buy when it comes time.)

If the **listing includes terms related to rent to own**, this may indicate a seller willing to work with you.

If the **home has been on the market for several months**, this could indicate that the seller is having difficulty selling the home, which means they may be more open to the possibility of a rent to own arrangement.

If the **home is vacant**, it probably won't sell as easily as one with someone living in it. Vacant homes are harder to sell, so the seller of a vacant home (especially one that has been sitting for a while) may be more open to working with you on a rent to own deal.

A real estate agent can be very useful for your housing search. The trick is finding a qualified real estate agent who will be knowledgeable in the area of renting to own!

Option #4: For Sale By Owners

Another option to find quality rent to own deals is looking for homes that are "for sale by owner".

Not all for sale by owner homes will be rent to own candidates, but there are cases where an owner may have had trouble selling the home and needs to do so sooner than later. If a person is about to give up on their "for sale by owner" plan, your "rent to own" proposal may be just what they need to stay in the game.

The downside to a "for sale by owner" is that most sellers using this approach are doing so, at least in part, to avoid paying commission to a real estate agent. This means that if you want to use a real estate agent in a "for sale by owner" rent to own deal, you may have trouble finding a willing seller who will be willing to pay the real estate commissions.

Option #5: Real Estate Investors

When we talked about the process of buying foreclosed real estate, we mentioned the method of going to the winning bidder and buying from *them*. Some of the people that bid at foreclosure auctions are real estate investors who buy real estate for as low a price as possible and fix the property up, and then resell it.

These are the types of real estate investors that can be great contacts when you're looking for a rent to own deal. Most real estate investors that fix up properties and try to sell them quickly are fairly motivated to sell once the property if fixed up, and a number of them will have done rent to own agreements before.

If you can find an honest, reputable real estate investor, this can be a great way to find a rent to own deal. Sometimes real estate agents will be helpful in this department because of their contacts in the area of real estate.

Other Ways To Find Rent To Own Deals

While the above 5 methods are the best that I know of, there yet other ways that you can search for and find rent to own deals. One simple way is to answer classified ads that sellers place online and in newspapers, and pitch them the idea of a rent to own agreement. (One author[3] and rent-to-own advocate suggests the tactic of placing classifieds of your own, which can work too!)

The problem with these methods is that they don't offer much help in the area of weeding out potentially bad-news deals.

---

[3] Wendy Patton, Rent-To-Buy

Making The Most of Your Search

When searching for a rent to own deal, the most important things that you should remember are:

- look for a home that you can afford
- stay away from sticky situations and questionable sellers, and
- look for a home that you will *want* to live in.

A home that you can afford should be fairly obvious, but sometimes people forget this and end up with dreams bigger than their wallets can reasonably handle.

Remember when we talked about the ratios and percentages relating to your income and your debt? These are good things to keep in mind when you're searching. Even better, if you **can improve your income and expense situation** and become intimately familiar with your own finances, you'll be far ahead of the game. You need to know what you can and can't afford, and ideally you need to shoot for something well within your affordability range.

Staying away from sticky situations is another obvious but big one... and exactly what constitutes a sticky situation isn't always necessarily *obvious*. Generally speaking, short sales, houses in the foreclosure process, and houses where the owner is behind on the mortgage won't work for a rent to own agreement. To the third option there may be an exception where the owner is willing or able to catch up the mortgage payments and then allow you to pay the mortgage payments directly as part of your rent. An arrangement like this complicates matters, though, so if you're looking for a clean deal you probably want to keep looking.

As for looking for a home that you do now and *will in the future* **want** to live in, this is something you can't afford to overlook. Buying a home is a big step, and it's important to find a home in the right neighborhood, with the right schools, with the right neighbors, with the right layout, and the right features to fit your needs. I recommend coming up with a detailed wish list of what you want in a home, and use that as your measuring stick during your search. We'll talk more about how to do this later in the program.

Before You Sign Up...

This chapter I've given you some good ideas on how to find leads for rent to own deals. There is a good chance you've already done some research and searching along these lines.

Before you sign up for anything, we need to talk about something of utmost importance: the paperwork!

Next chapter we'll talk about what paperwork is involved in a rent to own deal. We'll talk about contracts, what goes into them, and what you do and *don't* want in yours.

15 RENT TO OWN: CONTRACTS AND PARTS OF THE DEAL

This chapter we're going to get more into the nitty gritty details of rent to own deals by diving into the topic of rent to own *paperwork*.

Maybe this doesn't sound particularly exciting to you, but believe me—you don't want to skip this one!

The paperwork can make or break a rent to own deal, and there are some **very important** details that you *need* to know!

So let's get to it...

The Three Main Pieces of The Rent To Own Paperwork Puzzle

There are three main pieces to rent to own paperwork. These include:

1. The Rental Agreement
2. The Sales Contract
3. The Lease Option, or "Option to Purchase" Agreement

In one way or another, the aspects covered in these documents will need to be covered in a rent to own agreement. Some may involve more paperwork and addendums, others less, but the points covered by the rental agreement, the lease option agreement, and the sales contract *should* be covered in any rent to own agreement.

For the sake of simplicity and clarity, it's best to have the three portions of the paperwork defined clearly as separate but related agreements.

Now let's talk in some detail about each piece of the rent to own paperwork puzzle. As we discuss these details, please remember that there are state and local laws that can affect various aspects of rent to own agreements and the paperwork and processes involved. It is always advisable to work with professionals such as attorneys and qualified real estate professionals to avoid potential problems.

The Rental Agreement

The rental agreement is much like any other rental agreement. It specifies the lease term (i.e. how long you will or can rent the home), the rent amount, deposits and other fees, and more.

It also includes any required notices (such as those about led based paint) as required by law.

There may also be addendums regarding your rights and responsibilities. These are *important* to pay attention to. Some landlords may want addendums about your use and care of the property or other similar stipulations. Some of these rental agreement add-ons may give the landlord the right to evict you in certain circumstances that may not be obvious or expected, which is why you need to pay attention.

> SIDE NOTE: There have been issues in the past with dishonest landlords using minor infractions set up in the rental agreement to evict a tenant who has signed up for a rent to own deal, in which case the tenant loses any option fees paid and any other money (and time) they have put into the deal. You need to **protect yourself** by paying close attention to the rental agreement and other aspects of the paperwork, up to and including by having an attorney review the paperwork before you sign up.

One thing that a rental agreement covers that you will want to pay special attention to is about how rent is to be paid. In a rent to own agreement, it is **very** important that the seller (the landlord) pay the mortgage. Sometimes they don't, which means you could put a lot of work and money into a deal that is ultimately doomed. One simple way to avoid this problem is to pay your monthly payment (or a portion of it) to the lender directly to cover the mortgage payment. It is also advisable to check your landlord's credit ahead of time, get references, and take the other steps I have suggested in the previous chapters to protect yourself and give your rent to own deal the best possible chances of success.

The best advice I can give about the rental agreement is to go into the rent to own deal with an agreement of your own that you know has the clauses and stipulations that you can live with. **Don't just accept what the seller or landlord asks you to sign as many (if not most) people do.** Especially in the context of a rent to own deal, you have a right—no, a responsibility—to make sure that the rental agreement is customized and shaped in such a manner that it protects your interests as much as (if not more than) those of your landlord (the seller).

The Sales Contract

The sales contract portion of the rent to own paperwork specifies things like the sale price of the home, the terms of the sale, and details about title insurance, inspections, and more.

There are also state-specific details and clauses that must be part of a sales contract.

Most of the time the sales contract in a rent to own agreement specifies a price that the buyer will eventually pay for the home. It doesn't *have to* be that way necessarily—the buyer and seller can agree that the buyer will have the option to purchase the home at the fair market value—but generally speaking, for you as the buyer, it is better if you can get the sale price set up front.

This gives incentive for you as the buyer to keep the property up, and to make improvements if that is part of the agreement, and also means that if the property increases in value in during the rental period you will get into it at a lesser-than-market-value price. Most of the time, you as the buyer will want to lock in the sale price based on the current market value (which is one of the advantages, for you, of a rent to own agreement).

In a rent to own agreement, the sales contract will usually refer to the rental agreement and the option agreement to fill in certain details, such as the time period in which the renter has the option to buy the house.

Usually the sales contract should include certain clauses to protect you as the buyer, and also the seller. A default clause, for example, will say what happens in the event that you don't purchase the home (usually you simply forfeit any option fee paid), or in the event that the seller defaults and causes you to be unable to buy the home in one way or another (it would be preferable that the seller be required to refund your option fee in this case.)

The Lease Option Agreement

Of the three elements of a rent to own agreement, the "lease option agreement" or "option to purchase agreement" is the one that is unique to the rent to own scenario.

Before we get into the details of the lease option agreement, let's talk a little about some semantics issues.

Traditionally, there are two types of agreements: a lease *option* and a lease purchase agreement. A lease *option* agreement would give you the option to purchase the home at a later date, while a lease *purchase* agreement would require you to do so. For obvious reasons, you want a *lease option* agreement and not a *lease purchase* agreement.

However, the matter is complicated somewhat by the fact that some people use the two terms interchangeably. This could create a situation where there is some ambiguity in a contract or agreement between two parties if the terms are not defined clearly. The simple solution to this is to make sure that there is a clear and thorough "definitions" portion of your lease option agreement, and make sure important terms such as the title of the agreement (i.e. "lease option agreement") are clearly defined.

Now that we've got that out of the way, let's talk in detail about what the lease option agreement covers. A lease option agreement will include information about:

- ✓ The option fee amount, how it will be applied, and how it will be paid
- ✓ The term of the option agreement (how long it is valid)
- ✓ How and *if* option credits will be applied
- ✓ Stipulations and clauses related to the option fee and option credits

The Option Fee

The option fee is the amount of money you pay to the seller for the right to buy the house at a later date. This could be an amount as much as 1% to 2% of the purchase price of the home, or there may be no option fee at all. The option fee is non-refundable (except perhaps in cases of a seller default, which would have to be provided for in the contract). This means that you will <u>NOT</u> get it back if you decide not to purchase the home.

Note that an option fee is not the same as a security deposit, and you may have a separate security deposit required under the rental agreement. The security deposit would be returned to you at the time of purchase similar to any rental scenario, where once an option fee is paid, you won't get it back.

How The Option Fee Will Be Applied

The option fee usually doesn't go towards the purchase of the home in any way, but some agreements can be structured so that the option fee does go towards the purchase price of the home or towards the down payment.

How The Option Fee Will Be Paid

The option fee may be paid all at once up front, or broken up and paid with the month's rent over a period of time. This is something that should be specified in the lease option agreement.

The Term of the Option Agreement

This is what specifies the period of time in which the option to purchase remains in effect. This will be a date range, and will be the period of time in which you have the option to purchase the home. A typical option period or rental period is 2 years. From your perspective, the longer this term is, the better.

How and If Option Credits Will Be Applied

The term *option credits* refers to the portion of your monthly rent (if any) that will be applied towards the purchase price of the home. Obviously, it is to your advantage to have a portion of your rent be applied to the purchase of the home. This could be as much as 50% or more of the rent amount, and is something that will have to be negotiated with the seller.

Other Stipulations And Clauses

Other stipulations and clauses that are included in a lease option agreement usually include things like a requirement for the buyer to have the exclusive right to buy during the option period. This is a protection for you that forbids the seller from selling to anyone else while the lease option agreement is still in effect. Also included might be stipulations and clauses about the renter/buyer's right to pay any payments directly to the lender or the appropriate tax entity. This protects you from the seller defaulting by not paying the mortgage, taxes, insurance, etc.

Other Paperwork

An optional part of the rent to own paperwork that provides protection for you as the buyer is the *memorandum of option*. This is basically a document that is recorded with the county clerk's office that gives public notice of the option agreement, and essentially prevents the seller from selling the house to anyone else or refinancing their loan.

You want to have this as part of your rent to own agreement if you can get it.

What You Need Most When It Comes To Rent To Own Paperwork

Real estate transactions can be tricky all on their own. It is very easy to miss something crucial in the course of any real estate deal, including a rent to own agreement.

For this reason, I highly recommend enlisting the help of a qualified real estate agent or attorney who can assist you with navigating through the paperwork and covering your bases.

The seller may also have an attorney or expert helping them, and that's fine, but their attorney isn't there to help you. You need someone to look out for <u>YOUR</u> interests in this transaction.

How Easy It Can Be

I know that all this legal talk may make the rent to own process sound complicated, so next week I'm going to make things a little easier by breaking down the entire process from beginning to end, and show you all the necessary steps that you need to take in order to make the most of a rent to own opportunity. I'll show you just how easy it can be, and you'll come out of next chapter with a step by step walkthrough that you can use as your own personal map and checklist as you navigate the road to home ownership through renting **to own.**

16 RENT TO OWN: THE 12 STEPS FOR SUCCESS USING RENT TO OWN

This chapter I'm going to give you the 12 steps for success when using rent to own programs. Like many things in life, there is a right way and definitely a ***wrong*** way to use rent to own. We're going to learn the *right way*.

The big key to making a rent to own program work for you the buyer is to make ***improvements*** to your situation both **before and during** the rental period.

Knowing this, you might expect for the "improvements" to be a big part of this plan... and they are.

I will try to keep this chapter material as *practical* as possible, and give you concrete tools and strategies that you can use throughout the rent to own process to make it go as smoothly as it possibly can. This chapter isn't about theories; it's about *action*. It's about what **really** makes a rent to own approach work.

Now let's get into it. Here are the 12 steps necessary for success using rent to own programs!

☐ STEP 1: <u>Evaluate</u> Whether Rent To Own Is Right For You!

Don't skip this step! You need to know going into this whether or not a rent to own approach might be a good option for you. *Are you the right buyer?* (Don't go on until you know the answer to this question!)

Here's a little checklist to help. The more of the following items you can check, the more likely it is that a "rent to own" scenario will work for you.

<u>RENT TO OWN EVALUATION CHECKLIST</u>

- ☐ I have **bad credit**.
- ☐ I don't have a lot of available cash for a down payment.
- ☐ With my current circumstances I am unable to qualify for a home loan, or to get favorable terms.
- ☐ I am *capable* of taking the steps necessary to improve my credit and my finances.
- ☐ With my income, I can reasonably expect to afford house payments on a home in my area.
- ☐ I know I am going to have to rent for a while, but would like it if I can make progress towards home ownership while I do it.
- ☐ I am *willing* to **work** to get my finances into shape so that I can afford the home of my dreams.
- ☐ I am planning on living in the same area (and home) for a long time, <u>OR</u> I am moving to a new area and would like the *option* to buy the home I am renting if I decide to stay.

The more items on the RENT TO OWN EVALUATION CHECKLIST that you check off, the more likely it is that "rent to own" is right for you. If you are confident that this choice is for you, proceed to STEP 2!

☐ STEP 2: Start <u>IMPROVING</u> Your Income And Expenses!

This step has two parts.

The first part is to improve your **income**. The second is to work on your **expenses**. This will improve your cash flow and put you in better shape to afford not only a home, but everything else in your life.

I believe you should start this step **before** you sign up for a rent to own agreement for two reasons:

1. It could take longer than you think to improve your finances.
2. You will help insure that you can afford to **rent** and ***buy*** the home you want to live in, and avoid problems that would otherwise get in the way of that goal.

It's also important to realize that this step is NOT a "one time event". This is something you should commit to doing *continually*. Not only should you do it before you sign any paperwork, you should continue to work on your income and expenses during the rental period and beyond.

The more attention you give to this area, the better off the other areas of your financial triad (i.e. your credit and your net worth) will be!

Coming up in the program we will be going into great detail on how to improve your income and your expenses. For now, you can use the following checklist to get started with some ideas.

IDEAS FOR INCOME AND EXPENSE IMPROVEMENTS - CHECKLIST

- ☐ Did you complete the **income** tracking exercises from earlier in this program?
- ☐ Possible to get a raise at work?
- ☐ Able or willing to get a part time job doing _____?
- ☐ Look into other ways to make extra money?
- ☐ Find ways to make the most of existing income and "make more" without actually changing your income (don't worry, I'll tell you how to do this in about 5 chapters.)
- ☐ Did you complete the **expense** tracking exercises from earlier in this program?
- ☐ Did you keep a spending diary to find out what you really spend?
- ☐ Try to think of ways in each of the 5 categories of expenses that you can cut back. List some ideas here (don't worry; we'll talk about this in detail later!):
    - _____
    - _____
    - _____
    - _____
    - _____
    - _____
    - _____
    - _____
    - _____
    - _____

☐ STEP 3: Get Your Debt Under Control!

What does your debt situation look like? Are you buried in debt and barely making it? Do you have more debt than you'd prefer to have? Do you need to improve your net worth by increasing your savings and paying off debt?

This is another important *preliminary* step.

Debt problems can be difficult to overcome, and if you're having trouble, you need to tackle the problem **now** rather than later.

You should look at your debt situation at this stage (rather than later) for a couple of reasons:

1. You may need **TIME** to pay off or otherwise deal with your debt.
2. If your situation is such that you need to do debt negotiation or file for bankruptcy, you'll want to get it out of the way as soon as possible so that you can start repairing the damage right away. (Don't wait until you've signed a rent to own agreement to file for bankruptcy... then it's too late and will hurt your ability to take advantage of your option to buy!)

In order to evaluate your debt situation, you need to get a clear picture of "where" you are. You need to know the answer to this question:

"How bad is it?"

Here are some questions you can ask yourself that can help you develop an answer to the above:

- Am I behind on my debt payments?
- Am I in danger of a repossession on an auto loan?
- Do I have any open and unpaid collection accounts?
- Am I currently being sued by any creditors or collectors?
- Am I having to make serious sacrifices just to get my minimum payments paid?
- Am I struggling to afford the basic necessities of life such as food, water, and shelter?

The more of these questions that you answered "yes" to, the more serious your debt situation is.

If you are truly buried and seriously struggling, you can't expect to enter a rent to own agreement or buy a home until these issues are resolved. *(Even if you could get into a home in this state, could you continue to afford it?)*

For those who are buried beyond belief, there are two options that belong at the top of the list:

1. Debt settlement, and
2. Bankruptcy

The "bankruptcy" word might scare you, but remember... you CAN get approved for a home loan after a bankruptcy. You CAN improve your credit score (even dramatically) within a year or two of a bankruptcy.

But if you haven't filed for bankruptcy yet **and you need to**, then this is the time to get down to business.

If you want to avoid bankruptcy or don't think you're quite at that point yet, *debt settlement* can be a worthwhile option to explore for some. Debt settlement is the process of working out settlements with your creditors in which they agree to accept less than you actually owe to pay off your unsecured debts. This allows you to pay off your unsecured debts for (usually, on average) somewhere around $0.40 on the dollar.

Debt settlement still hurts your credit, and can take longer than bankruptcy to complete. If you decide to use the debt settlement approach for your debt it could delay your rent to own plans some. (This is why

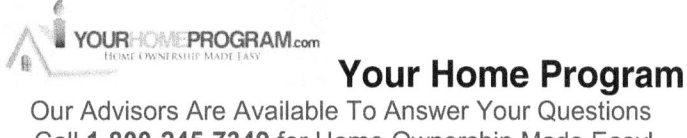

you need to start as soon as possible if you're going to!)

The good news is that if your rent to own agreement is structured properly (i.e. allowing enough time in the rental period), you should have plenty of time to repair the credit damage that will result from either bankruptcy or debt settlement.

If you aren't absolutely buried in debt and can see yourself (realistically) paying off your debts without the bankruptcy or debt settlement processes, then this is the time to get your debt game-plan together and start paying off debt.

Remember the debt ratios that we talked about earlier in the program? You need to, at the very least, have your debt to income ratios within the required range.

To get the current debt to income ratio requirements for FHA loans, go here:

Video Resource
Video Name: How does Bankruptcy affect your Credit?
www.YourHomeProgram.com/BookResource

Video Resource
Video Name: Is Bankruptcy a Credit Score killer?
www.YourHomeProgram.com/BookResource

http://www.fha.com/fha_requirements_debt.cfm

Once you know your *required* target, you can develop a debt elimination plan that goes at the pace you need it to.

I'll provide some strategies later in the program for dealing with debt and paying off debt faster.

For now, here's a checklist to help you get your debt situation under control:

DEBT SITUATION CHECKLIST

- ☐ If bankruptcy is a possibility, consult with a qualified expert.

- ☐ If you think you may be a candidate for debt settlement, then do some research on the subject and consult with an expert to find out whether it is right for you.

- ☐ Check the debt to income ratio requirements for FHA and other potential lenders.
- ☐ Develop a tentative plan to get your debt well within the ***most restrictive*** requirements from those you looked up.

☐ STEP 4: Start The House (And Seller) Hunt!

The next step in your rent to own program is to start the hunt for the *right home* and the *right seller*.

Some people might choose to start with this step much sooner. Just remember that you need to get your financial ducks in a row before getting too far into the house hunting process.

House hunting is a pretty big subject in itself, and we'll devote a whole chapter to the topic of choosing a home later in the program. *Seller hunting* is almost as important when you are looking for a rent to own opportunity. You need to find a (preferably *honest and trustworthy*) seller who is willing to work out a rent to own deal with you.

> For both the house hunting and the seller hunting aspects of this step, you will probably have the most success if you enlist the help of a qualified real estate agent in your area.

Remember that first and foremost, the "right home" is a home that you ***want*** to live in. It also needs to be a home that you ***can afford*** to live in. Using the information already covered about debt to income ratios, your knowledge of your financial situation and your spending habits, and the help of your real estate agent, you *should* be able to come up with a pretty clear idea of what you can and can't afford.

Here's a short checklist to get you started on choosing the right home:

THE BASICS OF CHOOSING A HOME - CHECKLIST

- ☐ Develop a "wish list" that describes your ***ideal*** home. (I'll help you with this in more detail later in the program.)
- ☐ Decide on a price range that you can reasonably and comfortably afford. Be sure to take your spending habits and your lifestyle into consideration.
- ☐ Enlist the help of a real estate agent with the goal of finding a home that fits the following criteria:
  - ✓ The home is as close as possible to fitting your wish list
  - ✓ The home is in your price range
  - ✓ The seller is willing and able to do rent to own
- ☐ Come up with as many candidates as possible for your potential future home, and start contacting sellers with your rent to own proposal.

As for the seller, you need to find a seller who is *willing* to do rent to own, who *can* do rent to own, and who is *not likely to default* on your rent to own agreement.

Here are some checklists to help you find and choose the right seller:

FINDING AND CHOOSING A SELLER - THREE CHECKLISTS

Use the following 3 checklists to help you along the path of finding and choosing a seller. The first checklist is for "FINDING" a seller, and the second and third checklists are about "CHOOSING" a seller.

#1 FINDING WILLING AND ABLE SELLERS:

- ☐ Check with friends and family
- ☐ Check the "for rent" ads
- ☐ Follow up on leads from your real estate agent
- ☐ Develop a list of "For Sale By Owner" candidates and contact them with your rent to own proposal
- ☐ Find ways to get in touch with real estate investors in your area.

#2 THINGS YOU WANT IN A SELLER:

The more things you check off here, the better the potential candidate might be.

- ☐ Is the seller *motivated?*
- ☐ Does the seller have more than one home or are they paying two mortgages?
- ☐ Did the seller put out a "for rent" ad?
- ☐ Has the seller successfully completed a rent to own deal before?
- ☐ Does the seller have references that they are willing to provide?
- ☐ Is the seller someone that you know?
- ☐ Is the seller someone with whom your real estate agent has worked before?
- ☐ Can the seller provide a clear title?

#3 THINGS YOU DON'T WANT IN A SELLER:

These are some things that you don't want. Anything checked here should be a big red flag. This list isn't necessarily all inclusive, but should give you some ideas to get the ball rolling.

- ☐ Is the seller having financial problems?
- ☐ Is the seller behind on the mortgage?
- ☐ Does the seller have signs of serious past or current credit problems?
- ☐ Is the seller unwilling to share certain information or do they seem to be avoiding topics related to their financial status or the status of the property?
- ☐ Does the seller have any tax problems?
- ☐ Is the seller unable or unwilling to provide evidence of their own financial responsibility?
- ☐ Is the seller going through a major life change (such as a divorce)?
- ☐ Does the seller seem dishonest or of questionable integrity? *(What's your gut feeling on this person?)*

☐ **STEP 5: Do Your Due Diligence!**

Does Your Landlord Measure Up? Are there any red flags with the seller or the property?

This is the stage at which you follow up on any possible red flags with the property, the seller/landlord, or anything else that has come up.

By this time you should have picked one or two serious candidates for your rent to own plan, and you should already have one or two sellers that will work with you on a rent to own deal.

> **This step is about *protecting* yourself. You <u>cannot</u> afford to skip it!**

Here is a "due diligence" checklist that should get you well on your way to a clean and worry-free rent to own deal:

<u>DUE DILLIGENCE CHECKLIST:</u>

- ☐ Check the seller's references.
- ☐ Check the seller's credit.
- ☐ Talk to people with whom the seller has completed rent to own deals in the past, if possible.
- ☐ Verify that the price of the home is comparable to other similar homes on the market.
- ☐ Are you likely to come up with a contract that will meet your needs and those of the seller?
- ☐ Get a home inspection.
- ☐ Do a title search on the property.
- ☐ Write yourself a note to buy title insurance when the time comes.
- ☐ If you have a start on your rent to own paperwork (such as a contract to use as a starting point), <u>READ</u> <u>IT</u> and make sure you understand it. Note the areas that need amended or changed.
- ☐ Find out what you can about the seller's equity in the home, how long they have owned the home, etc. (Note: This information should be obtained (preferably) from <u>verifiable</u> sources.)

Depending on the situation and circumstances, there may be more things you need to add for your own "due diligence" checklist. The important thing is to be thorough and to leave "no stone unturned".

Don't be shy about checking up on <u>EVERYTHING</u> related to your pending rent to own deal. Leaving something out could come back to bite you.

☐ STEP 6: Evaluate Your <u>Goals</u>!

Now is a good time to take a step back and make sure you are on the right track.

Considering everything you know about yourself, your income and expenses, your net worth, your credit, your financial habits, and your lifestyle, answer this question:

Are your goals realistic?

Here are some more questions you can ask yourself to help better answer this question:

- ☐ Can I realistically expect to get from my current credit score of _____ to the required/needed credit score over _____ ? (Note: If you aren't sure of this, one good way to find out is by consulting with an expert in the area of credit repair.)

- ☐ Am I willing and able to do the necessary work to improve my finances and my credit?
- ☐ Is my down payment goal a realistic one?
- ☐ Is the house that I want to buy a reachable goal considering my **current** income and expenses?
- ☐ Can I afford to *rent* a house like the one I want to buy?
- ☐ Can I realistically expect to get my debt under control within the timeframe I'm thinking of?
- ☐ Am I allowing myself enough time to get my finances and my credit in shape?

☐ Is this goal within reach enough so that if things don't go as planned, I may have enough "wiggle room" to still make it happen? (In this regard, the more within reach your goal is, the better.)

☐ **STEP 7: Create A <u>Credit</u> And <u>Down Payment</u> Plan of Attack!**

Now you need to develop a plan of attack for your goals of improving your credit and coming up with your down payment funds. You will need time and effort for both of these goals, so it is important to have a specific plan describing <u>HOW</u> you plan to reach them.

Your credit plan should include your current credit score, your target credit score, your negative items and other credit barriers, and what you plan to do to address them.

Your down payment plan should be an outline of how you plan to implement the "down payment push".

Here are a couple of checklists to help you through the process of planning for your credit repair and down payment efforts.

<u>CREDIT REPAIR PLAN - CHECKLIST</u>

☐ Know your current credit score. (My current credit score is _____.)
☐ Know your target credit score. (My target credit score is somewhere above _____.)

Your Home Program
Our Advisors Are Available To Answer Your Questions
Call **1-800-245-7349** for Home Ownership Made Easy!

☐ Review the items on your credit report that are holding your credit score back. List them here:
_____
_____
_____
_____
_____

☐ Decide on a preliminary strategy for tackling your credit situation and the above items. (How are you going to improve your score? Are you going to try "credit repair" yourself or enlist the help of a professional?)
☐ Make note of any other possible credit problems, such as debt-to-credit ratio issues and outstanding debts that haven't yet appeared on your credit report.
_____
_____
_____
_____

☐ Decide on a plan of attack for the above-listed items.
☐ Consult with an expert in the field of credit repair if needed.

DOWN PAYMENT PLAN - CHECKLIST

- ☐ Know how much money (approximately) you are likely to need for a down payment. Amount: $_____
- ☐ Consider family, friends, and other possible "easy" resources for down payment funds.
- ☐ List the steps you are willing and able to take as part of a "down payment push" plan. (Savings plans, part time jobs, seasonal work or odd jobs... list all of your ideas here!)

_____
_____
_____
_____
_____
_____
_____
_____
_____
_____

- ☐ Based on what you listed above, choose three things that you can start to take action on beginning **now**. Take action!
- ☐ Map out your "down payment push" plan for (roughly) a year from now.
- ☐ Take action on your "down payment push" plan.

☐ STEP 8: Double Check Everything!

For this step, you simply double check everything you have done so far. *Do your numbers make sense? Are your goals realistic? Have you crossed and dotted everything accordingly?*

Double check everything and make sure everything is in order. Now is a good time to have your real estate agent, and perhaps a friend or family member look over your rent to own plan.

☐ STEP 9: Sign Up!

By now you should have a firm verbal agreement and a contract ready to be signed with a seller. You should have a home that passed the inspections and title work, and that you both *want* to live in and *can afford* to live in.

Everything should have been checked and double checked by this time. You *should* be ready to sign the paperwork and move in.

NOTE: If you haven't already, you will want to have a qualified real estate agent and/or real estate attorney review your paperwork for you at this stage, **BEFORE** you sign anything!

Here's a short checklist covering a few important points for this stage in the process...

THE SIGN UP AND MOVE-IN CHECKLIST!

- ☐ Have an attorney or <u>qualified</u> real estate professional review the paperwork.

- ☐ Double check the rental agreement and the lease option to make sure it is clearly spelled out who is responsible for what with regards to repairs and maintenance.
- ☐ Sign the paperwork, including the Rental Agreement, the Sales Contract, and the Lease Option Agreement.
- ☐ If you are using a Memorandum of Option, go through the necessary steps to complete and file it with the county clerk.
- ☐ Make sure the details about title insurance are spelled out in the agreement.
- ☐ Make sure you have the ability to pay the lender directly if possible. This should be provided for in the lease option agreement.
- ☐ Make sure the *term* of your option agreement allows you enough time to repair your credit and save for a down payment.
- ☐ If there is an option fee required, pay it.
- ☐ Make sure it is clear how your option credits will be applied.
- ☐ Move into the home once you've signed up.
- ☐ Make sure you pay your rent on time!

Your Home Program
Our Advisors Are Available To Answer Your Questions
Call **1-800-245-7349** for Home Ownership Made Easy!

☐ STEP 10: Repair Your Credit!

By now you will have moved into your future home and should be paying your rent every month. Now it's time to get to work on your credit! **Remember that in order for a rent to own program to really work, you MUST work on your credit and your financial situation during the rental period.** This step is *non-negotiable*. (The success of your rent to own plan could hinge on your success or failure at executing this single part of the plan.)

I'll spend several chapters covering credit repair later in the program for those who wish to repair their own credit. If you plan to go this route and do your own credit repair, make sure you pay close attention when we get to the credit repair module!

If you plan to have a credit repair professional help with your credit repair, now is the time to find one (if you haven't already) and get signed up for their service.

It is also a good idea to check the references of the credit repair professional you're working with. (This is a good general practice when dealing with any professional or company that will be working in areas related to your finances!)

You want to be sure that you are working with a reputable credit repair professional or credit repair firm.

☐ STEP 11: Save For Your Down Payment!

Almost as important as repairing your credit is setting aside funds for a down payment during the rental period. Your *option credits* may help with this, depending on how your agreement is structured, and by now you should have a plan in place for your *down payment push*. (Hopefully, you've already started it!)

To review, the steps that you need to take for the "down payment push" plan are:

1. **Know** what your down payment requirement is likely to be.
2. Use every possible method to **save** for a down payment over the course of one year.
3. **Evaluate** where you are in relation to your goal.

Know. Save. Evaluate. Rinse and repeat. That's really all there is to the *down payment push*.

At this stage, you should ideally be at the "SAVE" step or the "EVALUATE" step.

For further review, here's a list of suggestions I gave you earlier in the program when we introduced the "down payment push". You can use this list to check off any strategies you are using or planning to use. (I've also included a couple of blanks where you can add your own ideas.)

DOWN PAYMENT PUSH STRATEGIES - CHECKLIST

- ☐ Automatic savings plan(s)
- ☐ Part time job(s)
- ☐ Odd jobs and seasonal work
- ☐ Tax refunds
- ☐ Sell stuff
- ☐ Get a roommate
- ☐ Spend less
- ☐ Family gifts and friendly loans
- ☐ Retirement funds
- ☐ _____
- ☐ _____
- ☐ _____

☐ **STEP 12: Buy Your Home!**

If you've made it this far, then congratulations! You're ready to buy your home.

At this stage, you should have made plenty of progress on your down payment funds and your overall financial picture (including but not limited to your credit). You should be ready to get qualified for a loan, get your financing together, and act on your **option to buy** the home you are living in.

I don't have a long checklist to give you at this stage in the process. If you've done your homework and followed all the suggestions I've provided up until this point, you ought to be in pretty good shape.

The only thing left to do is to **take ownership** of your home!

The One Last Thing You Should Know About These Steps

Before I sign off this chapter, there is one last thing that you need to know about the steps we've covered this chapter. Here it is:

Some of them can be somewhat *complicated!*

Yes, some of the steps we've covered this chapter really involve quite a bit of work.

Take credit repair for example... anybody who has ever worked on their credit will probably tell you that the process of credit repair is <u>NOT</u> always easy.

Getting out of debt and getting your finances under control may prove to be quite challenging, too.

> **And these things (meaning credit repair and improving your finances) are things that you <u>need</u> to do, quite frankly, whether you plan to use the rent to own approach or not!**

For this reason, we're not quite done with these topics. I couldn't possibly pile all of the necessary information into this chapter, so in the coming chapters we're going to be talking in detail about each of these "complicated" but necessary steps.

We'll talk about...

- ✓ How to repair your credit
- ✓ How to get out of debt
- ✓ How to (really) make more money
- ✓ How to achieve dramatic effects by addressing each of the 5 categories of expenses
- ✓ And a whole lot more!

You'll probably see as we go through these "complicated" items that they aren't quite as complicated as you may have thought. There will be challenges, for sure. But the goal of this program is to give you the tools you need to *overcome* the challenges that you will face.

17 IMPROVING YOUR INCOME – GETTING A RAISE

Our focus for the next 4 chapters is a going to be all about your **_income_**. We're going to talk about several possible ways to improve your income, some of which you may not have thought of.

Income is (obviously) an extremely important part of financial success. Without income, you could not possibly have a healthy positive cash flow.

The more income you have, the more it will ease the burden on the other aspects of your financial life. Debt will become easier to pay off, bills will be easier to pay, your credit will be easier to manage, and it will be easier to accumulate money in savings.

For the first chapter of our "Income" series we'll be talking about a strategy that many, MANY people out there just leave up to _chance_. We're going to talk about _getting a raise_. Some jobs are easier to earn raises at than others. Some companies have a more subjective process than others. For some, getting a raise is often a matter of simply asking, and doing so in the right manner.

We'll talk about all this and more, starting right now...

A Go Somewhere Job

Some jobs have a salary cap. Not every job has endless earning potential. But just because a job has limited earning potential, doesn't mean it's going to be impossible to get a raise.

The thing you have to ask yourself is this:

"What am I doing that deserves an increase in pay?"

Maybe you're a secretary and you're already making pretty good money for a secretary. _Are you stuck?_

Maybe not. Maybe you're a secretary that has been building relationships with customers for a few years. Maybe you just got xyz customer to buy 1000 widgets on the phone last chapter. Maybe you've been doing that every chapter or two for a year or more.

Can you demonstrate that you are saving the company money, making the company money, or improving customer retention?

If so, then even your "go nowhere" job may actually be a _"go somewhere" job_.

Be That Person

Before you can make the claims that you're saving the company this or that amount of money, or making the company this or that amount of money, you (obviously) need to actually be doing it.

In other words, you need to be a great employee.

If you drag in every morning 5 minutes late, leave 5 minutes early every day, spend your lunch time whining about having to go back to work after lunch, and commit other similar (but common) minor offenses, you may have a hard time selling yourself and your worth to your boss.

Instead, you need to be the person who shows up a few minutes early every morning. Don't whine about the work load, the customers, or the management, but find something else to talk about. Be willing to take on extra duties now and then, even if they aren't paid duties. Be willing to take on extra responsibilities to fill in for others, even if others "should be able to do it themselves."

Be *that person.*

Be the person that cares about the company you work for. Act like an owner instead of an employee. Doing this will almost always help to move your salary in the right direction. (That is, up!)

Three Case Studies

In just a moment I'm going to give you some practical principals, steps, and advice for getting a raise. First, I think it will help if we look at a couple of case studies.

Each of the following case studies is based on a true story. These case studies are about real people, with real jobs.

John At McBurgers

> John was 24 when he got a job working at a local fast food chain that we'll call McBurgers. McBurgers was known for hiring high school kids and students, and didn't exactly have a reputation of being the highest paying job in town. Most of the high school kids working at McBurgers made minimum wage. Managers made about $13 an hour. John started at $7 per hour and worked part time.
>
> It was immediately clear to John's supervisors that he wasn't like the high school kids working at McBurgers. He acted responsible, he checked food before it went out, he worked hard to leave a good impression on customers and to make sure he did his part to make McBurgers operate smoothly and efficiently.
>
> Once when some of the high school kids failed to do their jobs, John stayed late with the shift manager and worked hours into the night to pick up the slack.
>
> He also identified a couple of problems, including one potential health code violation, which the management was able to act on and fix.
>
> John found out eventually through talking with other employees that people who had worked at McBurgeres for years were making, on average, about $1.50 to $2.00 per hour more than John.
>
> John decided he was worth at least that much, and decided to approach the management team and ask for a raise. He had only been working there a few months, but he believed that had been enough time to demonstrate that he was *worth it.*
>
> John started with the shift manager that he helped late into the night. He talked to him, mentioned some of the things he had done that helped the restaurant and saved the company money, and asked the shift manager if he'd support him if he asked the restaurant manager for a raise.

The shift manager was very supportive because he appreciated the (now numerous) times that John had stepped in to help.

John and the shift manager went to the restaurant manager, and John explained what he'd been up to for the last few months. The restaurant manager had heard about him and some of the things he had done to go above and beyond the call of duty, and was therefore happy to give him a raise.

John walked out of the manager's office that day with a $1.50 per hour raise, which was quite substantial for someone who had worked at McBurgers for only a few months.

Sally at ACME Office, LLC.

Sally started at an entry level position working at ACME Office, LLC. She worked on a team that included several staff who all answered to the same direct supervisor.

Sally was extremely organized in her work which was reflected in her performance. It didn't take her supervisor long to notice that she had strong organizational skills and a good solid work ethic. Sally showed up on time, worked hard, and was always willing to fill in when needed.

On several occasions Sally filled in when her supervisor was absent. Not only did she handle her own duties well, she handled her supervisor's duties well too.

After about a year of this, Sally decided she needed something more. She approached her supervisor and the department manager about what the possibilities may be. Sally had hoped to come out of this with a $1 per hour raise.

As it turned out, a supervisor position had opened up just recently, and the manager and Sally's direct supervisor thought she'd be perfect for the job. Sally came out of the meeting with a $3 per hour raise, and a promotion!

Virginia at So-So Communications, INC

Virginia worked as a receptionist in the busy offices of So-So Communications, INC, a small software engineering firm specializing in a certain type of communications software.

Virginia was responsible for answering the phones, routing calls, greeting people who came in the door, managing vendors for many basic services, and ordering office supplies.

One day, Virginia had some free time and decided to use it to do something useful. She had thought for a while that the company may be paying too much for office supplies from the current supplier. She did some research and shopping around, and found a new source for office supplies that would save the company about $1,000 per year.

Encouraged by that, she made a few other phone calls, and managed to save the company another $1,000 per year by simply asking their current vendors for better pricing.

Virginia was excited to have saved the company $2,000, and thought she deserved to be recognized for it.

> She wrote a short, respectful letter to her manager explaining what she had done, and describing how she had been managing her duties at the office for some time.
>
> She then requested a meeting with her manager in which she handed him the letter, and requested that he read it then and there.
>
> When he finished reading it, she said to her manager:
>
> "I feel that I'm a valuable asset to this company, and I was wondering if I could possibly have a raise?" Virginia had hoped to get $1.00 per hour raise to match the $2,000 that she saved the company. She didn't get it. She did get a $0.50 per hour raise though, and her manager gave her a $500 bonus to reward her for her extra effort.

Video Resource
Video Name: Income versus Saving
www.YourHomeProgram.com/BookResource

The 5 Pay Raise Earning Principals

Now I'm going to talk about the **5 key principals** that will be necessary for most people to demonstrate in one way or another if they are to be as successful as they possibly can in their efforts to make more money at their current work.

Here they are:

Ownership

Ownership is the first principal necessary to be the most valuable employee you can be to your company.

This doesn't mean you need to own stock, or to "walk around like you own the place."

What it means is that you should *think* and *act* like an **owner** rather than an employee.

How does an owner act?

Take our case studies of John and Virginia as an example. Both John and Virginia were concerned about saving the company money and serving the company's interests.

Owners look out for the company.

If you're going to act on this principal of ownership, you need to act like an owner. You need to act like you *care* about the success and the future of the company. (Obviously, it is better if you *actually do* care!)

If you think, act, and *work* like an owner instead of an employee, then this will be reflected in most if not all aspects of your work. Usually this is something that managers and *actual* owners will notice!

Relationship

Relationship is an important principal to keep in mind at almost every job.

The relationship principal is about building meaningful (but appropriate) relationships with the people you work with, from the bottom of the company to the top.

The more positive relationships you build at work, the more you will be liked and viewed with favor by those you work for. Statements like "She is well liked..." and "His supervisors love him..." are born out of positive and healthy working *relationships*.

If you have an established positive relationship with a manager or supervisor and you go to that person to ask for a raise, your relationship is going to affect their *feelings* on the matter. Your existing relationship will be a **positive frame** in which your manager or supervisor can more easily see your **merit** which warrants the raise.

Without that positive frame, the person making the decision about your raise may have to work through their impressions of you first, and those will most likely be a factor in whether or not you get the raise you deserve. If you've already established the necessary positive working relationship, there are no more impressions to work through—as that part is *established*—and the only thing left is the **value** you bring to the table. *(Why you deserve the raise!)*

Work Ethic

If you are lazy and have poor work ethic, you can't possibly expect any supervisor, manager, or owner to be excited about giving you a raise. They may be excited about firing you, but that's about it!

For this reason, **work ethic** is a raise earning principal of utmost importance.

You need to be a hard worker. You need to be productive. You need to *try hard* at your job, and not just for the two or three chapters before your performance review.

Work ethic is about working hard regardless of who is watching. Work ethic means you can work on your own when necessary, and you don't have to have someone looking over your shoulder constantly in order for you to keep working.

Work ethic is a must. If you don't have it, *develop it*... and don't even think about asking for a raise until you get there!

Value

You will have the best chances of earning raises and making more money at your "day job" if you can clearly demonstrate to your employer that you are a **valuable** asset.

And believe it or not, this starts with you valuing <u>yourself</u> and <u>the job you do</u> for the company. You need to see yourself as worth it, and you need to understand how and why the job you do is meaningful and valuable to the company. First find your meaning and value to the company. Then, increase it!

The second part of value is that you need to be able to <u>demonstrate</u> your value to your supervisors and managers, and (ideally) demonstrate your ***increased value*** to the company as time goes on. Are you worth more to the company today than you were 6 months ago? Prove it!

Value yourself and your job. Know your value. And don't flaunt it necessarily, but be willing and able to document, describe, and demonstrate the value of the work you do.

Integrity

The next raise earning principal is *integrity*. Integrity means doing the right thing when nobody is watching. To understand why integrity is important when you're considering asking for a raise, it may help to understand just how *lacking* a lot of employees are in this area.

Your employer is probably used to employees who show up a few minutes late and leave a few minutes early (stealing time). They are probably used to having to buy more pens than they actually use because their employees take pens from the supply closet home and think nothing of it (stealing office supplies). They are probably used to having to check up on people and watch closely to make sure the company's computers aren't being used for personal internet surfing and games (stealing time / misuse of company resources).

Integrity means that when someone checks up on you, there won't be anything for them to find. Integrity means that you won't have anything to hide.

Integrity means that when you mess up, you fess up. If you make a mistake, rather than hide it you should highlight it. No, *seriously*. It might sound strange, but with integrity you can turn *even your mistakes* into positive traits. All you have to do is bring attention to them before anyone else does, and preferably as quickly as possible.

> *"Oops. I messed up. Here's what I did. Here's what I'm going to do to make sure I don't make the same mistake again."*

An attitude of integrity like this will go a long way towards building your status and eventually your salary in just about any company where status and salary can possibly be built.

The results of your confession will be <u>MUCH</u> better than if you waited until your performance review and let your superiors discover your mistake(s) on their own!

Have integrity. Show integrity. Doing so will be good for your company, your relationships, your value as an employee, and (ultimately) for *you!*

Before You Go Asking...

Before you ask for a raise, there are a few things you should know:

1. **Company policies vary.** You need to know your company's policies on raises before asking. If you don't have an employee manual you can look in, then simply ask a supervisor or someone in HR what the policies are. There may be a specific way in which the employee manual dictates that employees ask for a raise. If there is such a specification, then it is advisable that you follow it exactly.
2. **Some companies <u>only</u> give raises at review time.** This might also fall under the subhead of "policies vary", but deserves attention of its own. If your company has a policy of only giving

raises at regular review times, then you can still apply the principals and ideas from this chapter to the extent that this structure allows. One simple approach: about a month before your review, submit a letter of "self-review" to your supervisor. Highlight your value, your accomplishments, and anything else that will help your case. Explain that you believe these things should be considered in the process of your next performance review. Bring a copy of the letter to your review, just in case they lost their copy or the person performing the review hasn't seen it.

3. **Questions can be an important foot in the door.** Here are three important questions that you can ask that can lead to an eventual raise:
    a. "What other responsibilities can I take on?"
    b. "What can I do to grow in ***and with*** the company?"
    c. "What can I do that will make me more valuable to the company?"
4. **Be reasonable. Be realistic.** Research salaries (or hourly wages) in your field and geographical area, and see how yours compares. Don't expect magical results. Expect a realistic level of compensation to match your value to the company.
5. **A letter by itself just won't do.** Letters alone are not enough. Some people find it easier to communicate via a letter or email, but these communications are very limited in their effectiveness when asking for a raise. When you send a letter, or even an email, it does not demand an immediate response. If you do manage to get a response, "no" is a lot easier to say in writing. When you are sitting in front of a boss or supervisor asking them for a raise, you can see their reaction, they can see yours... an immediate response of some kind is necessary to keep the conversation from getting weird! If you are afraid of not being able to make your case verbally, then you can get the best of both worlds by first writing a letter, then requesting a meeting with your supervisor or boss at which you give them your letter and request that they read it. You can say something like "Here's a letter I wrote to ask for a raise. I'd like to know what you think, and I can wait a minute for you to read it right now so that we can discuss it." Whatever you do, don't just use a letter alone if you can help it. A letter and a meeting, or at the very least a letter and a phone call, will be much more effective.
6. **You have to sell yourself.** You need to sell yourself when you ask for a raise like you should sell yourself when you go to a job interview. Maybe you have an outline of your achievements on the job. Maybe you have a chart showing how much money you have saved or made the company. However you do it, you need to sell yourself. *(Consider something more than just, "Can I have a raise?")*

Steps To Asking For (And Getting) A Raise

Here are some practical steps you can follow if you want to get a raise at work. A raise isn't "guaranteed", of course, but with these steps and the information from this chapter you'll have the best chance possible.

STEP 1: Master The 5 Raise-Earning Principals!

At the risk of sounding repetitive, I need to bring up the 5 raise earning principals again. Mastering and applying these principals will make you more **valuable** to the company you work for. And your *value* as an employee is what is at the core of your request for a raise.

STEP 2: Do Your Homework

Research what other people in your field and geographical location with comparable education and experience are making. Make note of this, and save it for when the discussion comes up later.

At this stage you should also research your company's policies on raises and reviews if you don't know them already.

It's also wise to look at the atmosphere at work currently. Have there been recent management changes? Is the company struggling financially? *(If things like this are going on, now might not be the best time to ask for a raise, or your justification may have to be stronger to meet with success.)*

STEP 3: Create a List of Reasons You Believe You Deserve A Raise

Note that we're not talking about why you *need* a raise—i.e. "My wife just had a baby that I need to support"—but instead why you **deserve** a raise. This is about work <u>performance</u>, not your personal situation.

Make a list of the reasons why you deserve a raise. Your list might include things like:

- ✓ Your length of time with the company
- ✓ The length of time since your last raise
- ✓ Projects you've completed
- ✓ Ways in which you've become more efficient or otherwise improved at your job
- ✓ Ways in which you've saved the company money
- ✓ Ways in which you've made the company money

Try to highlight things that other employees couldn't also say. For example, rather than say "I landed 5 new accounts last month", you could say, "last month I landed our second largest account ever." *(Obviously, you'd only say this if it were true!)* The point is to highlight things that make you *uniquely valuable* to the company.

Once you have your list together, proceed to the next step.

STEP 4: Request A Meeting With Your Boss or Supervisor

Now is when the time comes to ask your supervisor for a meeting. This could be as simple as a phone call or email saying, *"I was wondering if we could meet for a few minutes to talk about my salary. When is good for you?"*

STEP 5: Go To The Meeting, and Make Your Pitch!

Now is when you go to the meeting that you've set up with your boss to discuss your salary and how valuable you are to the company.

Don't worry too much about what to say or how to say it. Just relax, use your notes, and explain why you deserve to make more money.

What If I Get Turned Down?

If you get turned down after asking for a raise, it's not the end of the world. You have several options. First, a quick rundown of what **NOT** to do:

- Don't be or act embarrassed (Really, it's okay! No need to feel embarrassed!)
- Don't get angry
- Don't cry

- Don't say things you'll regret
- Don't threaten to quit
- Don't say you have an offer from somewhere else for more money (they'll probably tell you to take it!)
- Don't beg
- Don't act unprofessional

Okay, so maybe the last one kind of sums it up. Be professional, and accept the rejection of your request graciously.

So what *should* you do if you get turned down?

For one thing, now is a good time to ask what you can improve or change in order to make yourself eligible for a raise in the future.

Take note of the feedback, and make your plans accordingly.

There may be other options too with some companies...

Other Ways To Make More Money At Work

There may be other things you can do to make more money at your existing job. These will depend greatly on the type of work you do, and the type of company you work for, but here are some examples that have worked for people in the past:

- Request extra hours
- Request to be paid in whole or in part based on performance (rather than hours)
- Request more responsibility
- Ask if you can do things on the side for extra money or a stipend (such as cleaning the offices, or other similar responsibilities that might otherwise be outsourced)
- Offer to cover other people's shifts
- Offer to help out the sales department on a part time/commission only basis

When The Only Way Up Is Out

Unfortunately, there are jobs out there in which there is very little or no opportunity for growth.

Sometimes, the only way to move "up" is to move *out*.

In these cases, you have three options:

1. Quit and look for work elsewhere
2. Take no action, Keep working at the same job, or
3. Keep your day job and look for other opportunities to make money on the side

It's this third option that is going to be a likely possibility for many people out there.Sometimes, even if you CAN get a raise at work you'll still want to find ways to make extra money on the side. That's why for the **next two chapters** we'll be talking about real, legitimate ways to make **extra** money. Don't miss it!

18 MAKING EXTRA MONEY, PART 1 (OFFLINE MONEY MAKING)

This chapter we're going to talk about making extra money above and beyond what you make at your day job. To start with, we will be talking exclusively about <u>offline</u> money making strategies.

Next chapter we'll talk about the opportunities that are available online. For now, we're keeping it *offline*.

This chapter we'll talk about everything from part time jobs, to odd jobs, to starting your own business, and we'll discuss how these money making strategies can be used to improve your financial situation with the ultimate goal of buying (and *keeping*) a home.

This chapter is ultimately about ***ideas***... it's about ideas that can help you build a more secure and steady income, and a better financial future. If you find an idea this chapter that sparks interest or enthusiasm in your mind, then you might want to take it and run with it!

Part Time Jobs

Part time jobs are a common way to earn extra money. Common part time jobs include things like paper routes, working in coffee shops, and flipping burgers to things like part time office positions and temp jobs.

For our discussion we'll break part time jobs up into the following categories:

1. Ongoing Part Time Jobs
2. Seasonal Part Time Jobs
3. Temp Jobs

Let's talk about each of these in some detail.

Ongoing Part Time Jobs

An "ongoing" part time job is probably the first thing you think of when you hear the term "part time job". It's simply a job that you apply for with an employer and work at, and for which you are usually paid hourly.

Part time jobs in this category have a couple of main advantages in that they usually provide **steady work**, and that they usually have **flexible schedules**.

The disadvantage of this category of part time jobs is that they often don't pay very well, and if you have any kind of commute to consider at all, it can cut into what you gain from the job quite a bit. In other words, the meager hourly pay and small amount of hours may not be enough to justify the commute.

Work places that could offer opportunities for ongoing part time jobs include...

- coffee shops
- restaurants / fast food
- retail shops

- specialty shops
- construction cleanup/grunt work
- grocery stores
- home improvement stores
- school districts
- some churches
- hotels and motels
- gas stations / convenience stores

As with any job opportunity, if you have a college degree you may have more options available. For example, many school districts are always in need of substitute teachers. The pay is usually decent, and you can usually work as much or as little as you want. Some school districts will hire substitutes with only an Associate's degree or the educational equivalent.

Even without a degree, there are quality ongoing part time jobs out there (even at schools, such as substitute teacher's aide positions) where you can feel at home, feel fulfilled, and make the extra money you need.

Seasonal Part Time Jobs

Seasonal part time jobs are the kinds that come around only at certain times of year. These include things

Video Resource
Video Name: Get more Cash for Home Ownership
www.YourHomeProgram.com/BookResource

like the extra help the many retail stores hire around the holidays, and extra harvest workers that some farms and orchards hire for a few weeks each year.

Usually these seasonal opportunities involve a lot of hard work in a short period of time.

The advantage of these part time opportunities is that they don't usually require a long term commitment. You commit to a few weeks of hard work, and once it's done, you're done!

The disadvantage of this type of work for many people is that sometimes it will require more hours (even if just for a few weeks) than they can reasonably expect to spare.

Jobs in this category may include any of the following:

- Seasonal farm/harvest help
- Seasonal retail work
- Staffing at state fairs, county fairs, and other annual events
- Staff positions at summer camps

Many seasonal part time jobs, as you might guess, involve outdoor work. This will appeal to some people of course, but if you're not the outdoors type you may be limited mostly to the holiday/retail opportunities.

Temp Jobs

In many office settings, when someone is going to be missing for a few days, the company hires a "temp" to take their place. Temp agencies can be a good place for a person with the right skill set to find work on a non-full-time basis.

Temp jobs are the business world's equivalent of substitute teaching. You show up for a day or two, do your work, and move on. If they like you, the next time they need a temp they may request you specifically.

Most temp jobs require computer skills, clerical and office skills, and the flexibility to be available on a moment's notice. This "spur of the moment" nature of temp jobs is perfect for some people, while for others it creates problems.

If you need a predictable schedule, then a temp job is probably not the path for you. If you can't make a big commitment (for one reason or another) and enjoy variety, a temp job might be a good fit.

The way to find temp jobs, for those who are interested, is to sign up at one or more temp agencies.

Applying For A Part Time Job

I'm including this short section because sometimes when you've been working steadily at one job for a lot of years, you get a little rusty at the job application process. Also, for a career oriented adult, the less-corporate, less-formal nature of the part time job application process might be a little disorienting.

(If you show up for a fast food joint interview in a suit and tie, you'll probably be laughed out of the building!)

So let's talk about the basis of applying for a part time job before we move on.

DRESS: Don't over dress. Don't under dress. Look nice, cleaned up, but not overdone. A good rule is this: Plan to dress *one step above* what you will be required to wear on the job.

PREPARATION: For many part time jobs, there will be no need for a lengthy and detailed resume outlining your experience in software engineering or machine shop work. What is best is to bring a simple manila folder with a short, one-page resume that highlights the aspects of your personality and work experience that will be valuable for this part time job. (Things like "great with people", or "lots of sales experience", or "hard worker" come to mind here.) This is more than most of their applicants will do so you will stand out, but it is not so much that it makes you look desperate or ridiculously over qualified.

FORMALITY: Many part time jobs have a rather informal interview process. It helps to know this up front, because your persona and preparation should more-or-less match the interview style.

PERSISTENCE: In the corporate world and in many "big company" jobs, persistence doesn't always pay off. With a lot of part time jobs, however, it does. Has it been a week since you submitted your application with no phone calls? Call and ask about it. In fact, in many cases you can just **ask for an interview** and get it. *(You'll have to judge the feel you get on this one as to whether or not it is a good idea to ask.)*

Start Your Own Business

Starting your own part time or side business can be tricky. You often need to spend at least a little money up front, and your success isn't always guaranteed.

With that said, for the right person in the right place with the right amount of flexibility, a part time side business can be just what is needed to bring in some extra cash.

A side business has a lot of advantages, like greater income potential than a part time job, greater flexibility and freedom, and the possible option to grow the business and even eventually replace your full time job.

The disadvantages are that the income isn't guaranteed, and it isn't guaranteed that your business idea will work. Side businesses often require some money to get started, or at the very least, some hard work in the beginning for which you won't get paid.

There are really endless possibilities for what your side business could be, but here are a few ideas:

- house cleaning business
- office cleaning business
- window cleaning business
- booth at a flea market selling crafts or anything else
- food stand at local events and festivals
- lawn mowing business
- tree trimming business
- handyman service
- massage therapy service
- making and selling custom bags, clothing, jewelry, etc.
- credit repair business

Making it Work

A lot of businesses fail. A lot of side businesses fail too. A lot of people have a lot of great business ideas that never get off the ground. Here's how you can avoid being one of them.

5 RULES FOR MAKING YOUR BUSINESS IDEA WORK

1. **Choose your market FIRST.** In other words, know who you are marketing to BEFORE you design and refine your product or service.
2. **Don't spend money needlessly.** Don't spend money that you don't have to spend. A lot of business ideas fail because people spend money on their business idea but never bother to start making money.
3. **Do spend money when you have to.** Sometimes people have the opposite problem of #2. They go the cheap route and their business never gets off the ground as a result. An example of an acceptable and necessary start up expense: *advertising!*
4. **Sell first, perfect later.** Don't spend 6 months perfecting a product, service, or business idea that you don't know whether or not you can sell. Sell it first, offering your "minimum possible" product or service, and grow from there.

5. **Get your first customer.** Once you have your ducks in a row, all your effort should go into getting your first customer. Once you've done that, analyze *how* you did it, and then REPEAT and REFINE that process until you get your next customer. *Rinse and repeat.*

Doing these 5 things will help you make money. They may not help you grow your business for the long run (it gets a little more complicated as you grow), but they will help you accomplish what many part time and side businesses never accomplish: *earning a profit.*

If you are on a limited budget, some businesses can be started with very little money up front. It's difficult, but "bootstrapping" your business startup process is possible if you're willing to work at it.

For minimizing startup cost, just remember this ONE rule (of the above 5): Get your FIRST CUSTOMER!

If you can win your first customer, you can sometimes use the income from your first customer to finance the purchase of needed tools and supplies, and even the advertising budget to gain more future customers. Getting that first customer in this manner can be a lot of work, and require a lot of time and effort, but if you're on a tight budget it **can** be done.

You just have to be creative, and willing to work at it!

Video Resource
Video Name: Income for Home Ownership
www.YourHomeProgram.com/BookResource

Educational Gigs

Do you have special knowledge or a special skill that other people would want to learn? If so, an educational gig may be the thing for you.

This type of money making opportunity usually involves teaching other people *about something* or *how to do something* that you are an expert in.

The possibilities here are really endless. Here are some ideas:

For The Musicians Among You:

- Voice lessons
- Guitar lessons
- Piano lessons
- Drum Lessons

For The Computer Savvy:

- Basic computer skills classes
- "Build your own computer" classes
- Beginner's programming classes
- Tutoring for students taking computer related classes

For The Crafty:

- Community sewing classes
- Quilting classes
- Seasonal crafting classes (e.g. a kid's class to make a Christmas ornament, etc.)

For The Artistic:

- Pottery classes
- Painting classes
- Drawing classes
- Sculpting classes

For The Handy:

- Woodworking classes
- Basic car maintenance classes

For The Athletic:

- Private Swimming Lessons
- CPR classes (if you are certified to train in CPR)
- Aerobics classes
- Dance lessons and classes

For The Homemakers:

- Baking classes
- Cooking classes
- Child-oriented activities and classes

For The Entrepreneurial Spirit:

- Marketing seminars
- Sales seminars
- One on one sales coaching

Hopefully the above choices give you a good start on some ideas.

A lot of times people have an idea for a class or lessons but don't know how or where to look for the proper venue.

The venue could be something as simple as your home, or could be as formal as the "non-credit" classes offered at many community colleges. Some specialty shops and art retailers might be open to letting you teach a class for them in an area where you are qualified (it never hurts to ask!)

The downside to educational gigs like these is that the money isn't always very steady. A <u>LOT</u> of people sign up for music lessons, for example, but very few people stick with them for any length of time!

This can make the process of finding students both frustrating and difficult.

This doesn't mean there aren't opportunities for steady income in the area of educational gigs. You may just have to work a little at finding them.

Sales And MLM

There are a lot of part time and full time opportunities that operate on a commission-only basis. These sales jobs can be a fun, flexible, and easy way to make some money on the side.

The tricky part is finding a sales opportunity that is *legitimate*, as there certainly are scams out there.

Opportunities in this area might include things like:

- MLM (Multi-Level Marketing) Companies
- Dish System Sales
- Alarm System Sales
- Computer System Sales
- Various Product Sales (Vacuums, Knives, Vitamins, Cleaning products, you name it!)
- Insurance Sales (and related products/services)

The major downside to looking for these opportunities is that sometimes it is difficult to separate the wheat from the chaff. In other words, it's hard to find the good ones!

The best way to find good ones is often through a friend or acquaintance—i.e. someone that you know—because with someone you know you are less likely to get into something that is a scam or otherwise bad news.

Aside from that, if you stick with reputable products and companies with established networks of independent sales people, you are a lot less likely to get into a situation where you'll be taken advantage of.

The big plus of sales jobs of this nature is that they can be quite profitable for those people who are skilled at and enjoy sales. The competition can be brutal though, so if you aren't a skilled salesperson you may want to consider something else.

Odds And Ends

There are a lot of money making ideas that are hard to fit into any particular category. For the purposes of our discussion this chapter, I'm going to lump them into this appropriately named "odds and ends" category.

The odds and ends of money making ideas include things like...

- "Odd" jobs (go figure)
- Garage sales

- Flea Markets
- Buying and selling silver and gold
- Various forms of offline "arbitrage" that encompass any of the above
- Antique mall booths

This is kind of a difficult category to summarize because the opportunities are so wide and varied. I'll cover a few basics here, and leave the rest up to your imagination.

Some people use things like garage sales, swap meets, and flea markets as what essentially amounts to a side business. There are a number of ways this might work. Here are a couple of examples:

- They may buy items cheap or in bulk at auctions and sell them at flea markets and garage sales
- They may buy items at garage sales for cheap and sell them at flea markets or at their own garage sale(s)
- They may find antiques at auctions, estate sales, and garage sales, and sell them in a booth at an antique mall

Both of these examples, and many others that are similar in nature, are really a form of what you might call *"arbitrage"*.

Arbitrage is a term usually applied to investing where an investor attempts to take advantage of slight differences in price. The term arbitrage, when applied to these money making ideas, boils down to finding a cheap source of goods or services, and re-selling those same goods or services at a better price in a different venue.

Arbitrage is about being a middle man. *Joe wants x and expects to pay x for it, John knows where he can get x for less money, so he offers to sell x to Joe and make a profit.*

A lot of ideas in the odds and ends categories can be summed up as being a form of arbitrage. *Find a market that needs a middle man, and be that middle man.*

The plus side of many opportunities in this category is that they can be fun and can be executed in a laid back, relaxed manner. The downside is that the money may not be steady or consistent, and there could be a costly learning curve that involves learning what sells and what doesn't.

Keeping Your Sanity

When you commit to taking a part time job, or starting a side business, it is going to put more stress on you and your family. Your relationships could suffer if you don't attend to them. Your health (both physical and mental) could suffer if you don't take the steps necessary to take care of yourself.

You need to be prepared for this up front, and plan for and take the steps necessary to keep your family, your health, and your sanity intact.

The most important thing you can do is draw a clear distinction between work time and family time. Keep your family time sacred, and keep certain days and times "off limits" for anything work related.

This will do two things:

1. It will give you the time and space you need away from your work and business obligations to recharge and de-stress.
2. It will give your family dedicated time that they can count on with you (that will be much needed).

One good approach is to take one full day off every week. It's helpful if it can be the *same* day each week, and if you can do it, that day should be untouchable for any and all other obligations. It's a family day, and nothing else. This is important for you <u>and</u> your family. It will show your family that they have a place in your life too, and that your work isn't the only thing in your life capable of holding a "priority" position.

In order to maintain your mental and physical health, it is also important to take time to do things you enjoy. Family time is important, and "you" time is just as important. You won't be much use to your family if you lose your mind. So find ways to take personal "sanity breaks" of your own.

This might mean spending time with some hobby or project that you enjoy, or taking a night "out" on your own occasionally to sip coffee and read books.

Whatever you do, take your health and your sanity seriously. Don't over-extend, or over-estimate your ability to work without balancing work time with play time. <u>Everyone</u> needs a break. <u>Everyone</u> needs play time.

You might like to think you're a superman or superwoman sometimes, but the reality is that you're not! So give yourself a break, and take care of yourself, your health, and your family in the midst of your efforts to make more money.

Conclusion

This chapter we've talked about a number of offline money making options. A lot of the ideas presented this chapter offer considerable opportunity for a person who is willing and able to jump on it.

However, these ideas and opportunities are not without their drawbacks.

One of the major issues with finding ways to make money on the side is the problem of **<u>TIME</u>**. Simply put, time is limited... and some people just don't have the *time* to put into a part time job.

Offline businesses and job opportunities also usually involve the need for your direct, physical involvement. This might mean needing to be available at a particular time of day or night. As you can probably imagine, this creates road blocks for a lot of people who might otherwise venture into a side business or other money making opportunities.

Then, there is all the legal stuff. Some offline job opportunities are tied up in various local and state legal requirements, which can further complicate matters. The legal requirements and restrictions aren't necessarily deal breakers, but they certainly create another level of complication.

Luckily, for those who for one reason or another just can't pull off an offline side business or part time job, there are still options available. The internet has opened up opportunities that can help many people get around the time and "physical presence" requirements that offline money making opportunities entail.

This is why next chapter, I'm devoting the entire chapter to teaching you about how to make money online. Stay tuned for some exciting possibilities!

19 MAKING EXTRA MONEY, PART 2 (ONLINE MONEY MAKING)

Making Extra Money, Part 2 (Online Money Making)

Sometimes, for one reason or another, a person won't be able to make extra money through a traditional part time job or a simple side business. Whether it is money constraints, time constraints, or even something like not having the necessary transportation to pull something off, sometimes the "offline" money making strategies just won't work.

Luckily, for people in that situation there still may be hope. The internet has opened up doors for the homebody and the geographically constrained like no other opportunity before.

Before we start talking about all the possibilities, though, I need to let you in on a few downsides to the world of online money making.

The Downside(s)

"Make money online!" That's the promise. There are many, many, MANY people out there making that promise. Most of them want to SELL you something so that THEY can *make money online*.

The huge downside to the online-money-making world that most people will experience the minute that they start to look for "real" opportunities is that there is, quite frankly, a lot of **junk** to sift through.

If you don't already know, let me be the first to tell you:

A LOT of the money-making products and websites out there are complete *crap*.

Sure, some of them aren't. In fact, if you're picky there are a lot of products out there that offer a lot of great information that can help you *if you apply it*. There are also a lot of scams, however, and a lot of hype, and a lot of people who make their money by telling other people they can make money, but never giving them any real substance or instruction as to how to do that.

The good news is that this chapter I'm going to give you quite a few ideas for *legitimate* ways to make money online. Many of you won't have to look for new or other ways to make money online after this chapter. Instead, you can pick something from the ideas I cover this chapter and learn more about it, and learn how to make that work.

Even if you can find an idea that fits you nicely, beware... a lot of other people have probably found the same idea! Another downside to making money online is that there is a lot of competition out there. And in several arenas, you're not just competing with people in one geographical area. You are, instead, competing with people all around the world. This can be both exciting and *frustrating*, and certainly adds a degree of difficulty to the process.

Another downside to the world of making money online is that if you're not tech savvy, you will be at a disadvantage. You need to be capable of learning at least some basic computer and internet skills in order to survive in the online markets. You also need to be willing to change frequently and update your skills and knowledge when working online. Things change quickly on the internet, which adds an interesting dynamic for anyone trying to make a steady income on it.

And speaking of change, I should note that due to the nature of the online world, the ideas and information that we'll cover this chapter are all subject to change. (Sorry, it's unavoidable!)

Now let's get back to...

Making Money Online

Last chapter was all about ideas. I tried to give you a lot of them in hopes that one of them would spark something brilliant in your own mind.

This chapter is about ideas, too. We're going to cover a lot of them. Not all of them will apply to everyone, but I'll try to talk about a broad range of ideas to give you who are reading this the best chance of finding that *spark* you need.

Selling Stuff Online

In the year 1997, the owner of a small music store in a medium sized city in the Midwest was doing an interview. In that interview, the music store owner said this:

Video Resource
Video Name: Get more Cash for Home Ownership
www.YourHomeProgram.com/BookResource

*"When we first started doing eBay, we didn't expect it to go anywhere. We have since **doubled** our business."*

Some random store in some random town took the relatively simple step of listing their inventory on eBay, and **doubled** the amount of business they were doing.

From the earliest stages of the "internet business" idea, the most natural and obvious way to make money online has been by *selling stuff*.

So that's what we're going to talk about first.

Before I go into this, let me tell you that there are literally HUNDREDS of ways and places to sell things online. I'm only going to cover a few here for the sake of space and time.

Ebay

EBay (www.eBay.com) was the home of one of the very first internet gold rushes. Thousands (if not millions) of people heard stories like the one above (which is a true story, by the way), and flocked to eBay in hopes of making it big.

Not everyone was successful of course (nor is everybody now), but today eBay remains one of the most active (and profitable) online marketplaces there is.

One big advantage to selling on eBay is that it is a relatively easy and user friendly process. Their system, having been around for so long, is highly refined. It's a "well-oiled machine". There is also a huge built-in audience there (i.e. a LOT of buyers). That's a good thing!

The downside is that the competition can be fierce, especially in certain categories.

Here are some common approaches that people use to selling on eBay:

- Expand their offline business by posting their inventory to eBay
- Expand their *online* business by posting their inventory to eBay
- Buy stuff at auctions, estate sales, and garage sales, and sell on eBay (often these people are specialized, and sell things like antique cameras or watches, for example)
- Make things to sell on eBay (For example, one person made a healthy part-time income for several years selling homemade dog treats on eBay. Some people sell handmade bags, socks, quilts, you name it!)

craigslist

Craigslist (www.Craigslist.org) is a mostly free online classified service. One simple way to make some extra money is to clean out your closets, your garage, or your basement, and sell your stuff on Craigslist.

Note that listing an item on Craigslist is different than on eBay. There isn't as much competition since you're selling locally, but people don't flock to the site to bid either. It is much like selling something through a newspaper's classified section. People respond to your ad, you tell them the price (if you didn't in the ad), they may visit you or meet you on some middle ground to see the item, and they may or may not buy it.

Because of the steps that are often involved, Craigslist selling is probably better for larger and bigger-ticket items, such as cars, exercise equipment, and other larger items that you might have difficulty *shipping* if they were sold on a site like eBay.

One thing to watch out for with Craigslist is scammers. Since the money transactions don't take place *through* Craigslist, it doesn't have the built in protections that eBay has.

A lot of people have been scammed on Craigslist through the use of stolen checks, fake money orders, and more. For this reason, if you decide to sell on Craigslist a good policy is "cash only", and make sure you check to confirm that it's real!

Etsy

If you are crafty, you may want to consider selling your crafts on Etsy (www.etsy.com). Of the websites we're covering this chapter, Etsy is probably the newest.

It is a specialized site where many *unique* and *handmade* items are listed and sold. Etsy is a different kind of marketplace, and while there is competition, it isn't quite as inundated as larger places like eBay (or Amazon.com, which we'll talk about next.)

If you're into sewing, crochet, or other handmade crafts, you may want to look at what Etsy has to offer as an online selling platform.

AMAZON.COM

Amazon.com is a huge marketplace that now includes many things, including books, music, food, and more. Amazon.com offers the opportunity for sellers to list items of their own for sale on their website.

The most obvious choice for sales is books, and if you're a used-book guru, Amazon.com might be a place where you could make some money. There is a lot of competition, though, which makes the used book prices go quite low. (The side effect of this is that the only way to make any real money selling used books on Amazon.com may be through *large volume* sales, and not everyone can do that.)

Another more recent opportunity that Amazon.com offers is the eBook market. Authors can sign up and list their own eBooks for sale on Amazon.com, making them available on Amazon's growing e-reader platform. The website for selling your own eBooks on Amazon.com is http://kdp.amazon.com.

info products

Since we're on the topic of eBooks, it's probably time to talk about an important category of products that can be sold online, that has collectively come to be known as "info products".

An info product is really just what it sounds like: a product where the main thing of value is the *information*. Sometimes people have special knowledge or information that can benefit others. Sometimes those people compile that special knowledge into an eBook or special "members-only" website, and sell it to the people who need or want it. The product they sell, whether it's an eBook, a membership website with information, or even a printed book, is what we call an "info product".

Info products aren't just limited to text. They can also be (or include) CDs or MP3 audio, video, and more.

Some examples of info product topics that have been successful for some are:

- how to save your marriage
- starting a _____ business
- how to fix _____ (health problem, social problem, or something as simple as a golf swing)

An advantage of the info products market is that because much of the time the topic or subject is something in high demand (i.e. people REALLY want an answer/fix for their problem), the prices are generally higher. "Info product" eBooks and printed books have sold at pricing ranging from $10 to $300 and up.

You may be thinking to yourself, "yeah, I have special knowledge, but I don't think I can write a book!"

The good news is that you don't have to. There are ways you can create an info product without necessarily writing it. Here are some ideas:

- You could create notes on paper and/or audio about your knowledge and give them to a freelance writer who could then create the product for you.
- You could have someone interview you and record it, have it transcribed, and sell the transcript and the audio recording.
- You could record audio or video of yourself teaching a seminar or class on the subject, and sell that.

Those are just some ideas. Once you have an info product to sell, you have to figure out how and where to sell it.

Sites like Clickbank.com, e-Junkie.com, and other similar sites are set up in such a way that it makes selling your info products online quite easy. With e-junkie, all you'll need is a PayPal account and you can have your info product online in a matter of minutes.

Clickbank.com takes a little more setup, but with Clickbank.com you can accept all major credit cards and have access to their network of *affiliates*.

An affiliate is someone who sells someone else's products either online or offline in exchange for a commission. Since the subject of affiliates has come up, now might be a good time to talk about...

affiliate programs

An ***affiliate program*** is a program through which affiliates (as defined above) can sell products and earn a commission. You can harness the power of affiliate programs in two special ways:

1. Get affiliates to sell your own products
2. Earn money online *as an affiliate* without having *or needing* a product of your own to sell!

Working as an affiliate selling other people's products has the advantage of being extremely easy to set up and get started. Without any product creation steps whatsoever, you can have a product to sell tomorrow.

Being **able** to sell that product, however, may be a different story!

This is because the big downside to the affiliate marketing world is there is a ton of competition, and some people are very good at it. You will be competing with affiliates who have been doing it for years, and who make $10,000 or more per month selling other people's products.

The good news is there is a lot of potential and you don't need your own product. The bad news is, the competition can make it difficult to get your foot in the money-making door.

Working Online

Maybe you don't have any ideas for a product, don't want to make a product, or just don't like the idea of selling junk online. If that's the case, you may still be able to find **work** online where you can make a good part time income and do so from the comfort of your home.

The advantages of working online are huge: often no set hours, lots of flexibility, work in your pajamas, work independently on your own terms with nobody looking over your shoulder.

The downside, like many other online opportunities, is that it can be difficult to separate the "real" opportunities from the scams, and once again, in some areas there is considerable competition that you must contend with.

In this section we're going to talk about a number of ideas for doing real, actual **work** online. Some of these are "per hour" jobs, others are "per project", and others yet may be paid on other terms, such as "per word" or "per page" for writing and editing/proofreading.

Let's talk about some exciting online work opportunities now, starting with perhaps the most basic...

Telecommute Jobs

A telecommute job is probably the closest online equivalent to a "real" job. With a telecommute job, you do the same work you would normally do for what is typically a "normal" employer. You just do it from home.

Some large and small companies are starting to see the benefits of having telecommute positions.

These benefits include things like:

- (proven) increased productivity when working from home
- happier workers with less stress
- less office space requirements
- less equipment requirements

Telecommuting part time (or even full time) can be a very rewarding and enjoyable way to work. The trick is, of course, finding the right opportunities.

Admittedly, telecommuting opportunities for part time workers are not as common as for full time workers, but they do exist. To find telecommuting opportunities, the first thing to know is what NOT to do: don't search online for "telecommute jobs".

Why not?

Because, when you search online for "telecommute jobs" you are almost guaranteed to end up on a website that wants to charge you a fee to tell you how to get a telecommute job. They may even offer listings. The fee is a waste of money, however, and the listings are most likely junk.

Here is the real way to find a telecommute job:

1. Make sure you have **skills** (or start now developing a skill) that will allow you to work from home. You can't work construction and frame houses part time from home. It just doesn't work. At the very least you will need data entry skills, but the more skills you have the better off you will be. (Helpful skills may include (but are not limited to) basic computer skills, programming, graphics design, website design, clerical and office, phone skills, sales, bi-lingual/translation, transcription, and more.)
2. Start by looking on **Craigslist**. Don't just search your own area, either (remember, this is telecommute!) Get a resume together that highlights your skills (see point #1) and submit it to positions for which you are qualified. Remember that chances are, the companies you are applying to are getting MANY applications off of Craigslist, so your resume (and email message, if applicable) should not only stick out, but should be very professional and to the point.
3. Browse internet companies for telecommute job openings. It's a little known fact that many web hosts, online retailers, and other internet/online companies routinely hire workers for telecommute jobs. Most commonly these jobs are in the area of customer service.
4. If you are moving or otherwise forced to leave a regular part time or full time job that COULD feasibly be a telecommute job and you have a good relationship with your employer, then suggest the telecommute option as a way to "keep you on board." It would save your company the

expense of having to find and train someone new, not to mention the other added benefits that we've already talked about.

Freelance Work

What I call "telecommute jobs" are jobs where you are working for an *employer*, who "hires" you as an *employee*. The other big way of working online is through freelance work.

When you do freelance work, you are not hired but *contracted*. You don't work for an employer, but for *yourself*. Yes, you'll still answer to your customers. You'll still have work to do, and if you don't do it well (or at all), you won't last long as a freelancer.

Freelance work can span a broad range of categories. We'll talk about several areas in which online freelance work is possible in a moment, but for now let's focus on how to go about finding freelance jobs.

There are **four main sources for freelance work** where most of the opportunities that we're going to cover can be found. They are:

1. Freelance Websites
2. Craigslist and Classified Websites
3. Direct Inquiry Local Businesses
4. Direct Inquiry To Non-Local Businesses

Freelance websites like Guru.com, e-Lance.com, and vWorker.com are popular places to find freelance work of various kinds. One advantage of using freelance websites like the ones listed here are that they provide a ready-made market place of jobs where you can hand-pick jobs in your specialized category to bid on. Another advantage is that most freelance sites offer escrow services and other helps that are designed to make your freelance transactions go smoothly. These can help you avoid scams and non-paying clients.

The two major downsides to the freelance sites are COST and COMPETITION. The websites charge fees which are most often taken from the amount of your winning bid. Some charge the fee whether you get paid or not, others only charge it when you are paid. The fees range from 5% to 15%. Competition on freelance sites is also something to consider. Depending on your area of work, you may be competing with people in other countries who are capable of doing the exact same work for much less money. This, and the generally high amount of competition on these sites, often drives bid prices quite low. This is great for the companies buying the work, but not as good for the freelancer trying to make a living.

Craigslist is a great source for freelance work if you know what to watch out for. There are scammers on Craigslist. There are people who will "hire" you for work but will never pay you a dime. If you can avoid the ads posted by these people, Craigslist can be a great source for freelance jobs. The best advice to avoid the scams and find real freelance work on Craigslist is this: watch Craigslist ads every day in one or two areas for a month or two. Take note of any ads that have similar wording, obvious re-posts or repeats, and *especially* those that sound too good to be true. Tune in your "fraud" detector (the one in your head) to find and weed out these ads in the future, and you'll be on your way to finding the right kind of opportunities.

Finally there is the direct inquiry approach, which can apply to local or non-local businesses. With local businesses, the tactic is simple: walk in, introduce yourself, and offer your services. You can also take your time, develop relationships, identify needs, and suggest ways that you might help meet those needs.

The most common "direct-inquiry" scenario involving *remote* businesses is the process of getting freelance writing gigs for newspapers and magazines. If you're not a writer, there may still be opportunities available for you. The process goes something like this:

1. Find a company who might benefit from your service as a freelancer
2. Contact that company and tell them about your service

This is commonly done for anything from editing and proofreading, to more specialized services like indexing and book formatting. It's a viable approach for most (if not all) of the categories of freelance work we're about to cover.

Now, let's talk about a few possible categories in which you might do freelance work...

Website Creation

Website creation involves creating and editing websites for companies. There may be graphics creation and manipulation involved, programming, and even some "SEO" (search engine optimization) related stuff.

In order to best pull off freelancing in the area of website creation, you will need to have a wide array of technical skills at your disposal.

For those who have the skills, website creation can be an enjoyable part time freelance gig.

Graphics Creation And Manipulation

Graphics creation and manipulation is similar to the website creation, but is often more specialized. People focusing on this area in their freelancing efforts will typically have great skills in the areas of computer graphics creation and editing, illustration and drawing, and flash/animation. If you have a hobby of graphic art on the computer, or work with graphics in your "day job", then moonlighting as a graphics guru might be just the thing for you.

Programming

Programming is another specialized area requiring special knowledge and skills related to the computer. If you have any experience programming (whether professional or not), you can probably find freelance work as a programmer. The key is, as with many freelance opportunities, to find the jobs that match (and don't exceed) your skill level.

voice talent

If you sound like Morgan Freeman, then you might have a future in the world of professional voice-overs. The voice talent market is a competitive market, though admittedly not everyone can do it. Since, in many cases, companies seeking voice talent will be looking for Native English speakers with a very clear and professional sound, you won't necessarily have the huge amount of competition from all over the world like you would working in some other areas (such as data entry, for example). Even though your competition is *less*, it is still **fierce** competition. In the professional voice-over market you'll be competing with numerous professional and well-known radio and TV voice talents.

translating

Do you speak more than one language fluently? If so, you might be able to pick up freelance work as a translator. This specialized area is a common need for businesses trying to keep up with the ever-increasing levels of diversification among their clientele.

writing

Writing is an extremely popular and competitive area of freelance work. The term "freelance writer" has an almost romantic feel to it for many people. The reality may not be as romantic as the term feels, however.

Freelance writing is hard work, and again, is quite competitive. Depending on the market, rates can vary from as little as a penny per word, to over a dollar per word. The dollar-per-word might sound good, but you will typically work very hard for that dollar. Believe it or not, sometimes a few pennies per word can be more profitable to you as the freelancer.

If you are a skilled writer and willing and able to meet deadlines while putting out consistent quality work, freelance writing might be worth a go as a part-time money-making venture.

data entry

Data entry is a very competitive area of freelancing. Usually online data entry freelance jobs involve transferring data from one format to another manually and/or inputting data into an online form.

Data entry is probably one of the most competitive areas of online freelancing with perhaps the lowest pay for the freelancer. Because of the high level of competition, often the best places to find data entry jobs are places like Craigslist or other online classifieds rather than using the freelance sites. (Note: You can still find work for reasonable pay at freelance sites, but it may be more difficult to come by.)

transcription

Transcription typically involves taking information in one format (such as audio), and producing a written version of that same information.

Transcription work is done verbatim, and like data entry is a very "detail oriented" task. Accuracy and speed are the most valued traits of transcription freelancers. If you are a fast typist and a good listener, offering audio transcription services might be the foot-in-the-door you need to get into the freelance world.

virtual assistant

A virtual assistant may do any variety of online (or even offline) tasks for a fee. The tasks could range from answering phones, to checking email, to making reservations and other appointments. In many cases, companies or individuals looking for a "virtual assistant" are looking for a sort of online receptionist with the technical and organizational skills that can help them organize and maintain their online (and offline) business and/or life. If you are detail oriented, tech savvy, and an organizational guru, freelancing as a virtual assistant might be worth a try for you.

SEO AND RELATED SERVICES

There are a number of things involved in running a website or a business that is on the internet. One of those things is commonly called "SEO", which stands for "search engine optimization".

SEO refers to the process of taking various steps to increase the chances someone searching in a search engine will find your site.

To be successful in the area of professional SEO, you really need to be an expert. But even if you aren't skilled in all the aspects of SEO, there are specialized tasks involved in the search engine optimization process that you may be able to do.

Here are a few examples: article submission, press release submission/distribution, article writing, press release writing, editing websites for SEO purposes, and setting up social site profiles (i.e. Facebook, Twitter, online forums, etc.) that will be used for SEO purposes.

If all this is over your head, don't despair. Just move on to the next item on the list, which is...

ONLINE ODD JOBS

There are some opportunities for the freelancer that are difficult to categorize, or that are too uncommon to have their own category.

I call these opportunities online "odd jobs". Online odd jobs may include things like writing product reviews, editing term papers, or doing research on a specific topic for an individual or company. Online odd jobs also include things like taking surveys (for companies like Brand Institute), setting up or installing software for clients, and any other tasks that a company or individual might need that they are willing to pay for, and that you can do remotely from your home.

Even if you don't have specialized knowledge or skills, it may still pay to surf the online classified ads and freelance sites looking for your own special category of online odd jobs!

Hybrid Money Making Strategies

Before we close this chapter, I'd like to talk a little about what you might call "hybrid" money making strategies.

Some money-making strategies aren't ONLY online, but are offline too. Some of the best strategies for making a part time income involve both online *and* offline work.

One example is the practice of buying certain high quality items at estate sales, auctions, and garage sales and re-selling those items online via sites like eBay and Craigslist.

Another example is taking your online freelance work to local businesses. If you do graphics design and web design online, why not take to the streets and offer your services to local businesses?

These are just examples but hopefully you get the point: don't limit yourself by thinking that your part time money-making venture should necessarily be "online" or "offline" exclusively. It can actually be ***both*** if you want it to be.

Conclusion

As you can probably see from what we've covered this chapter, there are plenty of opportunities to make money online. The trick is, as has already been said, finding the **right** opportunities for *you*.

Even with the wide variety of online opportunities available, the "online" thing just won't work for some people.

You may be wondering what can be done about your income if you just don't have the TIME to commit to a money making opportunity either online or offline.

There is no getting around it, just about everything we've covered so far can end up taking you considerable *time*, whether to do the work itself, or just to find the work.

Is there anything that can be done to increase income for those who can't possibly handle the time commitment necessary for a part time money-making venture?

In many cases, the answer is **"yes!"**

Next chapter we'll talk about things that can be done to increase your income that don't involve getting a part time job or starting a side business. You won't want to miss these powerful income-increasing strategies!

20 MORE INCOME INCREASING STRATEGIES

Maybe you can't do the part time job thing, or the part time business, and you aren't tech savvy enough to do more than check your email online.

What are your options, then, for increasing your income?

Believe it or not, you may still have a few.

This chapter we're going to talk about a few options for those who may feel like they are running out of income generating options.

A Friendly Reminder

Before we get into the meat of this chapter's discussion, let me give you a friendly reminder about one important option that so many people overlook: asking for a *raise!*

Yes, I know we talked about it already. But if you're so stretched time-wise that you can't fathom taking on a part time income generating task, then perhaps you're working hard enough to earn a raise.

If you're at a job where a raise might be a possibility, I encourage you to go back to the material we covered about asking for a raise, and put it into practice.

Now on with the show...

Changing Jobs

Drastic times may call for drastic measures. If you're at a dead-end job with no possibility of earning more money in the near future and that dead-end job is sucking so much life out of you that you can't possibly put in the time and energy necessary to make money elsewhere, then maybe it's time to look for a ***new job***.

Don't sacrifice your life or your well-being for a job that gives you neither.

If you can find income elsewhere in the form of another job or even a different position in the same company, that's something you might want to consider.

A new job could give you the time and freedom you need to either get a part time job or pursue a part time business venture. The new job may also have other benefits that affect your income and expenses indirectly, and could benefit you substantially in the long run.

For those who can't change jobs or positions at their company, I'll offer a few more possibilities in the following paragraphs.

Make It A Family Affair

Maybe you don't have the time to tackle a side business, but your spouse or partner does. Make it a joint effort. You bring the idea, some knowhow, and maybe some friendly motivation, and your spouse or partner brings the labor.

Working this way can be tricky, but it can be a great way to make the most of your resources and ideas. Letting someone else be "you" can give you the freedom to explore money making ideas without having to put as much time into the ideas yourself.

Of course, the person needs to be rewarded. Ideally if a business idea makes money, the person helping you (be it a spouse, partner, roommate, or the teenager upstairs) will get a direct benefit from their work as your side business starts to make money. That could mean hourly pay or a percentage of the profits, and is something you'd probably want to work out ahead of time in order to keep everyone happy!

Only Give Uncle Sam What You Owe Him (Part 1)

Millions (and I *do mean millions*) of Americans give the government an interest-free loan every single year.

Video Resource
Video Name: Income for Home Ownership
www.YourHomeProgram.com/BookResource

The reason that they give the government this interest free loan is because they are giving the government more than they actually owe in the first place.

They are doing this through excess **tax withholding** on their pay checks, and proof of these interest-free loans can be seen every single year when tens of millions of Americans get their tax refunds.

You can stop giving Uncle Sam an interest free loan ***and give yourself a raise*** by ONLY giving Uncle Sam what you OWE him out of your paycheck! This is done by simply changing your tax withholding so that you are no longer getting a $3,500 refund each year.

That $3,500 per year that you are no longer loaning the government will amount to an almost $300 per month RAISE that you can give *yourself*.

Only Give Uncle Same What You Owe Him (Part 2)

I know this heading is just like the one above. Why? Because there are other ways in which many Americans frequently give Uncle Sam too much money.

Let me sum this section up by saying this:

If you're like most people, you probably pay too much taxes.

I'm not talking about withholding. I'm talking about what you actually end up ***paying***, even after your big tax refund.

Many Americans don't get all the deductions and credits they should simply because they don't know about them. The tax code is complicated, and people depending on software and books to get them through the tax return process may be short changing themselves.

Even if you have doubts, I recommend trying this just ONCE: have a competent accountant do your taxes for you.

You may find that you've been paying too much taxes all along.

You may be able to go back and amend past returns to get back some of that overage you've paid. At the very least, you can start saving money and **give yourself a raise** from here on out.

Giving Yourself A Raise

I've used the phrase "give yourself a raise" a few times now.

I'd like to talk a little more about how you can give yourself a raise. Here are a few ideas:

- ✓ **PAY OFF YOUR DEBT.** If you wipe out $300 worth of monthly payments on debt, then guess what? You just gave yourself a $300 per month raise!
- ✓ **CUT BACK ON YOUR EXPENSES.** Every dollar that you **don't** spend on a monthly basis is like a dollar raise. If you can find a way to save $100 per month on your regular expenses, then you can give yourself a $100 per month raise!
- ✓ **PAY YOURSELF FIRST.** No, really. A penny saved is really a penny earned. Eventually having a good chunk of money deposited in an interest earning account can give you a steady monthly income in the form of _interest_. By doing nothing but paying yourself first, you can give yourself a raise!

Video Resource
Video Name: Get more Cash for Home Ownership
www.YourHomeProgram.com/BookResource

I have some good news for you. Maybe you don't see any real hope of making more money the "old fashioned way". If that's the case, you are in luck. Over the next few chapters we are going to be talking about how you can give yourself a raise by doing the things I mentioned in the bullets above.

We'll talk about how you can improve your cash flow, effectively giving yourself a raise, by paying off debt and cutting back on your expenses.

You might think there is no room to cut back or reduce your expenses, but just wait. If you can implement the approach that I'm going to give you over the next few chapters, it will be *close to impossible* for you to NOT save money.

Beginning next chapter, we'll be talking about how to save money across each of the 5 categories of expenses, with potentially powerful results!

21 YOUR EXPENSES, AND HOW TO TAKE CONTROL OF THEM – PART 1

For the next few chapters, my focus is going to be showing you the *power* that you probably aren't aware that you have. I'm going to give you the tools you need to be **empowered** to take CONTROL of your own expenses (whether you think they are expenses you can control, or not).

The information that I'm going to share with you in this and the coming chapters is all about putting YOU in the driver seat.

You can take control of your expenses.

You can win back your financial life.

I'm about to show you how.

The 5 Categories Of Expenses

If you think back to earlier in the program, you might be able to recall when we talked about the **5 categories of expenses**. I broke your expenses up into 5 categories for you to analyze separately. The 5 categories I used may have seemed a little unorthodox at the time (and may still now), but we used those 5 categories for good reason:

Because expenses in each category must be dealt with **differently** if you're going to have the type of impact you want to have on your expenses.

In order for you to truly take control of your expenses, you need to tackle expenses in each of the 5 categories in the way most effective for that category.

> **The powerful thing about this approach is that if you can accomplish even a little across each of the 5 categories of expenses, your "little" successes will often add up into a substantial amount of savings!**

So let's do a quick review of the 5 categories of expenses so we're on the same page. Here they are:

1. **Required and Unseen Expenses** - Income Taxes, Property Taxes, and health insurance premiums (the ones taken directly from a person's pay check) would fall under this category for most people.
2. **Required Bills** - These are the bills that most consider non-negotiable. They include things like electricity, natural gas or propane, water, trash, car registrations, and car insurance.
3. **Negotiable Bills** - These are bills that can generally be reduced or eliminated. Included in this category are phone bills, mobile phone bills, long distance, internet, cable TV, gym memberships, and more.
4. **Regular Required Expenses** - These are the expenses that most people have that don't come as a bill in the mail. Things like groceries, school enrollment, oil changes for your car, and similar expenses would fall under this category.
5. **Extra Expenses** - This is the category of expenses that is most often out of control. This category of expenses includes all of the extra and unplanned expenses that many people have but never take

the time to track or plan for. Things like snacks and drinks, dining out, and entertainment expenses are included in this category. One could also include "emergency" expenses, because whether right or wrong, many people seem to treat emergency expenses as if they fall into this category (i.e. they don't plan for them, nor do they track them.)

This chapter our focus is going to be on the first two categories in this list:

Required and Unseen Expenses and *Required Bills.*

So let's get started with talking about...

Taking <u>CONTROL</u> of Your Required And Unseen Expenses!

Income Taxes

We've already talked a little about how the "required and unseen" expense of <u>taxes</u> can be dealt with.

When income taxes are taken directly out of your paycheck, sometimes it's difficult to understand the impact of them. Many people see that *big tax refund* in April each year as a *good* thing. The truth is, however, that there is <u>**no**</u> reason you should be giving the government that big interest-free loan every year. If you haven't already done so, you should take action now to <u>stop</u> giving Uncle Sam more money than he needs.

Here are some steps to take:

1. **Change your tax withholding** with your employer. I've actually heard HR people tell employees that they were not *allowed* to change their withholding. That's nonsense. The worksheet you fill out estimates what your withholding allowance should be. The bigger the number you claim, the bigger your refund is. If you were claiming "9" so that you could get a big refund, there isn't any reason why you can't *lower* that number so that you'll get more money in your PAYCHECK versus in your tax refund.

Video Resource
Video Name: Spending Habits, Budget and Home Ownership
www.YourHomeProgram.com/BookResource

2. **Have an accountant review your taxes.** I know the extra expense may seem like a lot. But just imagine this: If you do step 1 above, for <u>MANY</u> people that's going to mean about $200 or even $300 *or more* in savings <u>EVERY</u> <u>MONTH</u>. If you just added $200 per month to your cash flow, then I can't think of *ANY* reason why you shouldn't take $200 or $300 **just once** to have an accountant review your taxes. ***You might find that having your taxes professionally done can save you even more!***
3. **Get serious about deductions.** Do you give 10% (or more) of your income to a church or charity? Do you frequently make donations to Goodwill or the Salvation Army? Do you pay large

amounts of medical expenses each year? All of these things could be possible itemized deductions on your tax return, and could save you money. If you have doubts, take a piece of paper and run through a year in your mind. Estimate the amount of money you give in donations and spend on medical expenses. It will be helpful if you can look back through a check register or bank statements. You might find that if you just improve your tracking a little, you could save money by *itemizing* your deductions on your tax return.

Property Taxes

Since the whole purpose of this program is helping you reach the goal of home ownership, property taxes are an important expense to talk about. Sure, you might not have to worry about them *now*. But *eventually* property taxes will be part of your "required and unseen" expenses category.

When someone has a mortgage, they typically don't pay their property taxes directly. A portion of their monthly "house payment" goes into an escrow account to pay for insurance and property taxes.

Each year they get a property tax statement in the mail, which is usually confusing and difficult to read.

How property taxes are calculated varies from place to place (by county, actually), but one thing remains the same across the board:

The taxes are based on the *assessed* value of the home.

In other words, a homeowner may get a notice in the mail that their home has been re-assessed by the county and the value has been deemed to be $150,000. "Good news," they think... "that's up from $130,000 last year!"

Then their property taxes go up, and their house payment increases by $50 or $100 per month. Ouch!

What a lot of people don't realize is that the "assessed" value of their home is up for debate. Through a special process (which is admittedly complicated), they can **appeal** the assessed value of their home if they don't feel their home has been assessed fairly.

Here's the thing to take away from this:

You don't have to take the property tax assessment lying down. If you think you're getting the shaft, then fight it.

According to some statistics many people pay **over $1000 more than they should be paying** for property taxes. When the time comes, make sure that you're not one of them!

Health Insurance Premiums

Health insurance premiums are another "required and unseen" expense that many people rarely think about. Some people let the health insurance premiums be deducted from their paycheck, and ultimately *forget* that the money ever existed.

Depending on your health and your actual insurance needs, you may be paying too much for health insurance.

Here's an example to illustrate:

One young employee had $150 per week taken out of his paycheck for health insurance. He was on the "mid-range" plan, and his company paid part of his premiums. The $150 per week was his part.

That $150 per week didn't seem too bad since he never saw the money.

The young man typically only went to the doctor only once or twice per year.

One day, something occurred to the young man: *he was paying* **over $600 per month** *for the benefit of having only a $50 co-pay at the doctor's office when he went only twice a year. Sure, he was covered in the event of a serious illness or emergency, but the company offered cheaper plans that would cover that.*

When the next open enrollment came around, the young man changed his insurance coverage to the bottom tier plan. He had to pay the full expense of his doctor visits (which averaged about $200 per visit) and still had enough coverage to prevent a huge financial loss in the case of a serious injury or illness.

The young man's health insurance premiums went down to around $250 per month. That's a savings of over $4,000 per year!

Video Resource
Video Name: Function of a Budget
www.YourHomeProgram.com/BookResource

Sometimes there are cheaper plans available that offer "catastrophic" coverage for the people who don't have a lot of regular medical expenses and doctor visits.

Many people could save thousands of dollars a year by selecting one of these plans.

Sure, they'll have to pay more for doctor visits. Yes, they might have to pay for their own (occasional) prescriptions.

But in the long run, these people could save **huge** amounts of money in insurance premiums by taking on a few "extra" medical expenses.

The moral of the story: don't pay for more health insurance coverage than you need.

Obviously, you want the best coverage you can get, but if paying for your own doctor visits twice a year could save you $400 per month without sacrificing the "bigger" parts of the coverage (such as hospitalization), would you do it? *Of course you would!*

Taking **CONTROL** of Your Required Bills!

Now let's talk about how you can take control of your "required" bills. This is a difficult category of bills, and some of these have a tendency to leave people feeling *helpless*. Some of these bills have serious consequences if they aren't paid, and people often see them as set-in-stone and non-negotiable.

Let's talk about what can be done about them.

This category includes bills like electricity bills, natural gas bills, water and trash bills, alimony and child support. Auto insurance would also typically be included here. Certain things can't really be avoided. Sometimes, you can at <u>least</u> do things to better manage them, though. In this section we'll look at some of the big ones that most people have to deal with at one time or another.

Electricity

Reducing your electricity usage (and therefore your bill) may be easier than you think. Here are a few ideas to get you started:

- ✓ **Buy and Use A Programmable Thermostat.** If you're gone all day at work and the kids are in school, is there any reason you should be paying to keep your home at just the right temperature while you're *gone?* A programmable thermostat will allow you to set different temperatures for your home for different times of the day and the week. This can be an excellent way to save money by only using your air conditioner (or heater, if you don't use gas heating) when you need it the most. *(Note: if you are renting a house with central heat and air, most landlords won't object to you installing a programmable thermostat, but be sure to ask first!)*
- ✓ **Use energy saving light bulbs.** LED and compact florescent light bulbs can save you a ton of money on electricity in the long run. Replacing all of the lights in your house with their energy efficient equivalent can save you a bundle.
- ✓ **Turn off the lights**. Speaking of lights, learn to turn them off. Don't use electricity that you don't need. Turn lights off when you leave the room. Don't leave the TV or radio on when you aren't there to listen. *Do you frequently forget to turn things off at night?* Simple electrical timers (that can be purchased at most hardware stores) can be a great tool for helping the forgetful to be more energy efficient.
- ✓ **Buy a $25 electricity usage monitor** to see how much your appliances are costing you. These monitors are quite handy, and can tell you how much electricity a given appliance is using. You simply plug the monitor into the wall, and the appliance into the monitor, and watch the reading on the monitoring device. One consumer found that their outdated refrigerator was costing them $35 per month! They replaced it with an energy-efficient model and saved over $300 per year!

Natural Gas

The biggest natural gas expense is usually for heating a home or apartment in the winter. The second is for hot water. We already talked about how a programmable thermostat can help your electricity usage. If you use natural gas for heating, then the same thing can help to (sometimes drastically) reduce your winter heating bills.

Here are some other things that can be done to help reduce natural gas usage:

- ✓ **Winter Weatherization.** Buy inexpensive foam seals and plastic to keep the warm air in and the cold air out around doors and windows.
- ✓ **Don't turn your thermostat up as high.** Especially in colder climates, you can save a lot of money each winter by dressing warmer around the house and setting your thermostat a couple of degrees lower.

- ✓ **Make sure your water heater is insulated.** There are special insulation wraps that can be put around water heaters. Water heaters waste energy when they have to cycle on due to lost heat.
- ✓ **Turn your water heater down.** Having a water heater turned up too high can be a waste of money. Try turning it down some for a month or two and see what effect it has.

Water, Sewer, and Trash

Trash usage can be a tricky one because there aren't always a lot of choices (or <u>any</u> choices) when it comes to trash service. If you have a choice between multiple companies, then shop around. If you don't, then find out if your trash company offers a cheaper service, such as one with a smaller trash can, or perhaps a discount for pre-paying.

For water usage, there are things you can do to make your home more efficient and use less water, which should lower your water and/or sewage bill.

Here are some ideas:

- ✓ **Take shorter showers, or fewer showers.** If you're showering for an hour two times a day, now might be a good time to consider cutting back!
- ✓ **Take showers instead of baths.** A typical (short) shower uses about 30% of the water that it takes to fill a typical bathtub.
- ✓ **Use faucet aerators and water-saving shower heads.** Often you can reduce the amount of water you use by simply installing shower heads and faucet attachments that are designed to reduce water usage.
- ✓ **Fix leaky faucets, toilets and pipes**. If you have any faucets, toilets, or pipes that are leaking, those leaks can actually cost you a lot of money in the long run. Go to the hardware store and spend $10 to get the supplies you need to fix your leaks. Your water bill will thank you!
- ✓ **Only run full loads of laundry and dishes.** Using the washing machine and the dish washer only when you have a full load can be good ways to cut back on water usage.
- ✓ **Water your lawn less.** A lot of water is wasted watering lawns during rainy periods. You can save money by watering even just a little less. If you see rain in the forecast, then try skipping this week's watering and let the rain do its job.

Auto Insurance

Auto insurance can often be like health insurance. People frequently have more coverage than they need. Auto insurance is tricky, though, because you **don't** want to end up with <u>LESS</u> coverage than you need (which *does* happen!)

Here are some ways you can make sure you are getting the best deal on car insurance without sacrificing the most important aspects of your coverage:

- ✓ **Shop around and compare.** Do it <u>often</u>. Each time your policy comes up for renewal, call around and get quotes from a few other companies. Insurance rates frequently fluctuate and at any given time one company may have a drop in rates that could make them a more economical option for what amounts to the exact same coverage.

- ✓ **Raise your deductibles.** If you have $250 or $500 deductibles, you could consider raising them to $1,000. The higher deductible will mean lower monthly premiums. (You should always at least ask what the difference is so that you can make an educated choice.)
- ✓ **Get rid of the extras.** Some auto insurance policies come with extras (such as road side assistance) that many people don't realize are there, and never actually *use*. (If your work gives you an AAA membership, you don't need road side assistance from your insurance carrier.) Know what is on your policy, and know what you do and don't need. Stick to the necessities!

Imagine The Possibilities...

If a person were to implement every single idea from this chapter, the savings could be substantial.

Some people, by just taking steps to address their taxes and their health insurance premiums could save as much as $500 or $1,000 *per month!* That's a lot of money saved! If through following the steps from this chapter, you could save even a fraction of that (say $250 per month), it would still amount to thousands of dollars in your pocket in the long run. $250 per month is $3,000 per year.

Over 10 years, that's $30,000 in savings!

As you can probably see by now, there is actually a lot that can be done with these "required" expenses and bills... bills that many people consider to be "out of their control".

Just imagine what's possible with your other expenses!

This chapter was all about the non-negotiable bills and things that people don't often think about reducing. Next chapter, we'll talk about the "Negotiable Bills" category of expenses.

Trust me; you don't want to miss it!

22 YOUR EXPENSES, AND HOW TO TAKE CONTROL OF THEM – PART 2

Last chapter we talked about how to reduce expenses in areas that for some, aren't exactly obvious targets for big savings.

This chapter we're going to talk about your negotiable bills... bills that you probably know you can get for cheaper or that you may not need at all. Even if you think you don't have enough of these kinds of bills, or you think that you are already as "trim" as you can get... don't skip this chapter because there may be some strategies and tactics that surprise you!

So let's get on with talking about your...

Negotiable Bills

You may be wondering just what is meant here by the term "negotiable".

Negotiable bills generally refer to bills that meet one or more of the following criteria:

- ✓ The bill can be reduced one way or another
- ✓ There is competition (You can take your business somewhere else)
- ✓ It is expendable (You can live without the service if you need to)

As you can imagine, this covers a very wide array of bills that people pay.

Many of the bills in this category can be lowered just by making simple phone calls and asking some questions. Others are more complicated. Some are, simply put, services that you can live without and don't need, and you should therefore consider cutting them for the sake of your financial well-being.

Communication and Connectivity

The first types of negotiable bills that we're going to look at are those involving *communication* and *connectivity*.

This includes phone bills, mobile phones, pagers, internet service, and more.

Many families spend huge amounts of money on communication and connectivity without ever considering what can be done to spend **less**.

There are three main ways to cut back on communication and connectivity bills...

Negotiate

This means you call the company in question and say something like this:

> *"Hi, I'm trying to get my expenses under control and need to do something about this {insert bill type} bill. Is there anything I can do to reduce the amount I'm paying for this service?"*

If they say they can't help you, suggest that you can get a better price somewhere else and you're considering cancelling your service. Ask if they are SURE that there isn't anything they can do to help you LOWER your bill. If they still say "no", then move on to the next option, which is...

Compare

One important thing to do with services in this category is to **compare** what you can get for your money across different companies. Compare prices. Look at recent offers from the company you use and others and see how they compare to what you're paying now.

It is fairly common for phone companies and cell phone companies to change plans and offer new services and deals as time goes on. If you are on an obsolete plan, you may be paying too much. Ideally, the phone rep will tell you this when you call to negotiate, but if they don't, you can probably find out on your own by doing some basic online research and comparison shopping.

An example of how this can pay off: One family was paying about $250 per month for a 900 minute plan on 3 separate cell phones. After shopping around and comparing, they realized that several pre-paid carriers were offering plans that would allow them to get unlimited minutes on all 3 phones for a total of around $160 per month. That's $90 per month in savings, just for taking the time to look around!

Cancel

The third option for lowering communication and connectivity bills is *cancellation*.

You can **cancel the service** itself, or **cancel parts of your service** to make it more affordable.

Video Resource
Video Name: Function of a Budget
www.YourHomeProgram.com/BookResource

This might mean "downgrading" to a 500 minute a month plan on a mobile phone that you don't use very much. It might mean changing your internet to a slightly slower internet plan, or getting rid of some of the bells and whistles on your phone service.

How Much Can You Save?

Many people who have phone service, mobile phones, and internet service will be able to knock $50 to $100 off by simply thinking through what they are spending, what they really need, and how they can possibly spend less in this area.

A lot of people use mobile phones so much, they could probably cancel their home phone service and never notice. Others pay hundreds of dollars per year for mobile phone services that they don't really need or use. Taking a look at your communication and connectivity expenses could *easily* save you a lot of money!

But don't stop there. Move on to the ***next big one***, which is...

TV and Entertainment

There are an increasing variety of bills and services that fall under this category. These may include, but are not limited to:

- ✓ Cable or Dish TV bills
- ✓ Streaming Video Services, and
- ✓ Streaming Audio Services

In short, these are bills that are all about entertainment and relaxation. Maybe you subscribe to an online service to stream movies. Maybe you have cable or a dish system too.

Whatever your bills are in this category, there is a good chance that you can find ways to reduce them if you work at it.

Video Resource
Video Name: Spending Habits, Budget and Home Ownership
www.YourHomeProgram.com/BookResource

Want to know the biggest culprit for money wasting in this category?

The **TV Bill**.

Most people give their cable/dish company more than they need to.

When they sign up, they want the "good deal" with loads of channels and all the bells and whistles.

Many people, however only watch a <u>small</u> <u>subset</u> of the channels that they sign up for.

Here's how to find out if you are one of them.

1. Get a pad of paper, and write down the channels you watch on TV for at least an entire chapter, preferably two chapters.
2. Go to the website of your cable or dish company, and review their plans. Find the smallest/cheapest plan that includes all of the channels that you wrote down on your pad of paper. Take note of that plan.
3. Look at your bill, and see which plan you are paying for. Compare it to the plan you noted in step 2. *Are you paying for a bigger service plan than you are actually using?*

Besides this, you can also use the steps covered previously for communication and connectivity bills.

This means that you can <u>NEGOTIATE</u>, <u>COMPARE</u>, and <u>CANCEL</u> unneeded services or options to lower your bills for TV and Entertainment.

How Much Can You Save?

Using the "negotiate, compare, and cancel" approach, some people will be able to save substantial amounts of money on TV and Entertainment. Savings amounts will vary, but **many** people who pay for cable or dish TV can probably save $25 to $50 per month by simply cutting down their TV bills to match their actual usage.

Always use **negotiate, compare, and cancel** to its fullest with entertainment related bills and services. This is one area where *most* people will have options, and it often truly does pay to take the time to compare.

Activities, Memberships, and Subscriptions

This is the "fun" category. It's where many people get a fair amount of exercise, socialization, relaxation, and enjoyment. It's also where a lot of people spend a lot of ***money***.

That makes this a prime target for your efforts at cutting back on your expenses.

What's included in this category?

The list is long, but here's a sample:

- ✓ YMCA Memberships
- ✓ Gym Memberships
- ✓ Club Memberships
- ✓ Magazine Subscriptions
- ✓ Newspaper Subscriptions
- ✓ And more!

There are a few things that we'll talk about in this category that *could* also be classified under "entertainment". That's okay. The point of this process is to systematically go through your expenses across the 5 different expense categories, and do what we can to have the greatest impact possible on your finances and your cash flow.

The most important thing that can be done to lower your bills for items like those listed above is to remember to **Negotiate**, **Compare**, and **Cancel**. Yes, I know we've already mentioned that a couple of times. I also know it's really important to actually DO! Don't skip this step for your activities, memberships, and subscriptions. Things like newspaper and magazine subscriptions are often negotiable, especially if it means they can keep your business. Shopping around for less expensive Gym Memberships, or skipping the Gym and buying some home work out equipment could end up saving you a bundle.

One key to consider in many of the activities, membership, and subscriptions that are included in this category is *exactly what your **usage*** *of the service/membership/subscription is*. **Simply put: *are you getting your money's worth?***

If the answer is no, then maybe it's time to move on.

A LOT of people have Gym memberships that they don't use. A LOT of people have newspaper subscriptions for newspapers that they don't even read or use coupons from.

*Evaluate your actual **usage**, and decide if the money might be better spent elsewhere.*

A Side Note: Keep Your Sanity Amidst Cutbacks!

You may be thinking by now...

> *"Okay, so I have to cancel my gym membership, get the slowest internet I can find, drop all those cool mobile phone features, and downgrade my TV channels. Am I allowed to have any fun???"*

Yes. In fact, it's <u>important</u> that you have fun.

In order to keep your sanity when you start tightening your budget, you're going to need to keep one thing in mind:

You need to be able to <u>enjoy</u> life and de-stress.

Don't think that you have to cut back or cancel every single "extra" that you have and go live in a box for awhile. That's not the point.

We're working towards something that is quite the opposite, in fact.

If you follow the instructions I'm giving you for reducing expenses across <u>ALL</u> <u>FIVE</u> CATEGORIES OF EXPENSES, there is a high likelihood that you will be able to make a **<u>substantial</u>** dent in your expenses without completely sacrificing your lifestyle.

Rather than make a huge cutback in one area, we're hoping that you can make smaller (perhaps seemingly insignificant, in some cases) cut backs across a wide variety of areas. Doing so, you probably won't "feel it" as much when you make these changes... and *that* should help you to better maintain your sanity and peace of mind through this process!

Other Negotiable Bills

You may have other negotiable bills that don't fall into any categories covered so far.

For any bills that you have that you'd consider "negotiable" based on our definition from this chapter, you can simply follow the three most important strategies for negotiable bills.

- <u>NEGOTIATE</u>
- <u>COMPARE</u>
- <u>CANCEL</u>

If you put these three ideas to work every chance you get, you will have a good chance of making good positive progress towards reaching your goal of better financial health (and ultimately, home ownership!)

Debt Payments

One type of negotiable bills that we haven't talked about yet this chapter are bills that would fall under the category of ***debt payments***.

The "negotiate, compare, and cancel" strategy more or less applies to debt payments like it does other negotiable bills. There are more possibilities with debt payments, though, and the ones we've already covered can become a lot more complicated when it comes to debt.

For this reason, I'd like to talk just a little about lowering your debt payments here. (Note: we'll talk a lot more about your **debt** when we devote an entire chapter to it in a few chapters!)

DEBT PAYMENT REDUCTION STRATEGY 1: LOWER YOUR BALANCE

This is an obvious one, admittedly, but it's worth covering because some people just don't realize the impact. On a credit card where the payments are for 3% of the balance, you can lower your payment by $30 for every $1,000 that you pay towards the credit card.

If you can pay off $4,000 worth of credit card debt on which the minimum payment is 3%, it's like giving yourself a $120 per month raise.

Lowering your balances and/or eliminating your debts is a smart way to reduce your expenses. There are numerous ways to go about reducing your debt. We'll talk about them in more detail later in the program. (Note: Debt settlement is one way to do this. Bankruptcy might be another if your debt situation is serious.)

Your Home Program
Our Advisors Are Available To Answer Your Questions
Call **1-800-245-7349** for Home Ownership Made Easy!

DEBT PAYMENT REDUCTION STRATEGY 2: NEGOTIATE YOUR TERMS

In cases where you can't quickly pay off or pay down a loan balance, or even if you can, you may want to consider attempting to re-negotiate the terms of the account.

The most obvious way to do this is to call the loan or credit card company and ask them what can be done. Maybe you can ask them to lower your interest rate. Maybe they have other special programs that could help you. Whatever the options are, you won't know about them until you ask!

DEBT PAYMENT REDUCTION STRATEGY 3: COMPARE YOUR OPTIONS

Comparison shopping applies to debts too. If you can't get anywhere with the terms of your current account, shop for better terms elsewhere if possible. This might mean using debt consolidation or balance transfers to get your account(s) moved to a more affordable place. Chances are, if you have accounts that are in good standing but not very affordable payment-wise, you probably have other options available. You just have to look around, ask around, and *compare*.

DEBT PAYMENT REDUCTION STRATEGY 4: CANCEL/CLOSE YOUR ACCOUNT

Sometimes when you tell a credit card company that you want to close your account, they will send you to a special department where the whole purpose is to try to SAVE the account. This can be a good way to get back to strategy 2 and attempt to re-negotiate your account terms.

If you're falling behind on payments, some credit card companies offer special programs that involve closing your account. Typically with these programs they will close your account, stop charging you interest, and allow you to pay off the account under whatever the then agreed-upon terms are.

Closing your account can also be used as a last-resort method to help reign in your spending on credit.

For secured debt payments like those on auto loans, you usually don't have the option to just "close the account". You may still have options though, including refinancing, selling the car, and perhaps a few other creative tactics.

If you have serious debt problems, then it's something you are going to need to get under control before you buy a home. Debt problems now (pre-home-ownership) will just translate into bigger (post-home-ownership) debt problems later if you don't do anything to fix them.

Besides, paying off debt or otherwise adjusting your debt payments could save you tens or even hundreds of dollars per month.

So don't miss it when we discuss the details of paying down debt in a few chapters!

Starting To Add Up...

If you're keeping score, the potential savings across the 5 categories of expenses is probably starting to look substantial.

Last chapter, we talked about how making adjustments to your "required and unseen" expenses and your "required bills" could result in huge savings. Some people could save thousands of dollars per year!

This chapter, we just added to the possibilities. By working through all of the negotiable bills we've covered, including debt, some people will no-doubt find ways to save hundreds of dollars. And we're not done yet!

Next chapter we're going to talk about another big one: your "regular required expenses!"

There are hundreds of dollars on the line... so don't miss it!

23 YOUR EXPENSES, AND HOW TO TAKE <u>CONTROL</u> OF THEM – PART 3

Your Regular Required Expenses!

Now it's time to talk about what can be referred to as your "Regular Required Expenses".

Last chapter we talked a lot about Negotiating, Comparing, and Canceling. *Unfortunately those steps don't apply to your regular required expenses!*

So this chapter we are starting fresh more or less, and we're going to have to come up with new and unique strategies to save money in this tough category of expenses.

A lot of this chapter will involve comparing services and cost of items, but there will be some more legwork involved than you had for last chapter's category. (More on that in just a moment.)

Just because the options are different, doesn't mean they are necessarily limited. You can't go into the grocery store and ask them to lower your grocery bill for you, but you can bring a pocket full of coupons and lower it yourself.

For this chapter's discussion I encourage you to keep an open mind. *Be open to the possibilities.* Remember, you can accomplish a great deal by taking little steps to save across each of the 5 categories of expenses (and their sub-categories). The same idea applies this chapter. You may not knock off $500 per month this week, but $100 or more is certainly possible.

So let's get started!

Groceries

Whether you have a family and do big weekly grocery shops, or you are single and take hit-and-miss trips to the store down the street, *groceries* is probably one of your <u>required</u> expenses.

This expense includes food, obviously, but also includes basic household supplies such as cleaners, toiletry items, and more.

Since *everyone* buys groceries, this is one area of expenses that all of us <u>should</u> pay attention to.

Price Matching

Obviously, you can't "negotiate" your grocery prices like you can some other expenses, but some grocery stores offer *price matching* which is almost just as good.

Price matching means that if you can find a lower price for the same item at a competitor, then the store will match that price. It usually has to be an *advertised* price.

If a local store offers price matching, doing some research into the competition can pay off. Get the ads and flyers from area grocery stores and bring them shopping with you. If you find a better price on something you're going to buy, circle it in the ad and take it to the register with you.

If your store doesn't offer price matching, the next best approach may be to...

Go Where The Money Isn't

In other words, if an item is cheaper at one store, buy that item there. Often times one store will always have better prices on one item or another. This approach involves buying groceries only at the store where you can find them the cheapest. This might mean you get your meats from Joe's Foods down the street, and get your bread and milk from the WalMaybe Grocery Superstore in town.

If you look around, you may find that it's worth a little extra gas and a little extra effort to track down the best prices on the things you buy frequently. Some people save a lot of money shopping this way.

When you're shopping like this, you are more likely to find pleasant surprises and deals that you might not otherwise find.

Discount Grocery Stores, Ethnic Markets, and Other Alternative Shopping Venues

One of the surprises you might find is that of the "alternative" shopping venue. By "alternative", I mean a grocery store or market that is typically specialized and targets a certain ethnicity, food type, or demographic.

There are some places to shop that aren't well advertised (or aren't advertised at all), that hide great bargains on certain items for those who take the time to look.

> As an example, one woman in Anaheim, California once told of how she always bought her olive oil at the local Indian Food Market, because she could get a full gallon jug for only $10.

Ethnic markets and discount grocery stores can be great places to find unexpected deals.

The difficulty is usually in finding the right places to shop with the right deals. Rural locations obviously aren't going to have the choices that big cities have, so your ability to find stores of this type may be limited.

(Just about everyone can do the next thing though.)

Buy In Bulk

Maybe you live in a small community without a lot of shopping choices. If that's the case, buying things in bulk when they go on sale might be a good way to save money.

The idea here is simple: when an item that you use regularly goes on sale, buy 3 to 5 times more than you normally would, as long as the item will keep long enough to be used. If it's a really good deal, consider buying several months' worth of it if you can.

> One mom bought organic milk for her son for school each week. The usual cost of the shelf-stable, serving-sized milk containers was about $1.25. One day there was a large display case and the milks were on sale for "4 for $1.00". Since the expiration dates allowed enough time, the mom was able to buy enough milk to cover most of the school year.

If her child drank 5 single-serving milks per week, which would amount to a savings of about $20 per month. That's not bad!

Buying in bulk can save you substantially if you buy the right items at the right times.

Coupons

Using manufacturer and store coupons is another good way to save money. Some families save as much as $50 per week on their grocery bill through the use of coupons. Even if you aren't a "mega-coupon" shopper, you could still easily save $5 or $10 per week by taking a little extra effort in preparing for your regular grocery shops.

How To Get The Coupons

One trick with coupons is knowing where to find the coupons you need for the items you buy most. Here are a few ideas:

Video Resource
Video Name: Spending Habits, Budget and Home Ownership
www.YourHomeProgram.com/BookResource

Video Resource
Video Name: Function of a Budget
www.YourHomeProgram.com/BookResource

- **Buy the newspaper.** Many community and local area newspapers feature manufacturer's coupons for commonly purchased food and household items. You can usually save substantially MORE than the price of the paper if you put the coupons to good use.
- **Ask for them.** Many big brand names will gladly send you coupons if you just ask for them. Visit their website, find the contact us form, and ask! You may be surprised at what you get!
- **Subscribe To Mailing Lists.** If you can get on mailing lists and email lists of the companies that produce the brands of food you use, you will probably receive special offers and coupons in the mail (or via email).
- **Don't Forget Store Coupons.** Some stores offer coupons for use in their store only. However, some grocery stores will accept the coupons of their competitors. So don't forget to check the ads at local stores for store coupons that offer big savings!

Using coupons consistently can save you a lot of money in the long run. Even a few dollars a week will add up to quite a bit over time. What if you could lower your grocery bill by just $10 per week using coupons? That's over $500 per year in savings!

Buy Generic And Store Brands

Generic and store brands can be a good way to save money on certain items. Sometimes, the "name brand" is definitely better. Other times, it doesn't matter.

Many store/generic brands are expanding to offer organic foods, too, which makes these an even better choice.

Frugal Meals

Another way to save on groceries is to think in terms of *meals*. Some meals are less expensive than others. By paying attention to what you buy, you can make your home meals a lot more affordable. For example, maybe frozen vegetables or meat will be cheaper than the fresh ones you normally use (or vice versa).

Another way to make meals more frugal doesn't involve WHAT you buy at all.

Whatever it is, just make *less of it*.

Does your refrigerator have leftovers from 2 weeks ago sitting in it?

Does this happen frequently?

If so, you're probably preparing too much food. Try to save some money by trimming down the amount of food you make for meals

Eat Healthier

A lot of people claim that eating healthy is more expensive. In some ways, it's true. Fresh, organic foods usually cost more than their "regular" and canned counterparts.

However, there are certain ways in which eating healthier can save you a lot of money.

A lot of people buy a lot of unhealthy extras when they go to the grocery store. Cutting these out could add up to substantial savings.

Some examples include:

- **Soda/Pop** - It is not uncommon for a family to spend $10 or even $15 per week on their favorite sugar-filled carbonated beverages. Making tea, Kool Aid, or just drinking water is much more economical!
- **Cookies And Other Sweets** - It's usually cheaper and healthier to make your own cookies than it is to buy them at the store. Skipping the cookies and sweets can save you a lot of money in the long run, not to mention improving your health.
- **Potato Chips** - You can usually make several batches of popcorn for the price you pay for a single bag of your favorite potato chips. (Popcorn is arguably healthier, too.)

Even if you aren't planning on becoming a health nut anytime soon, your body will eventually thank you if you decide to cut back on some of the unhealthy (and expensive) junk food now.

Your wallet will thank you, too.

Dump The Bad Habit(s)

This program is about home ownership, not health. Right?

Right.

But some bad and unhealthy habits are *also* **extremely costly**. And our purpose right now is to get your FINANCES in order. If that means your health improves too, then that's just an added bonus.

So let's talk about one favorite bad habit: *smoking*.

I know you've probably seen the commercials on TV. I know you may have already tried to quit. I understand that it's probably easier said than done.

But I want *you* to know what the **financial impact** of a long-term smoking habit may be.

The price of a pack of cigarettes varies from place to place, but the average is probably somewhere around $7 as of this writing.

The "average" smoker smokes about 1 pack per day.

One pack per day is $7 per day.

That's **$2,555 per year**.

> **That means that in 10 years of being a smoker, smoking one pack of cigarettes per day, you'll spend over $25,000!**

You can do the math. You don't need me to tell you how serious that cost is.

Automobile Expenses

The automobile expense that we most often think about is that of gasoline. How can you save money on gasoline?

The FTC offers a few ideas on their website[4] that might be helpful. Here they are...

- **Start driving right away.** Don't wait for the engine to warm up.
- **Don't speed.** Most cars start losing gas mileage once you pass 60 mph.
- **Avoid idling.** If you are going to have to wait in your car for a while, turn it off.
- **Use your cruise control.** It improves highway mileage.
- **Let up on the gas and minimize the need for braking.** (Basically, slow down!)
- **Don't accelerate or decelerate too quickly.** You'll use less gas and your brakes will last longer.
- **Don't over-use the air conditioner.** It does increase your fuel usage. However, driving down the highway your air conditioner will probably waste less gas than the drag created by having the windows open.
- **Combine and consolidate errands.** Make your trips to the store and other places count.
- **Dump the excess weight.** Yep. Time to remove those concrete blocks you like to carry around in your trunk.

---

[4] http://www.ftc.gov/bcp/edu/pubs/consumer/alerts/alt064.shtm

- **Don't load your roof rack.** Like having your windows down, this can create drag that will reduce your gas mileage.
- **Use a credit card that offers cash back.** This is great if you can do it. Just make sure you pay off the balance every month!
- **Keep your car running well.** Do regular tune ups and oil changes.
- **Mind your tires.** Your car will get the best mileage when your tires are properly inflated and your wheels are properly aligned.

Another way to save on gas is to reduce your commute time or commute costs. This might mean carpooling, or leaving for work a little early to avoid the traffic. Think creatively, and you can probably come up with more similar ways to save that will work for you.

You can also save money on automobile maintenance by taking advantage of local specials, sales, and coupons.

Some mechanics advertise in local media with offers of discounts, coupons, and other specials. For them, it's a way to get more business. For you, it's a way to save money.

If you're capable and have the necessary tools, you can usually save a fair amount of money by doing the regular maintenance on your cars yourself.

Regardless of whether or not you're a mechanic, you may be able to save as much as $15 to $50 per month on automobile expenses if you put a little effort into it.

Childcare

One cost that can be substantial for working parents is that of *childcare*. Childcare is a *required expense* that can really put a dent in your finances. You might not think there is much that can be done about the cost of childcare. After all, you can't negotiate new rates with your childcare provider, *right?*

Probably not. (Though it never hurts to ask.) But there are things that can be done to reduce the financial impact of childcare.

Here are a few ideas:

Taxes, Credits, And Other Special Programs

The first thing you can do about childcare costs is make sure that you are taking advantage of any local, state, and federal government programs that are designed to help ease the burden of those costs.

For example, you could check if your employer offers Flexible Spending Accounts (FSAs) for dependent care. These are special accounts funded with pre-tax dollars with which you can pay for certain allowed expenses (such as licensed daycare).

Make sure you are taking advantage of any tax credits that you can claim on your tax return, and any other programs that your state or local government may offer.

Many people will be able to save up to 15% on their childcare costs by taking advantage of the available programs.

Work Schedule Changes

If your employer can and will allow you to adjust your schedule, you may be able to save significantly on child care costs. This might mean you'll work from home one day a week, or work 10 hour days instead of 8 hour days so that you can avoid the cost of childcare one day a week.

You or your spouse could also consider working different shifts or days to help share the burden of taking care of the kids.

Some people will be able to reduce or even eliminate their childcare costs by making changes to their work schedule.

Collaborate

Another approach that some people use to lower the costs of childcare is to work together with other parents. This might include things like:

- Splitting the cost of a regular babysitter or nanny with a friend or relative.
- Let the kids go to grandma's house one day a week (only if grandma's okay with it!)
- *Trade* childcare responsibilities: consider a baby-sitting co-op.

Working together with family and friends can help ease the burden of paying for childcare. Some people could save 50% or more on childcare costs by collaborating with others.

Shop Around

Obviously, you don't want to skimp on childcare costs and sacrifice quality, but the more expensive childcare isn't necessarily the best. Shop around and compare prices. Visit other childcare facilities and see what else is out there. You might be surprised at what you are able find.

Quit Your Job

There are two options here:

1. Quit your job and start a business out of your home, or
2. Just quit your job!

Quitting your job to save money might sound crazy, but with childcare costs often ranging from $400 to $800 (or more) per month, you may want to consider this option because of...

The Cost Of Employment

Automobile costs and childcare costs bring up an important point.

For families, the cost of earning a second income (i.e. when both parents are working) can sometimes be so substantial that you may want to reconsider whether the second income is actually worth it.

Childcare costs can easily be $500 or $600 per month. Commute costs can be substantial too.

Do you have a second car to drive to your job? Would you need the second car if you didn't have the job?

Some people might be able to save $300 on a car payment by ditching the second car (and the job that they drive it to).

Then there is gas money, added insurance costs, maintenance on your car, snacks on the way home from work, lunches out, dinners out (because everyone is too tired to cook), and more.

Especially if your childcare costs are high, this is a possibility you might want to give a closer look.

What does your second income cost you?

To find out, add up all the expenses associated with your second income (childcare, car payment, insurance, gas, etc.) and subtract those from your monthly net income.

If your net income for the second income is $2,000, and you pay $900 per month in childcare costs, $300 for a car payment, $100 for insurance for that car, and $200 in gas to drive to and from work, without considering the extra spending like meals and snacks that often go with a second job, you're already netting only $500 per month from your second job.

You could easily earn that $500 per month working part time on the weekends somewhere! If you are in a situation like this, you may want to consider the true value (and cost) of your second income, and think about making some serious changes!

Conclusion

So far we've talked about how to lower your *Required and Unseen Expenses*, your *Negotiable Bills*, and this week we covered your *Regular Required Expenses*.

If you're keeping track and comparing your own situation, you may be finding a number of areas where you can make changes that will save you money.

Many people could save $3,000 per year or more by making changes to *their Required and Unseen Expenses* and their *Required Bills*.

Many people could save another $3,000 per year or more by making changes to their *Negotiable Bills*.

Some people with childcare costs could save $5,000 or more per year by making changes to their schedule and their approach to childcare. (Not to mention what they might save if they take steps to save on Groceries and Automobile Expenses!)

As you can see, the numbers are really starting to add up.

Taking a serious look at your finances and applying the strategies and ideas that we're discussing could result in ***drastic positive changes*** in your financial life.

Next chapter we'll dive into your extra expenses, and look at strategies that will help you **plan** for and **take control** of your extra spending. If you want to add thousands more to your potential savings, then don't miss next chapter!

24 YOUR EXPENSES, AND HOW TO TAKE <u>CONTROL</u> OF THEM – PART 4

Your Extra and Unplanned Expenses

This chapter we're going to be talking about your extra and unplanned expenses. Hopefully by now you have an idea of what those expenses are.

If not, now is a good time to figure it out.

A Quick Review On Tracking

If you recall, earlier in the program we talked about how to track and calculate your extra spending. The steps went something like this:

1. Write your expenses in a spending diary (i.e. a notebook) for two or three weeks. Include money spent on dining out, snacks, and any extra expenses you put on a credit card.
2. Total up your expenses for the 2 (or 3) weeks, and divide the total by the number of weeks you kept your spending diary. Here is the worksheet we provided:

Total of Expenses From Spending Diary:	/	Number of weeks the spending log was kept	= Spending Per Week
	/		
			▲▲ Use this number for STEP 3.

3. To get your average monthly extra spending, take your result from step 2, multiply it by 52 (the number of weeks in a year), and divide that number by 12. This will give you an estimate of your **monthly extra expenses**. Here's a worksheet for this step:

MONTHLY EXTRA SPENDING ESTIMATE			
SPENDING PER WEEK	TIMES 52	DIV. BY 12	= **MONTHLY**
	x 52	/ 12	

Another great way to track your expenses is to enter them all into financial software such as Quicken or Ace Money. This way you can categorize your transactions as you enter them and get a breakdown of your "extra" spending by categories.

Looking For Places To Cut Back

The main purpose of tracking and analyzing your expenses is to find areas where you might be able to cut back. Taking a close look at your extra spending may surprise you. Some people are shocked to find out how much money they spend on things like snacks and dining out.

Once you have this information, you can use it to adjust your budget and to help yourself make better financial decisions in the future.

Let's talk about some ways you can cut back on some of the more common extra expenses.

Reducing Your Extra Expenses

Here are a few ideas for reducing some common extra expenses:

- Use coupons when you dine out. Many restaurants offer "buy one get one free" deals for entrées, which can save you a bundle in the long run.
- Dine out for lunch instead of dinner. Many restaurants offer cheaper options at lunch than at dinner.
- Cook more. Brushing up on your cooking skills could save you a lot of money that would otherwise be spent at restaurants.
- Give yourself a snack budget, and stick to it. Sometimes people's snack spending gets out of hand simply because they don't plan for it. Give yourself a few dollars a week to spend on snacks, and take that out in cash every week. When the cash is gone, you're done!
- Rent movies instead of going to the movie theatre. The snacks are cheaper, and so is the admission.
- Put off impulse buys. If you come across something you "want" to buy that you weren't planning on purchasing today, put the purchase off until tomorrow. Often times, you won't want it anymore if you just wait a day.
- Plan your meals and snacks for the week. A lot of people make extra trips to the grocery store each week resulting in more over-budget and impulse spending. Planning ahead and making no more than one trip a week can reduce the costs associated with the extra trips.
- Make your own coffee. A lot of people spend $30 to $80 per month (or even more in some cases) buying coffee at gas stations and coffee shops. You can buy good (fancy) coffee for around $10 per pound. Even $20 per month spent on high quality coffee is less than you'll spend buying it by the cup.
- Make the most of local events. High school football games, musicals, and similar local events can provide good entertainment at a relatively low cost.

Converting Extra and Unplanned Expenses To <u>Planned</u> Ones

Remember the save and spend cycle and the "debt fund" cycle? Just in case you don't, here's a quick recap:

<u>SAVE AND SPEND CYCLE:</u>

> The save and spend cycle is when you struggle to save a little money in a savings account (or a jar), and then something comes up that immediately drains the fund you just saved. You get discouraged; you put off saving for a while, and then eventually muster up the gumption to go at it again. Once again, something comes up that creates a setback, and the cycle starts over.

DEBT FUND CYCLE:

> The debt fund cycle is similar to the save and spend cycle, except it happens using credit and debt. You work hard and manage to pay off a portion of your debt. Then some unexpected expense comes up, for which you have to use a credit card and undo the progress that you just made on your debt. Discouraged, you put off working on your debt for a while, until eventually you muster up the gumption to go at it again. You manage to pay off a portion of your debt once again, when suddenly another unexpected expense comes up. The cycle starts over.

A lot of people spend a lot of their lives in cycles like these.

As we discussed earlier, there is a way to break this cycle. It also happens to be one of the best methods there is for getting a handle on your extra and unplanned expenses.

Here's how it works:

1. Document your extra and unplanned expenses as they come up. Do what you can to reduce the common ones (covered above).
2. When a new extra or unplanned expense comes up, PLAN for that expense to come up again. ADD IT TO YOUR BUDGET. This is probably best accomplished using financial software such as Quicken or Ace Money. You can add the "unexpected" expense as a "scheduled transaction" either next week, next month, or next year (whenever you expect it to happen again).
3. As you do this, continue to look at your cash flow, subtracting your regular expenses from your income. Eventually, you will start to get a true picture of what your finances look like, and you will be caught by surprise less and less.

This process is all about converting extra and unplanned expenses to budgeted and planned ones.

Things come up. Life gets in the way. When that happens to you, track it, "count the cost", and PLAN for it to happen again in the future. The more you do this, the more you will be prepared for your own spending habits and the various financial hiccups that come along.

Preparing For Emergencies And More

As you get your extra spending and other expenses under control, you'll want to start setting some money aside in an emergency fund. A lot of people are intimidated by the idea of saving up 6 months or a year's worth of income in an emergency fund.

If you're one of those people, do yourself a favor and aim a little lower. Take baby steps.

Rather than set a large and lofty goal, start small. Plan on creating a $500 or $1,000 emergency fund to begin with. A small emergency fund is better than none at all. Perhaps you could plan on setting aside at least enough money for rent and utilities for one month as an emergency fund. This will help you to be better prepared for the unexpected, and could save your rent-to-own deal down the road, if that is the path you choose for yourself.

Another strategy that is helpful for many people is that of creating "funds" for other expenses besides emergencies. Couples might have a "date" fund. Families might have a "pizza night" fund. It may be nothing more than a jar that sits on the counter that everyone drops their extra change in now and then. This approach can be helpful to give you some breathing room and allow you (and your family) to enjoy life a little while planning and controlling expenses at the same time.

Ever Increasing Options

All this talk about "funds" and "savings" brings us back to an important point:

The other aspects of your financial triad (i.e. your **credit** and your **net worth**) will be affected in a positive way when you improve your expenses and cash flow.

If your expenses are out of control, chances are your debt (net worth) and your credit will be too. As you start to get your expenses under control and make improvements, it is inevitable that you will begin to show signs of improvement in the areas of net worth and credit.

The more your expenses get under control, the more likely it is you will be able to improve your net worth. In other words, you'll have ***more money!***

The more money you have, the more financial options you will create for yourself.

Money is <u>NOT</u> the answer for everything, but it can certainly make a number of things in life *easier*.

Working on your expenses using the ideas and strategies that we've covered in the last few chapters will certainly help you gain some financial momentum. *You can't help but improve your net worth if you follow the strategies we've covered.*

If your net worth is negative, you'll want to pay attention to what's coming next chapter. Starting next chapter we'll be looking at what can be done in a number of special situations, including "net worth problems", or simply put... *too much debt*. If you are buried in debt then you will no doubt want to stick around for next chapter's discussion on debt!

25 DEALING WITH DEBT AND NET WORTH PROBLEMS

Knowing what we know about the financial triad, it may be easier for us to see how a person can get in over their head with debt.

Imagine the scenario...

> *A person struggles with their income from week to week and month to month. They're trying to make it but life's unexpected events always seem to get in the way. They're barely making enough to support their family, when finally they get some breathing room... in the form of an almost magic little piece of plastic called a credit card. They use the credit card to fill in the gaps as needed, but before long, the bill for the credit card starts to grow. It becomes another expense that is quite difficult to keep up with. This person now has a debt problem. Soon, they develop credit problems too due to their inability to keep up with their credit card payments.*

Things like this *really do* happen.

Sometimes, debt problems are really just side effects of other financial problems. Maybe the core problem comes down to cash flow, as in the case above. Maybe it's net worth (lack of savings). Or maybe it's credit, and the lack of affordable credit puts too much pressure on an already struggling cash flow scenario.

Sometimes life just happens, and we end up with all kinds of debt and credit problems as a result. I heard a story recently of a little girl who had died after a long and painful fight with cancer. The doctors tried everything, but her little two-year old body finally gave out. Her parents, already distraught, were left with medical bills like you and I can't imagine—not to mention the cost of a funeral for their 2-year-old daughter.

As sad and horrible as it is to think about, things like this happen all the time. People get sick. People get injured. Tragedy *just happens*... and it often leaves a big bill behind when it does.

If your debt problems aren't due to such a tragedy, you should be thankful for that.

It doesn't make them any easier to overcome, however.

Whether it's half a million dollars in medical bills, or $50,000 in credit card debt, out-of-control debt can seem like an impassible barricade between you and your future. I'll never forget the story (I believe it was on PBS Frontline) where a college kid who got sucked into the credit card game ultimately ended up committing suicide over his debt and credit problems. His debt was probably only a small fraction of what many people have in medical bills. Still, it was *too much*.

It was a problem that seemed impossible to overcome.

However you got to where you are, and whatever your debt situation looks like, there is something that you should know:

There IS a way out. In fact, there are *multiple* ways out.

Sure, some are stressful. Some are difficult. But as you travel this road you should keep in mind that ultimately this is all "just money", and money is NOT the most important thing in life. Debt problems do not have to be the end of the world. (Most of us have enough to worry about without adding debt into the mix!)

So let's get started with talking about how to get your debt situation (no matter how bad it is) under control.

Getting Things Under Control

We've already talked a great deal about income and expenses. Often one of the keys to getting your debt situation under control is getting your **CASH FLOW** under control <u>**FIRST**</u>.

If your expenses are too high, or you aren't making enough money, it will be difficult to overcome your debt problems. For some people, this will mean that the only real options they have left are debt settlement and bankruptcy. Those aren't horrible options, by the way, if it turns out that they are your only options.

In any case, getting your debt under control really starts with your *cash flow*. If you're going to pay off your debt the old fashioned way then you need to be able to make the payments.

The Debt-Control Plan

Here's a simple outline that many can use to navigate through the process of getting out of debt:

1. Take **all** of the steps possible that we've covered in this program to ***increase your income***.
2. Take **all** of the steps possible that we've covered in this program to ***decrease your expenses***.
3. Once you've done everything you can do, are you able to make your payments on your debt?
    a. If Yes, then good. Things are under control for now. You can consider all the options and decide on a strategy for becoming debt free.
    b. If no, then your situation is more serious. You will probably want to give serious consideration to debt settlement, credit counseling, or bankruptcy.

Notice that the first two steps have nothing to do with debt directly. *See how important cash flow is?*

The question really boils down to: "Can you afford to pay your payments on your debt as they are right now?"

If not, and if you've tried every trick in the book to make your debt affordable, then it may be time for drastic measures.

Speaking of making debts affordable, I should mention that you can target your debt payments directly for this purpose, as we discussed previously when we talked about "negotiable bills".

In our negotiable bills discussion a couple of chapters ago, we talked about 4 strategies for lowering debt payments. The strategies we discussed were:

1. Lower your balance. On credit cards, a lower balance means *lower payments*. Obviously, if you're struggling to figure out how to get out of debt, this one is probably easier said than done.
2. Negotiate your terms. Simply call and ask for help.
3. Compare your options. Shop around for better terms, basically. (If you're falling behind, this may not be a workable option. Still doesn't hurt to try, though.)

4. Cancel/Close your account. This might get you to a department that can do something about your terms, or a credit card company might agree to "freeze the interest and fix the payments", allowing you to pay off the remainder of what you owe with zero interest.

It's possible that one or more of these approaches could be used to give you some needed breathing room with your debts. If your debt is out of control and you are struggling to afford your payments, perhaps a good place to start is with the *payments themselves*.

If you can't do that, don't worry. No matter what, you have to remember that...

You Have Options

The 5 most popular options for overcoming debt (in no particular order) are: Debt Reduction ("just paying it off"), Debt Consolidation, Credit Counseling, Debt Settlement, and Bankruptcy.

Let's talk about each of these in a little more detail.

Debt Reduction

Debt reduction is a term that can be used to describe any number of methods for paying off debt. The most common debt reduction strategy is what is commonly called the "roll up" or "snowball" strategy.

Video Resource
Video Name: Cash Flow, Savings and Debt
www.YourHomeProgram.com/BookResource

The idea goes something like this: Pay whatever *extra* amount you can afford to pay towards the first debt you plan to tackle. Once that debt is paid off, take your "extra" payment funds <u>AND</u> the payment that was going towards the now-eliminated debt, and put those towards the *next* debt on your list. Do this until your debts are paid off.

There are obviously problems with this approach (and many similar approaches) for people in certain situations.

Imagine, for a moment, being in your thirties and having gone through a medical catastrophe that left your finances in shambles.

Your debt might look like this:

- $30,000 in credit card debt (you maxed your credit cards out in the beginning in an effort to pay your doctor bills)
- $100,000 mortgage
- $500,000 in medical bills

Now imagine that your take home pay is $40,000 a year.

Even when paying $10,000 (25%) of your income towards your debt each year, it would take **the rest of your life** to pay off the debt. If you're in a situation like this, the "debt reduction" strategy may not be feasible. (Your only options in this case may be debt settlement or to file for bankruptcy.)

So while debt reduction strategies can be powerful, they aren't perfect, and they aren't the answer for everyone. If you just have some credit card debt, a car loan, a mortgage, and maybe a student loan or two, you may want to give debt reduction a serious look.

Debt Consolidation

Debt consolidation is the practice of putting all of your debt-eggs in one big debt-basket, in hopes that it will be a *more affordable* basket.

I'm sure you've heard the old adage about not putting all your eggs in one basket. Well, if you are going to do debt consolidation, you'll have to set that small bit of wisdom aside. With the egg/basket idiom in mind, it's probably easy to guess what the big problem with debt negotiation is:

You forfeit control of your eggs, in a sense. If something goes wrong with your plan, your debts are all piled up into a single installment loan, and you won't have any other options but to default on that loan, and possibly file for bankruptcy. If it is a secured loan (such as when a person consolidates their debts into a second mortgage), then guess what? You're going to *lose something* in this deal.

Debt consolidation isn't always a nightmare, but it isn't always a great move either. Before consolidating all of your debts into a single "big basket" loan, it's important to weigh the pros and cons. Ask yourself questions that highlight what you have to gain and lose by using debt consolidation...

Your Home Program
Our Advisors Are Available To Answer Your Questions
Call **1-800-245-7349** for Home Ownership Made Easy!

Will you save money on interest?

Will you save money on monthly payments?

Will you be able to avoid racking up MORE *debt since your credit cards are now "freed up"?*

For some people, debt consolidation just results in **more debt** because they go back to using their credit cards once their debts are consolidated. (This is, by the way, one reason that it is very important to get your income and expenses under control before you try to tackle your debt.)

The only way debt consolidation will work as a method to "get out" of debt is if you *stop adding to your debt*. A lot of people find that hard to do.

There is another "big basket" method that tries to address this issue, and it's called...

Credit Counseling

A lot of credit counseling services are non-profit. Don't let that fool you, though. Credit counseling isn't perfect, and as with many other so-called non-profits, you can rest assured that *someone* is making money *somewhere*.

Credit counseling services work by arranging agreements ahead of time with certain creditors, through which consumers who sign up for the service can pay off their debts. So the credit counseling service may have an agreement with Capital Three Credit Card Company through which they pay a whole collection of debts at once (the debts of their customers). Each new person who signs up for the credit counseling service pays their payment to the service, and the credit counseling service lumps the payment for that consumer in with all of the other funds to be paid towards Capital Three Credit Card Company at whatever terms the credit counseling service managed to work out.

They charge the consumer a monthly fee for the use of their service, and they require that the accounts of the consumer that are included in the service be *closed*.

This "closed accounts" thing is the part of credit counseling that is designed to keep a person from messing up again. To put this in terms of eggs and baskets: *You put all your eggs into one basket (the credit counseling service), and that basket destroys all of your other baskets (by requiring you to close your credit accounts)*.

Credit counseling services, when used in this manner, are really *debt settlement* in disguise. They have their strengths, of course, but they also have a fair number of *limitations*. Because of these limitations, if you feel you might be a candidate for credit counseling, it's also possible you should consider *debt settlement* as an option.

Debt Settlement

Debt settlement is the process of negotiating new terms with your creditors for **unsecured** **debt**. It usually involves negotiating lower balances (but doesn't necessarily have to). While debt settlement can damage your credit, for people who are in real financial trouble, it may be a more attractive option than the alternative (i.e. bankruptcy).

Ideally, debt settlement would take place when you're already behind on your bills. Many credit card companies, medical billing companies, hospitals, and doctors are willing to accept settlements in cases where a person genuinely needs help.

For credit card companies, the settlement process is often just part of the game. Some accounts are going to default. Some will be uncollectible. Some will want to pay what they can... and that's where debt settlement comes into play from the credit card company's perspective.

To use debt settlement, the basic approach is to write or call your creditors and tell them that you're having trouble paying your bills. Sometimes they will offer information about what options you have (such as "you need to stop paying for 2 months before we can help you", or "we may have a program that can help"). If they don't offer up suggestions or settlements on their own, you then write them with a reasonable settlement offer that shows in one way or another why it is good for both you and the credit card company. (Think along the lines of, "This settlement is important to me as I believe it will help me avoid filing for bankruptcy.") Once you have an agreement in place, you pay what you've agreed to pay.

Some hospitals and doctor's offices will forgive debts if you explain your situation and your hardship, and ask them what they can do to help. Even if they refuse to help, it never hurts to try. It could save you thousands of dollars.

There are certainly downsides to consider with debt settlement. One big downside is that the process can be downright *complicated*. There may be several rounds of negotiations. There may be collection agencies and even lawsuits involved. Another downside is that it doesn't provide any solution for *secured* debts. There are even some unsecured debts (such as student loans and tax debt) where the usual debt settlement tactics won't be much help. Obviously, there are costs involved in debt settlement too. In order to settle your debts, you have to be able to come up with the funds to do so.

Video Resource
Video Name: How does Bankruptcy affect your Credit?
www.YourHomeProgram.com/BookResource

With that said, debt settlement can most certainly be the right move for certain people in certain situations.

Bankruptcy

You might be wondering what can be done if you are buried beyond all hope of ever getting out.

Maybe your creditors are refusing to settle. Maybe your ability to work and earn has changed and there is no possible way of digging out or being able to pay for settlements to creditors in the foreseeable future.

There are certainly cases where bankruptcy is truly the best option.

We're going to dedicate an entire chapter to bankruptcy in a couple of chapters, so I won't go into the details here, but for now here is the one thing you should remember:

Bankruptcy exists for your protection.

Before bankruptcy came along, debtors who couldn't pay up were abused in all sorts of ways, including (but not limited to) prison, torture, starvation, and even death. Bankruptcy allows you to be released from your debt obligations.

While the consequences for not paying today aren't as severe as they once were, the protection that bankruptcy provides is still valuable.

Bankruptcy prevents creditors and collectors from suing you, getting judgments, garnishing wages, and similar activities. Again, bankruptcy exists for your *protection!*

So if you are in a situation where bankruptcy is your best or only option, don't despair. It isn't the end of the world. Those laws are there for a reason, and there is no shame at all in using them when your situation warrants it.

In a couple of chapters we'll talk more about the bankruptcy process, the costs involved, and what you need to do to minimize the damage.

Overcoming Your Debt Problems Once And For All

There is one place where virtually everything you ever do must start... one place where every change, every movement, every *moment* you live and breathe has its origination.

That "one place" is in your *mind*.

One of the biggest changes necessary in order for you to overcome your debt problems once and for all is a change in your *thinking*!

"Change your mind, change your life!"

If I were going to slap an advertising slogan on this idea, that's what it would be.

> **You need to change the way you think about money if you are ever going to stop being a slave to it.**

When you realize that making more money allows you to save more money, and saving more money does nothing but give you *more and more options*, you will be on your way to the kinds of mental changes that are necessary for true financial freedom.

And speaking of financial freedom, it's time for us to talk about an important key to gaining it: SAVINGS. Now I'm going to introduce you to something you will surely want to jot down and remember. It's called...

Video Resource
Video Name: Is Bankruptcy a Credit Score killer?
www.YourHomeProgram.com/BookResource

The Ultimate Savings Strategy

I'm going to introduce you to a savings strategy that has helped **many** people to take control of their finances and improve their net worth.

Many people have saved thousands, even *millions* of dollars using the strategy I'm going to tell you *right now*. The strategy can be summed up by a simple one-word acronym: *SAFE*.

A "SAFE" savings strategy is one that is...

Systematic
Automatic

Forgettable, and
Enough.

Now let me explain each of these points just in case they aren't clear.

Systematic - Your savings should be *systematic*. This means that first of all, you need to actually **have a plan** for saving money. This could be as simple as "I am going to save $50 per week."

Automatic - The ultimate savings strategy is one that can be *automated*. The less you have to think about it, the better. So to add to the above statement, we might say... "I am going to save $50 per week through an automatic bank draft to my savings account."

Forgettable - Even better than automatically saving the money, is if it is so "auto-pilot" that you are able to completely forget that you ever put the savings plan in place. To continue with our statements from the previous two points, we might say something like, "I am going to save $50 per week through an automatic bank draft to my savings account paid directly from my employer out of my regular paycheck." Some employers who do direct deposit will segment off an amount or percentage of your check to a different account if you ask them to. You'll never see the money, and as far as your checkbook is concerned it's as if you never had it in the first place.

However you accomplish it, a savings plan that you can "set <u>and</u> **forget**" is best.

Enough - In order to be effective, the amount you save has to be ***enough***. You aren't going to get very far on $1 per week. The amount needs to be substantial enough to build on, and to gain momentum as it starts to earn interest. It's okay to start small, but you should build increases into your automatic plan if possible (for example, by making the amount a percentage of your income). If you are unsure of what amount you should use, 10% of your income is a good place to start.

Your Home Program
Our Advisors Are Available To Answer Your Questions
Call **1-800-245-7349** for Home Ownership Made Easy!

The SAFE strategy can yield amazing results for those who put it into practice.

The reason it works so well is because it remedies some of the issues that often inhibit savings, such as procrastination, forgetfulness, and laziness.

One way or another, I highly recommend that you come up with a savings plan for yourself that fits the SAFE criteria as covered above. Doing so could be a truly life-changing move.

Conclusion

Getting your debt and your savings under control is important.

"Net worth", as part of your *financial triad*, is an important key to your overall financial health.

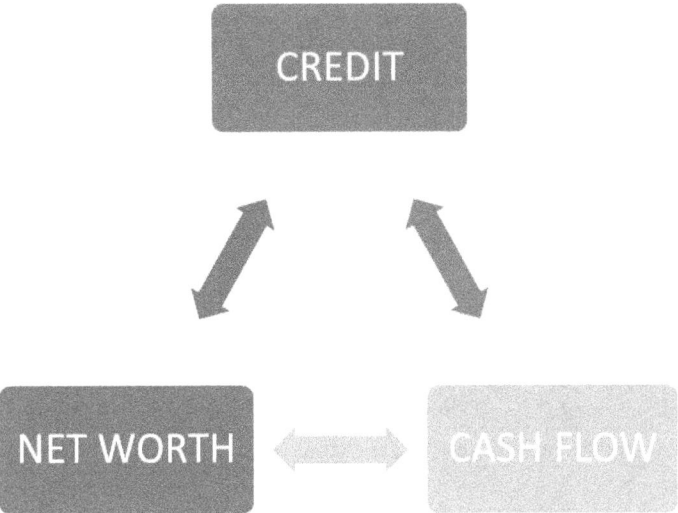

When you have money in reserves (thanks to your SAFE savings plan), unexpected hiccups won't be as likely to result in more debt. This means you'll have less credit payments, and healthier cash flow. Better cash flow of course makes it easier to save more, to avoid debt, and to better manage your credit.

I know I've talked about this a lot but it's important so it's worth repeating. Your financial triad is thoroughly intertwined, and the more you can improve upon each area, the more your overall financial health (and your ability to maintain it) will improve.

Coming up next chapter, we're going to talk about a special type of financial problem *that many people have* that can negatively affect cash flow, net worth, AND credit. It's one of the worst kinds of financial problems to have, but it's actually quite common. *Want to know what it is and how to overcome it?* If you're smart you do... and I'll tell you all about it next chapter!

26 TAX-RELATED PROBLEMS

> *"Our new Constitution is now established, and has an appearance that promises permanency; but in this world nothing can be said to be certain, except death and taxes."*
>
> *Benjamin Franklin*

Nothing can be said to be certain, except death and taxes. These are the famous words of Benjamin Franklin written in a letter to Jean-Baptiste Leroy in 1789.

We can't do anything about the death part, but this chapter we're going to do what we can to tackle the part about **taxes**.

Because of the seemingly unstoppable certainty of taxes, **tax problems** are among the most stressful, difficult, and costly financial problems a person can have.

A serious tax problem can hurt your net worth, your cash flow, *and* your credit. Because of the negative impact that tax problems can have on your financial triad, we're going to take an entire chapter to talk about how to address them, and perhaps more importantly, how to **avoid them**.

The most common tax problems are tax debt, tax liens, and chronic underpayments and overpayments.

Before we get into the details of each type of tax problem, let's talk about a most important point: how to avoid them in the first place!

Avoiding Tax Problems

*In 2006, actor Wesley Snipes was charged with (and ultimately convicted of) a number of crimes all boiling down to one key issue: **taxes**.*

Among the claims were allegations that Mr. Snipes used what is known as the "Section 861 Argument" as his justification and reasoning for believing that he did not have to pay taxes. Also, according to the indictment, the accountants used by Mr. Snipes had a history of filing fraudulent or false returns in order to get tax refunds for their clients.

Snipes was eventually convicted and after the appeals failed, reported to prison in late 2010 to begin serving his 3 year prison sentence.

There are two main things I want to bring up about this case: The accountants that Mr. Snipes used, and the so-called "section 861 argument".

First off, let's talk about the section 861 argument. This is, simply put, an argument used by some "tax protesters" based on a small portion of the tax code that they believe excludes them from having to pay income taxes. Most people who act on the idea of the 861 argument eventually end up with serious tax penalties or, as in the case mentioned above, *jail time*.

If you don't know or haven't heard, let me be the first to tell you: the "861 argument" is complete B.S. It's not a loophole. It's not a magic bag of tricks. The IRS and the government are well-aware of the various arguments against taxes and the reasoning behind them, and the courts have consistently upheld the **government's side of the argument**.

> Do yourself a favor on this one. Take the advice of Benjamin Franklin, and count on the fact that you will most certainly have to pay taxes.

People, by nature it seems, often **want** to trust other people. And it's very common for people to hold *distrust* for the government (sometimes with good reason).

So when an average Joe finds a person (whom they naturally want to trust) who reinforces their distrust of the government by telling them about secret tax conspiracies and little known "loopholes", they may find themselves **wanting** to believe what they are told. It's interesting, in the story of Wesley Snipes from above, that he was somehow able to find accountants who, according to the allegations, "had a history of filing fraudulent or false returns in order to get tax refunds for their clients".

I've mentioned earlier in this program the fact that you should, at least once, have a competent accountant look over your taxes to make sure you aren't paying too much.

But not all accountants are created equal. Anyone can find a *crooked* accountant who will save them money. That's what crooked accountants do. They *cheat*.

Using an accountant who is willing to cheat can lead to all kinds of problems, including jail!

How can you avoid such trouble?

For starters, use only a *reputable* accountant.

And if you don't know or aren't sure, here's a good general rule:

> Never follow advice that goes against your *common sense* or otherwise seems too good to be true.

One of the good and bad parts of the Internet is just about anyone can post anything online. If you have an opinion (even a *wrong* opinion), you can tell the world about it, and maybe even convince a few people that you're right.

Because of the *free-information-flow* nature of the Internet, some people end up taking advice from individuals whom they would not normally take advice from.

For example, they might see a video about taxes from a random guy on YouTube that *seems* authoritative, which happens to have been produced by a guy named Matt Foley who lives "in a van down by the river". Matt Foley[5] is fictional, if you didn't catch the reference, and that's really the point:

You don't <u>know</u> the random guy on YouTube.

You have no idea who he is, what he stands for, or what his hidden motives might be. He may be a few beers short of a twelve-pack, "living in a van down by the river", eating a "steady diet of government cheese"[6]. *Sounds like a great place to go for financial advice, right?*

---

[5] Matt Foley is a fictional character played by the late Chris Farley on the comedy sketch show, "Saturday Night Live".

[6] "Living in a van down by the river" and "eating a steady diet of government cheese" are both quotes from Chris Farley's fictional character named Matt Foley.

Not quite.

Why would you take tax advice (or any other financial advice) from a person like that?

It probably sounds absurd, but people do it all the time.

And sometimes following that bad advice, when it deals with their taxes, leads them into all kinds of tax problems and legal trouble.

The moral of the story here? Don't follow any tax advice that goes against what you (and Benjamin Franklin) know to be true.

Getting Things Under Control

Sometimes tax problems are truly accidental. There are accidental underpayments and overpayments, there are what we might call "chronic underpayments" and "chronic overpayments", in which people pay either too much or not enough in taxes year after year. (Do you have a big tax bill every year, then you're a chronic under payer. Do you get a huge refund every year, then you're a chronic over payer.)

Sometimes people don't realize certain income is taxable or should be reported. Other times they have difficulty keeping good records, and as a result, either end up paying too much tax or not enough.

The first step to getting things under control, short of realizing that you must pay taxes and making an honest effort to pay them, is getting your record-keeping and your finances under control.

The more involved you are in your own finances, the better equipped you will be to understand your tax obligations.

Most tax problems that people experience could be avoided by doing a few relatively basic things:

- ✓ Understand and accept what Benjamin Franklin knew... that taxes are *for certain*.
- ✓ Have a tax strategy and plan. Know *how* you will manage and pay taxes. Will you itemize deductions? Then your recordkeeping *must* be up to par. Are you self-employed? Then you should keep a separate account and keep track of receipts and business related expenditures.
- ✓ Don't try to get away with something or otherwise cheat the tax system. *Just pay what you owe.*
- ✓ Get an estimate of how much tax you should be paying, and take steps to make sure you are paying the right amount. (Not too much, not too little.)

Paying The Right Amount

We've already talked about how reducing the amount of the "interest free loan" that you give the government each month can improve your monthly cash flow.

It's also important to not *underpay* your taxes, which can lead to underpayment penalties, tax debt, and more.

When making changes to your tax withholding, seek advice about what your withholding *should* be in order to minimize your refund, but not end up owing a bunch of money either.

When itemizing deductions, be careful to only take deductions that you can legally take. Don't inflate values of donations or use other tactics to "maximize" deductions. Be honest. Have integrity. Sure, take advantage of whatever deductions you can, just don't try to do *more* than that.

Dealing With Tax Debt

Of all the entities that a person might end up owing large amounts of money to, the IRS is probably the worst. Nobody wants a big pile of tax debt.

However, sometimes people mess up. Sometimes they mess up big, and end up with a huge tax bill as a result. Sometimes they make payment arrangements with the IRS and make monthly payments. If they start to struggle with those payments, things can go downhill even more.

One might say that the best way to deal with tax debt is not to have it in the first place.

If you can't avoid it, the next best thing may be to move the debt elsewhere using something like debt consolidation, a friendly loan, or even credit cards. The downside to this is that if you are already struggling to keep up with your bills, moving the tax debt into another form of debt may be difficult to do, and may not really help you much.

What exactly you do with your tax debt, and how you tackle it, will depend a lot on your situation. If you're struggling to keep up, you could consider trying to settle with the IRS. If you can make the case that you are in financial trouble and that paying the debt would create a serious hardship, you may be able to settle the debt for less than you owe. Instances where this might be workable are cases where you've lost your primary source of income, or had some other major financial setback.

If you have problems with tax debt, and you are absolutely buried and struggling to make the payments, you may want to consider the following step.

Offer in Compromise

An "offer in compromise" is the official IRS version of *debt settlement*. It allows you to settle your federal tax debt for less than you owe under certain circumstances.

There are certain requirements that must be met for an offer in compromise. As of this writing, they include:

- You cannot afford to pay your full tax liability, or doing so would create a financial hardship.
- You must be current with all tax returns (i.e. have filed all tax returns as required by law) and payment requirements (such as estimated tax payments).
- You must not be in the process of bankruptcy.
- You must pay a $150 application fee, unless you are submitting an individual offer in compromise and meet the "low income certification" guidelines. (Note: fees are subject to change; always check www.irs.gov for the latest information.)

When you submit an offer in compromise, the IRS will look at your entire situation in order to determine whether or not to accept your offer. Here's what the IRS website says about offer in compromise approval:

> *"We generally approve an offer in compromise when the amount offered represents the most we can expect to collect within a reasonable period of time."*

With an offer in compromise, you have to tell the IRS how you intend to pay them, and even start paying them according to your selected plan, unless of course you meet the "low income certification" guidelines.

Obviously, it's best if you can avoid a situation in which you would need an offer in compromise altogether. Even the IRS website says to try every other option first.

For smaller amounts of tax debt which you could reasonably expect to pay off or even settle elsewhere, moving the debt somewhere else is the best option.

If your situation is such that you need to file for bankruptcy, it is *possible* that your tax debt could be discharged in the bankruptcy. (Note: this does NOT apply in all cases!)

If you think an offer in compromise is for you, then check out the official paperwork on the IRS website: http://www.irs.gov/pub/irs-pdf/f656b.pdf

Tax Liens

If you have a federal tax lien on your credit then you know how damaging they can be.

There are a few things you might need or want to do when you have a tax lien on your credit. The main ones are:

- Pay the amount owed in full or make payment arrangements with the IRS, then request a withdrawal of the lien.
- *Settle* with the IRS, in which case it will be "released" but not "withdrawn".
- Apply for a withdrawal of the lien for other reasons.
- Appeal the filing of the lien

Of particular interest is the first part, which is how *most federal tax liens* can be removed from credit reports.

When it comes to credit reporting, a "withdrawn" tax lien is a tax lien that never happened. It should be removed from your credit report and never show up again.

The process doesn't happen on its own though.

In order to obtain the withdrawal of a tax lien and get it removed from your credit report you must take the following steps:

1. Pay the tax lien in full or enter into a qualifying installment agreement.
2. Submit a special form (IRS FORM 12277) to the IRS to request withdrawal of the lien. Along with the form, include the names and addresses of the credit bureaus and the IRS will notify the bureaus of the withdrawal for you.
3. Wait for a response from the IRS. You should get a form notifying you that the lien has been withdrawn.
4. If, once you've received the IRS notice of withdrawal, the lien still remains on your credit report, copy the withdrawal form and send a copy to each of the credit bureaus along with a letter requesting that they remove the tax lien from your credit report.

It's important to remember that only paid-in-full tax liens can be withdrawn in this manner. If you enter into a settlement agreement with the IRS, the lien will be *released* but will remain on your credit report for 7 years.

Conclusion

Once again, I have to say that the best way to deal with tax problems is to not have them in the first place. Obviously, that isn't always possible... and some people end up with serious tax problems due to no *real* fault of their own. Mistakes just happen sometimes. People unknowingly get information from questionable sources. People act on bad advice... sometimes from sources that *should* be reliable.

If you find yourself with some income and you are asking yourself the question, "is this taxable?" the answer is, in most cases, a resounding "yes".

Think I'm kidding? Here's a partial list of items from the IRS that fall under the category of "income the IRS wants to know about so that you can pay taxes on it."

- The value of goods or services received in bartering arrangements.
- Forgiven debts
- Money received as a *bribe*.
- Certain expenses of yours that are paid by other people
- Property you find that was lost or abandoned that did not originally belong to you
- Free tours received from travel agencies
- Income from gambling, lotteries, and raffles
- Income from dealing illegal drugs, prostitution, and other illegal activities (report on form 1040, line 21!)

Hopefully you get the point.

If it's money, and it's coming to you in one form or another (even if not in the form of "money", but of goods and services—such as in the case of bartering), the IRS wants to know about it.

If you've already got serious tax problems, you may be wondering what your options are for relief. We've discussed a few of them this chapter, but if you're in real trouble financially it may be that bankruptcy is going to end up as your best option. Sometimes starting with a clean slate really is best.

But what will bankruptcy do to your tax obligations? Can your federal and state tax debt be discharged in bankruptcy?

The answer is: it *depends*.

There are several laws and requirements that dictate whether or not your tax debt can be included in your bankruptcy. Generally speaking, the main guidelines are as follows:

1. The tax debt itself is at least 3 years old
2. The associated tax returns were filed at least 2 years ago
3. It's at least 240 days from the date of the tax assessment
4. The return or returns were not fraudulent and the taxpayer was not guilty of tax evasion.

Those are the basics, but there are many variables that can change the outcome and affect the qualification of tax debt for bankruptcy. If you are considering bankruptcy and you have tax debt, it is highly recommended that you consult with a qualified attorney, preferably one that specializes in tax bankruptcy.

If you are in a situation where bankruptcy is a serious option, then don't despair. Next chapter I'm going to devote the entire chapter to the subject of **bankruptcy**. *(And it's not as bad as you think!)*

Your Home Program
Our Advisors Are Available To Answer Your Questions
Call **1-800-245-7349** for Home Ownership Made Easy!

27 WHAT IF I NEED TO FILE FOR BANKRUPTCY?

This chapter's discussion isn't going to apply to everyone directly.

However, even if you don't see bankruptcy in your future, it is wise to pay attention to what we're about to cover.

Video Resource
Video Name: How does Bankruptcy affect your Credit?
www.YourHomeProgram.com/BookResource

Why?

Several reasons, really.

For one, you don't know what will happen tomorrow, or next week, or 6 months from now. We all hope to be fine and financially fit of course, but if things don't go your way at some point in the future it will be beneficial for you to have been educated about the available options.

Another reason you should pay attention has a lot less to do with *you*. Bankruptcy carries a social stigma with it. Chances are, at some point in your life you are going to know someone who either is going through or has gone through a bankruptcy, and that person will no doubt appreciate having someone nearby that not only understands what they're going through financially, but understands the emotional and social impact as well.

So for whatever reason you choose to, I do believe you should stick around for this chapter. We're going to talk about bankruptcy and what it really means if your situation is such that the big "BK" is your best option.

The Cost Of Bankruptcy

When a lot of people think about the cost of bankruptcy, what they are really thinking about is what it will do to their ***credit***. In reality, there is much more to the cost of bankruptcy than just credit. Let's talk about those costs...

The Financial Cost

One cost that many people overlook when first considering bankruptcy is the *financial cost* involved. If a person is filing for bankruptcy, they are probably already struggling financially. Sometimes people are unprepared for the costs of the bankruptcy process itself.

The total cost of filing for bankruptcy (including all attorney fees, court costs, etc.) is somewhere in the range of $1,200 to $3,000. Sure, you might see ads by bankruptcy attorney's advertising for inexpensive bankruptcy filings, but there are more fees and costs involved than just attorney fees. You probably also don't want to go after the cheapest attorney you can find. (Remember, you get what you pay for.)

There's also the "DIY" method in which a person skips the attorney, completing and filing the forms on their own... but you're better off with a competent bankruptcy attorney than some cheap software or forms you found online.

The Personal And Emotional Costs

Florida bankruptcy attorney Lori Patton says on her website[7]...

> *"Experts say that filing a bankruptcy is one of the top 5 most traumatic events that can happen in an American's adult life, right up there with death of a loved one and divorce. It's a big deal."*

There are considerable personal and emotional costs involved in bankruptcy. The process can be stressful and emotionally taxing.

Video Resource
Video Name: Is Bankruptcy a Credit Score killer?
www.YourHomeProgram.com/BookResource

Emotions that people might experience and deal with in the bankruptcy process include feelings of failure, defeat, and even guilt. It may help to be prepared for this up front, and to remember that bankruptcy is there for your *protection*. It's part of our legal and financial system for a *reason*, and the fact that you are using it to get control of your finances isn't something to be ashamed of or to beat yourself up over.

The Social Cost

Bankruptcy proceedings aren't exactly private matters. In fact, they are matters of *public record*. This doesn't mean, however, that everyone in the area will necessarily know (or care) that you filed for bankruptcy. Still there is a social stigma that comes with the word "bankruptcy".

Earlier in the program we discussed how having bad credit, especially a bankruptcy, can hurt your chances of getting a job. This is, in many if not most cases, because of the stigma of bankruptcy and nothing else. The supervisor or manager who doesn't know better sees the bankruptcy and immediately makes a judgment, albeit an unfair one, about who you are.

You can minimize the social costs of bankruptcy by keeping your private life as private as possible and being prepared to re-frame your experience for things like job interviews and other situations where your bankruptcy may come into the picture.

---

[7] Source: http://www.loripatton.com

Another thing that might help reduce the perceived social impact is to understand this point: **you aren't alone**. Hundreds of thousands of people file for bankruptcy every year. It's a part of life. Yeah, it's a tough part of life... but it's something that people go through. If you're human, and you deal with money and debt, there is a possibility that you will have to deal with it at some point in your life if not right now. And that's okay.

The Credit Cost

The credit cost is probably the one cost involved in bankruptcy that people think about more often than any other.

Ironically, the argument could be made that the **credit cost** is the one cost that matters the *least*. The reason I say this is because, as we've already covered in this program, there are systematic methods and tactics—ones that actually *work*—to deal with the credit costs of bankruptcy.

I won't say that there is no effect on your credit score. Bankruptcy does hurt your credit. However, I *will* say that bankruptcy probably hurts your credit **less** than you think.

Let's take a quick look at the effects that bankruptcy has on your credit:

- Your credit score will go down, in part due to the bankruptcy itself.
- Your credit score will go down even more due to negative items not listed correctly as included in the bankruptcy.
- The bankruptcy will stay on your credit report for 7 to 10 years.
- The effect of the bankruptcy on your credit will be greatest in the first 12 to 24 months. (This is because most credit scoring algorithms put more weight on the last 2 years of history.)
- You will be scored according to a "bankruptcy" scorecard, which means you will be scored in comparison with other people who have filed for bankruptcy.

The systematic plan (that I've called the "Post Bankruptcy Credit Score Improvement Plan") to dealing with the post-bankruptcy credit blues takes most of this into account, and dare I say more than adequately addresses the biggest issues.

Credit after bankruptcy won't be easy. There is certainly some work and some cleanup to be done. But it is far from impossible, especially if you use the Post Bankruptcy Credit Score Improvement Plan. (Don't worry, we'll review it below!)

Minimizing Your Costs

We already talked a little about minimizing the social costs of bankruptcy. *What about the emotional costs?* These are the costs that few people consider but almost everyone is impacted by. How can you lessen the emotional impact?

One way is to simply be prepared. If you know what's coming and aren't taken by surprise, you'll be better off. Expect feelings of guilt and shame, and be prepared to counter those with facts: bankruptcy is a part of life. It isn't the end of the world. Hundreds of thousands of people do it each year. There is **no shame** in doing the responsible thing to get your finances under control.

Dealing with the social/stigma costs probably deserves further discussion as well. Employment is the biggest place that people feel this one (even if they don't know it). If you are applying for a job that involves a credit check and you have a bankruptcy on your credit, there is a very high likelihood that you will be turned down for the job based on your bankruptcy, but will never be told (as you legally should) that the bankruptcy was the "real" reason.

How can you combat this?

The best approach is to be up front. If you know there is a credit check involved, talk about the bankruptcy up front. Re-frame the bankruptcy as an obstacle that you had to overcome, and show how you have worked through it and are a better person now because of it. Using this strategy, your credit problems can actually become a *selling point* rather than a stumbling block!

Why Bankruptcy Isn't As Bad As You Think

The reality of the situation is that bankruptcy, while bad, is <u>NOT</u> anywhere near as bad as you probably think. It's not as bad as you think because for every problem associated with bankruptcy (i.e. credit, social/employment), there is a <u>solution</u> that works.

Because of this, bankruptcy isn't the end of your financial story. It's just a turn of the page into a new chapter.

What I'm saying is that as long as there are methods to deal with the madness, you need not despair!

We've already talked about the post-bankruptcy credit score improvement plan earlier in the program. The credit problems associated with bankruptcy—the cost that people consider most—can be dealt with in most cases by following this simple plan.

The Post-Bankruptcy Credit Score Improvement Plan

Let's review the Post-Bankruptcy Credit Score Improvement Plan quickly. Here's how it works:

STEP 1: Keep your credit <u>CLEAN</u>.

Remember that in the credit system, you are graded on a curve. One of the effects of bankruptcy as far as your credit is concerned is that you will now be scored on a "bankruptcy" scorecard. This means your credit performance will be compared with other people who have filed for bankruptcy.

Having negative items pop up on your credit report after the bankruptcy is a sure way to keep your credit score down and out. If you're going to improve it, you MUST keep your credit <u>CLEAN</u> so that, in comparison with other bankruptcy cases, it appears as though you have learned your lesson and are making improvements.

STEP 2: Make sure the items on your credit report are being reported correctly as "included in bankruptcy".

A negative item that was included in the bankruptcy that isn't correctly listed as such on your credit report is especially damaging because of the "curve" grading and "scorecards" that we've already discussed. Go through your credit reports and make sure that <u>everything</u> that was included in the bankruptcy is listed correctly as being included in the bankruptcy. If you find incorrect listings, get them corrected!

STEP 3: Build new credit history by adding new, positive credit accounts.

Now you've got to start building positive credit history. You might think: "How can I get new credit with a bankruptcy?" But it's probably easier than you think. However you do it, get credit lines that report to the credit bureaus and will start showing a new positive history. Do this as soon as possible after your bankruptcy is discharged.

Just 3 Steps!

Video Resource
Video Name: Home Loan after Bankruptcy
www.YourHomeProgram.com/BookResource

That is all there is to the Post-Bankruptcy Credit Score Improvement Plan. Three <u>SIMPLE</u> steps. If you follow these steps, the credit cost of bankruptcy will be minimal, and you'll soon be on your way to great credit and a bright financial future.

Navigating Through Bankruptcy

Your Home Program
Our Advisors Are Available To Answer Your Questions
Call **1-800-245-7349** for Home Ownership Made Easy!

Before you file for bankruptcy, you need to consider all possible alternatives. Look at all of your options. Consider the costs involved, and what you're getting yourself into.

If you think bankruptcy might be an option for you, I highly recommend consulting with an expert before you attempt to dive in. A qualified bankruptcy attorney can help you through the process, and can also advise you as to whether there might be better options.

Whatever you do, don't try to go through the process alone. Go to the trouble of finding qualified help. When it's all said and done, you will be glad that you did.

Conclusion

We started this week with a question: *"What if I need to file for bankruptcy?"*

I've spent some time now trying to sufficiently answer that question, mainly attempting to communicate to you that if you do indeed need to file for bankruptcy, it is **not** the end of the world. It is a serious undertaking, but not a financial-life-ending one.

In a couple of chapters we'll start talking about the details of credit repair, and I'll give you the tools and information you need to successfully dispute items on your credit report and clean up your credit (including bankruptcy related credit problems). You'll get to see and understand how the credit repair process works, and we'll even go over some sample disputes and examples.

Next chapter we'll review what we've covered so far, and take a look at your evolving financial landscape.

28 CHECKPOINT: IS YOUR FINANCIAL PICTURE CHANGING?

If you are taking steps to make changes as you go through this program, your financial picture *should* be changing.

This chapter we're going to review some of the key points from the last several chapters, and see what the affect has been (or *could be*) on your financial picture.

Next chapter we're going to start talking about the ever-important credit and credit repair, but before going down that road I want to be sure you have a firm grasp on the rest of your financial triad.

So let's review, starting with...

Income Strategies

We spent multiple chapters reviewing strategies for increasing your income. We talked about how to increase your income at your current job, and about tactics for making more money *outside* of your existing job.

Here is a quick overview. The strategy is listed on the left, and the potential ***increase*** in your monthly income is in the column to the right.

STRATEGY	POTENTIAL
Ask for a raise - You could increase your income by $150 or more per month by simply asking. You never know until you try!	$150+ per month!
Apply for a promotion - With more responsibility comes more money, and a step up can mean a $1 or $2 per hour raise, or more!	$150+ per month!
Request extra hours - Some employers will gladly give them to you. 1 extra hour per day at $15 per hour averages to an extra $325 per month!	$325+ per month!
Ask for side jobs - Some employers will let you take on extra projects on the side for extra money.	$200+ per month!
Get a part-time job - Whether ongoing, seasonal, or temporary, the income from a part time job can quickly add up!	$500+ per month!
Start your own side business - A part-time side business (such as a credit repair business or cleaning business) could generate up to $1000 or more per month!	$1000+ per month!
Teach classes or lessons - If you have a skill or special knowledge that you can pass on to others, why not make money at it?	$500+ per month!
Sales or MLM - There are a number of side sales jobs that are capable of generating a healthy second income.	$500+ per month!

Make money with odd jobs, garage sales, flea markets, and more! There are endless varieties of opportunities to make money for those willing to try.	$500+ per month!
Sell stuff online - There is a very long list of people who make a full-time living doing nothing but selling stuff online. You could do it too.	$3000+ per month!
Work online by telecommuting or doing freelance work - Again, a lot of people make a full-time living this way.	$3000+ per month!
Change jobs - If you're in a go nowhere job and can find better paying employment elsewhere, now might be a good time to give it a try.	$500+ per month!
Save money and collect interest - A penny saved is a penny earned. Enough money in interest-earning accounts can start to add up!	$50+ per month!

Did you happen to add up the numbers in the right hand column? If you did, you might notice that there are over **$10,000** worth of ideas here.

Sure, you might not be able to act on all of them, but it only takes one or two to make a difference. *Now on to your expenses.*

Expense Strategies

Here is a quick overview of some of the savings strategies we've covered. The strategy or idea is listed in the left hand column, and the potential *savings* is on the right.

STRATEGY	POTENTIAL
Change your tax withholding - If you're getting a big tax refund every year, change your withholding and improve your cash flow!	$300+ per month!
Have an accountant review your taxes - A qualified (and reputable) accountant may help you discover that you're paying too much taxes.	$200+ per month!
Don't buy more insurance than you need - You may be able to afford higher co-pays and deductibles in exchange for lower premiums.	$350+ per month!
Cut back on your electricity usage - Many people could save $50 per month or more on electricity bills by making a few simple changes.	$50+ per month!
Cut back on your natural gas usage - Many people could save $50 per month or more on their natural gas bills by making a few simple changes.	$50+ per month!
Cut back on your water usage - Things like fixing leaky faucets and taking shorter showers can add up!	$25+ per month!

Utilize the *Negotiate, Compare, and Cancel* strategy - A lot of people could save a lot of money by applying this strategy to as many bills as possible.	$100+ per month!
Pay less for TV - A lot of people don't use all the channels they pay for. Cutting back could mean saving big!	$50+ per month!
Pay off debts to lower monthly payments and interest paid - The less money you are throwing away on interest, the better!	$200+ per month!
Use debt negotiation to get better terms - Asking for better interest rates or payment terms could give a good boost to your cash flow!	$50+ per month!
Transfer credit card balances to cards with low introductory rates - You could easily save $20 or $30 per month in interest by transferring a balance.	$25+ per month!
Use coupons, price matching, and other methods to save on groceries - A lot of people save a <u>LOT</u> of money this way. You could too.	$200+ per month!
Stop buying so much junk food - Some people spend as much as $50 per week buying things like soda pop, chips, and sweets.	$200+ per month!
Stop smoking - Easier said than done, I know, but this is one *costly* habit that doesn't do much for your health, either.	$200+ per month!
Reduce automobile expenses - From oil changes to gas mileage, there are a lot of ways to save money. Why not give it a try?	$30+ per month!
Save on childcare - whether it's schedule changes or a babysitting co-op, there may be ways you can cut back on childcare costs without sacrificing quality.	$200+ per month!
Use coupons when dining out - Buy one get one free deals and other common offers can really add up!	$50+ per month!
Make your own coffee - Some people spend as much as $80 (or more) per month on fancy coffee drinks. You can make your own for much less.	$80+ per month!

If you add up the numbers in the right hand column, you'll see that there is over **$2,000** in potential savings listed on the table above. Obviously not everything applies to everyone in every situation, but if you did nothing else but go through the list above applying whatever strategies you *can*, how much money could *you* save?

Cash Flow Progress Meter

Has your cash flow improved since you started this program? If it hasn't, you need to ask yourself the question...

"Why not?"

The most common reason for lack of financial progress is a lack of ***action***. If you suffer from a chronic lack of action, perhaps it's time to make a change now and **act**. There are thousands of dollars in earnings and savings available to you, and I'm piling them all up into this one week for review.

What will you do with them? The choice is yours. All you have to do is act. Choosing to act and to make changes now (if you haven't already) could literally change your life forever.

In 99% of cases the following statement sums it up:

YOUR SUCCESS IS UP TO YOU!

Debt Strategies

Earlier we talked about several strategies for dealing with debt. We also talked about the "Debt-Control Plan," a simple outline to use that can help you navigate through the process of getting out of debt.

The key thing to understand with debt AND savings (covered next) is that they are both entirely dependent on the two major areas we've reviewed so far: your *income* and your *expenses*. I know it probably feels like I'm beating this "financial triad" thing to death, but I'm doing it for good reason. It's important!

Your debt and your savings (collectively known as your *net worth*) are highly dependent on your cash flow. As Forrest Gump might say, they go together "like peas and carrots."

If you'll remember, this interdependence was reflected in our "Debt-Control Plan" from earlier. Do you remember the steps? If not, here's a refresher:

1. Do everything you can to increase your income.
2. Do everything you can to decrease your expenses.
3. If you're able to make payments on your debt and your finances are under control, you can proceed with choosing the best strategy to get out of debt. If you still can't make your debt payments after steps 1 and 2, then you might be in trouble and it's probably time to consider debt settlement, credit counseling, or bankruptcy.

The first two steps, as you may have noticed, don't even mention the word "debt". They are all about *cash flow*.

What this all really means is that in order to have the best long term financial outlook with regards to your debt, savings, and even credit, you are going to have to get your income and expenses where they need to be.

The rest of your financial triad really pivots on ***cash flow***. The more money you have coming in, and the *less* money you have going out, the better off you will be.

We talked about several strategies for debt relief:

- Debt reduction
- Debt consolidation
- Credit counseling
- Debt settlement

- Bankruptcy

Generally speaking, the less cash flow you have, the less options you will have for dealing with debt. Once you have your cash flow in order you can start to tackle your debt and, in the end, improve your cash flow *even more*. Paying off debt creates a cash flow snowball effect. The more you pay off, the more cash flow you have, and the more debt you are able to pay off. It's a cycle that pays off!

And paying off your debt, freeing yourself from monthly payments will make it easier for you to SAVE money. It's like giving yourself a raise. Let's say you eventually eliminate $500 per month in debt payments. If you took just **half** of that and put it in savings every month, in just 10 years at 3% interest you would have over $35,000!

Savings Strategies

Do you remember the ultimate savings strategy?

If not, just remember the word "SAFE".

Systematic
Automatic
Forgettable, and
Enough.

The idea behind this strategy is extremely simple, but quite effective. It tackles head-on some of the main issues and barriers that keep people from saving money.

If you haven't already, maybe now is a good time to implement your own "SAFE" savings strategy!

Net Worth Progress Meter

Has your net worth improved since the beginning of this program? If so, then great. If not, then maybe it's time to consider doing something about your debt and your savings situation. Use the steps of the Debt-Control Plan to determine what your options might be, and if you think you need to consider bankruptcy or debt settlement, then it will be wise for you to consult with a qualified expert to see what your options are.

Conclusion

Well you might have seen it coming, but it's time to take another look at the financial triad...

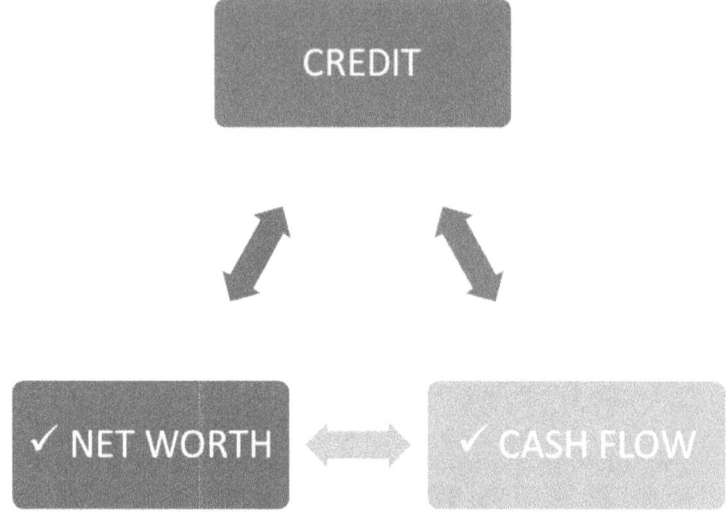

Did you notice that I changed the illustration slightly this time?

This is because, if you've been following along, you should be making some progress in the areas of **net worth** and **cash flow**.

The only area I don't feel like we can rightfully check off yet is the area of *credit*.

This means that it's time to dive into the topics of credit and credit repair!

For the next few chapters we will be going in depth on the topics of credit and credit repair, and what it all means for buying a home.

If you've got credit problems, then you'd be crazy to miss out on what I'm going to share with you over the chapters to come. (So stick around... you'll be glad you did!)

29 CREDIT REPAIR: THE CREDIT DISPUTE PROCESS

For the next few chapters we're going to come back to the process of *repairing* your credit. We'll start this chapter with talking about the dispute process itself. If you have bad credit and want to buy a home, credit repair is going to be an important part of your plan. If you choose the rent to own path, credit repair will be a crucial step during the rent to own period. *In other words, the next few chapters are important!*

When a lot of people think about "credit repair" or "credit disputes", they think of writing letters and sending them to each of the three credit bureaus. This is ***part*** of the process, but it is **not** the whole story.

There is more to credit repair than just disputing with the credit bureaus. (In fact, there is more to credit repair than just disputing, but I'm getting ahead of myself. For this chapter, we're focusing on the "disputing" aspect of credit repair.)

The FTC offers "help" on their website for the credit repair process. Even the FTC seems to believe that credit repair involves nothing more than sending disputes to the credit bureaus:

> *"Tell the **consumer reporting company**, in writing, what information you think is inaccurate."*
>
> *www.ftc.gov*

Tell the **credit bureaus** what you think is **inaccurate**.

This statement isn't anywhere near the **full truth** of the matter when it comes to credit repair. First off, in the credit repair process you may be dealing with the **credit bureaus**, the **creditor**, or a **bill collector**. Secondly, according to the FCRA (Fair Credit Reporting Act), any information that is found to be "inaccurate, incomplete, or cannot be verified" must be <u>removed</u>.

The FTC's website fall's short here by only mentioning a portion of what credit repair actually entails. To correct the above statement about credit repair from the FTC, we might change it to something more like this:

> *Tell the consumer reporting company, the creditor, or the collection agency, in writing, what information you think is inaccurate, incomplete, or unverifiable."*

There, that's more like it!

That is, in essence, the *credit repair process* as we are going to be talking about it this chapter. As you may have guessed, there is a little more to it than that, and we're going to get into those details starting now...

Dispute Process Basics

We've already talked about the fact that a dispute may be sent to the credit bureaus, the creditor, or a collection agency. You may be writing to dispute information that is inaccurate, incomplete, or otherwise can't be verified.

There are several things that your disputes should include in order to meet the minimum standards:

Video Resource
Video Name: Credit Repair Process
www.YourHomeProgram.com/BookResource

Video Resource
Video Name: What is Credit Repair?
www.YourHomeProgram.com/BookResource

- ✓ Your disputes should indicate which item or account is being disputed
- ✓ Your disputes should indicate <u>WHY</u> the item or account is being disputed
- ✓ Your disputes should indicate what action you want the bureau, creditor, or collector to take in response to your dispute
- ✓ Your disputes should include <u>documentation</u> to support your claim
- ✓ Last but not least, your disputes should be <u>factual</u>

Let's talk more about making a dispute *factual*, and why it is important.

Factual Disputes

A factual dispute is, simply put, a dispute that is based on **fact**.

More than that, a factual dispute is one based on the facts of your situation, based on factually incorrect reporting on your credit report, and based on the circumstances as you know them to be true.

There was a time when the standard approach to credit repair was a barrage of dispute letters, all sent to the credit bureaus, all saying the same basic thing: "This account is not mine." This was said regardless of whether or not it was true. It was the *sole method* of credit repair taught by many "experts". This approach doesn't work anymore, though. <u>Frivolous</u> disputes won't get you far, and even using ***legitimate factual disputes*** to repair your credit can be challenging. (More on that in a moment.)

> *With factual disputes, the only time in which you would write a dispute saying "this account is not mine" is if the account were indeed not yours.*

The reason that factual disputes are so important is because, in the event that the credit bureau, creditor, or collector doesn't comply with your initial dispute (which is common), the only real way you will have a "legal leg to stand on" is if your initial dispute was based on fact.

In other words, if the dispute was false or frivolous in the first place, you won't have much legal backup when push comes to shove.

Reviewing Your Credit Reports

Since disputes must be factual, *reviewing your credit reports* involves looking at your reports from each of the three credit bureaus, and looking for *factual errors*. Factual errors could mean anything from an account that is fraudulent, to incorrect amounts or dates on an account that is otherwise correct. You have a right to insure that the items on your credit report are accurate, complete, and verifiable. When you review your credit reports, you're watching for anything that may not meet those criteria. To the three criteria we might also add "timely", which means any items that are *outdated* should also be removed from your report.

Video Resource
Video Name: Incorrect Balances on a Credit Report
www.YourHomeProgram.com/BookResource

Here are some things you can look for that may warrant a dispute:

- Look for missing information and blank fields. One common example is that of a missing credit limit.
- Look for incorrect account types (does it say installment when it is revolving?)
- Look for incorrect account numbers.
- Look for incorrect dates.
- Look for incorrect balances and credit limits.
- Check the closed dates on accounts, and look for late pays that occur after those dates.
- Check the Date of Last Activity (or DOLA). This is the date that sets the clock for how long an item can stay on your credit. It is common for it to mysteriously change in such a way to keep a negative item on your report longer. If this happens, the account has been "re-aged", and it should be disputed accordingly.

Creating Successful Disputes

Once you know what you're going to dispute, you need to write a dispute that will get the job done.

Notice I didn't say you need to copy and paste a dispute from the internet.

Ideally, you should write you own. At the very least, you should start with a template and customize it.

Disputes should be either hand written or use strange fonts and colors. This might sound strange, but it's an important part of creating a successful dispute. The credit bureaus use special computer technology to "read" your disputes without any human involvement. Anything you can do to get around that will help to make sure your dispute at least gets seen by a human being. Here are some basics to help:

- Write your disputes by hand or use colorful and unusual fonts. Italics are good too.
- Use non-standard paper and pretty stationary. Background images on the stationary are a good idea.

- Include a lot of supporting documentation, and ideally staple it to your dispute using several staples, perhaps in non-standard places.
- Envelopes should be non-standard shapes and sizes when possible. Different colors may be good too.
- Make sure, in all of your efforts to customize your dispute that you keep it "human readable". You want to make it difficult or impossible for a machine to read your dispute, but if a human can't understand it you won't get anywhere! The dispute should still be in letter format, and should still include all the required information and documentation.

Taking these steps serves the purpose of reducing the *automation factor* when a credit bureau handles your dispute. In short, the more the credit bureaus are able to automate the process of handling your dispute, the less likely it is that it will get the attention it needs in order to be handled properly. So take the above steps to "de-automate" your dispute, and give it the best chance of reaching a human.

One thing to note: all of these "anti-automation" steps are currently only necessary when sending disputes to the *credit bureaus*. For collectors and creditors, it's okay to send disputes on standard paper using standard fonts.

Downsides to The Credit Dispute Process

There are some downsides to the credit dispute process that I want to talk about a little before we get into actual credit repair disputes and tactics.

First off, the credit dispute process can be downright *complicated*. The best way to go about disputing doesn't always jump out and grab you. And even if you go about things in the best possible way, you may still end up hitting road blocks that are no fault of your own, but are just the results of a somewhat corrupt and convoluted credit system.

For example, it is very common for the credit bureaus to deem disputes as frivolous or even ignore them altogether when a dispute is perfectly legitimate, factual, and authentic.

It is also common for the credit bureaus to "verify" items that are, in reality, incorrect, incomplete, or even "unverifiable". How could an inaccurate and unverifiable item come back as "verified"? Good question. The answer is a little beyond the scope of this chapter's discussion, but I can tell you this: the word "verified", when used by a credit bureau, creditor, or collector, should be taken very *lightly*. Just because an item gets "verified", does not mean that it is indeed accurate and should stay on your credit report. It just means you've hit another common road block.

This is just one of the many reasons that consumers often opt to seek professional help when it comes to repairing their credit. A qualified credit repair professional will know how to deal with all the ins and outs of the process, and won't be shut down by some of the common roadblocks and pitfalls of the credit dispute process.

Most of the downsides to the credit dispute process can be attributed to the fact that the credit bureaus, creditors, and collection agencies all ***profit*** from your bad credit. They are for-profit companies, and they are structured in such a way as to maximize profits, and if necessary, do so at the expense of your credit.

If you choose to do your own credit repair you will need to be prepared for this, and for the resulting road blocks and hiccups you are likely to encounter.

Now that we've got all that out of the way, let's move onto the fun stuff!

Credit Dispute Tactics

A credit dispute tactic is a method or tactic for improving your credit score through the credit dispute process. You may be dealing with a credit bureau, a creditor, or a collection agency when you use credit dispute tactics.

Some tactics are more-or-less useable across the board, and others only apply to one of the three types of companies you are dealing with (bureaus, creditors, or collectors).

Some tactics can be applied and adapted to a number of situations, and others are only of use in very specific circumstances.

In this section I'll try to stick to more general dispute tactics. Hundreds of pages have been written on this topic alone, so I can't expect to cover it in great detail this chapter. I'll try to hit the most important points though, so that you will be well equipped for your credit repair efforts (whether you choose to go the professional route or not).

Dealing With The Credit Bureaus

We've already talked about how dealing with the credit bureaus can be somewhat complicated. Unfortunately, it just isn't as straightforward as one would hope much of the time.

Your Home Program
Our Advisors Are Available To Answer Your Questions
Call **1-800-245-7349** for Home Ownership Made Easy!

With that said, some basic tactics can still accomplish good things for your credit. We'll cover them here.

Before we get started you should take note of the address information for each of the three major credit bureaus:

Equifax
P.O. Box 740241
Atlanta, GA 30374

Experian
P.O. Box 2104
Allen, TX 75013-2104

TransUnion
P.O. Box 2000

Chester, PA 19022-2000

These are the addresses you will write to when you send the credit bureau disputes. If you choose to use a credit repair company or credit repair professional, these are the same addresses they will use to contact the bureaus as well.

When creating disputes, keep in mind the notes we've already covered about "successful disputes." Following the given guidelines will not only help insure your disputes reach their intended destination, but will probably give you better results once they get there.

A Word About Frivolous Disputes

According to the FCRA (Section 611(a)(3)), one reason a credit bureau can deem a dispute to be "frivolous" or "irrelevant" is because a consumer fails to provide "sufficient information to investigate the disputed information."

What this means is that if you don't provide the information necessary for the credit bureau to "investigate" your claims, they can consider it frivolous and your dispute is dead in the water.

How can you avoid this?

Well, first I should say that sometimes it's easier said than done. It is fairly common for perfectly valid and well documented consumer disputes to be deemed frivolous. With that said, disputes can also be deemed to be frivolous because of simple mistakes and omissions. For review, here are some things we mentioned that your disputes should include:

- ✓ Your disputes should indicate which item or account is being disputed
- ✓ Your disputes should indicate <u>WHY</u> the item or account is being disputed
- ✓ Your disputes should indicate what action you want the bureau, creditor, or collector to take in response to your dispute
- ✓ Your disputes should include <u>documentation</u> to support your claim
- ✓ Last but not least, your disputes should be <u>factual</u>

If you are covering these basics, it will be difficult for a credit bureau to legitimately say your dispute is frivolous. You need to be detailed and thorough, but be mindful of the following fact:

There is a delicate balance between providing ***enough*** information and yet not providing ***too much*** information. If you provide too much information you may inadvertently do the credit bureau's job for them.

So be thorough, make sure your disputes cover the points above, but avoid self-incrimination at the same time. Sound tricky? It can be. That's one reason that consumers sometimes turn to professionals for help.

Basic Credit Bureau Disputes

When you send a dispute to the credit bureau, you are usually going to be tackling a negative item on your credit report based on the fact that there are errors in the reporting of the item (i.e. the information is wrong or inaccurate), <u>missing</u> information, <u>outdated</u> information, or <u>unverifiable</u> information.

The letters should be in a "human readable" letter format, but hand-written or use unusual fonts to avoid the credit bureau's "big-brother" computer system as much as possible.

Here is an example of a basic credit bureau dispute that you would use in cases where a creditor claims to have no record of the account (which does happen, believe it or not!):

Your Name
Address
City, State, Zip

Credit Bureau Name
Credit Bureau Address
Credit Bureau City, State, Zip

Date

Report #: [Credit Report Number]

Dear [Credit Bureau Name],

I am writing to dispute the account "[account name]" with the account number of [account number]. The creditor claims to have no record of the account. See the attached documentation which includes a phone log and written correspondence from the creditor. Please delete the account immediately.

Sincerely,

Your Name
Your SSN
Your DOB

You'll want to remember to include the information necessary to confirm your identity and current contact information when contacting the credit bureaus. This could mean a copy of your driver's license and a utility bill or similar documentation. If you don't send this, you give the credit bureaus an opportunity to stall the process and it will do nothing but slow things down... so don't forget!

Method of Verification Disputes

Your Home Program
Our Advisors Are Available To Answer Your Questions
Call **1-800-245-7349** for Home Ownership Made Easy!

What if, after sending a dispute like the one above, the credit bureau "verifies" the account? This happens frequently, even with completely fraudulent accounts.

The FCRA says that you can request what is called the "Method of Verification" from the credit bureau, and that they have to respond to your request within 15 days with a "description of the reinvestigation procedure".

The tricky part about the method of verification is that what the credit bureaus *actually do* doesn't *really* verify anything. The credit bureau sends a numeric code to the creditor who responds, often automatically, either saying the account is verified or that it should be corrected or removed. So when the credit bureau responds to your "method of verification" request, there is a good chance that their response will be a canned response that doesn't actually describe the true method of verification. You can then use this as fuel for another dispute demanding deletion.

Does this sound complicated?

I certainly understand how it could.

Again, this is why many people reach out to professionals for help. But if you don't want to go that route then you just need to remember the basic order of things. It goes like this:

1. Initial dispute
2. Verification by Bureau
3. Ask the bureau for the method of verification per the FCRA, which includes a request for the creditor address information AND a request for the method of verification.
4. Bureau sends canned response
5. When the bureau doesn't respond, or fails to respond with sufficient information, write them again stating that they have violated the FCRA by not providing the information they are required to provide, and demand that they delete the account again.
6. If the bureau still does not delete the account, then proceed to...

Secondary Tactics For Dealing With the Credit Bureaus

Let's say, for the sake of example, that you have followed steps 1 through 6 above and that the credit bureau is still not budging.

This is when you move into the realm of "secondary" tactics. A secondary dispute tactic is a follow-up tactic for use with the credit bureaus (or creditors or collectors).

There comes a point when the dispute process ultimately boils down to a matter of persistence... and if you've reached the point of using a secondary tactic, then persistence is probably going to be the name of the game.

One common secondary tactic is using a third party to contact the credit bureau on your behalf. This could mean going through your state Attorney General, the BBB, or even having an attorney send a letter to the credit bureau on your behalf.

Regardless of the path you choose, a secondary tactic is all about getting the credit bureau's attention and making it clear that you aren't a pushover who is going to easily go away when you meet a little resistance. You want to make it look like they'll have a fight on their hands (and waste a lot of money) if they persist... and often just giving that impression is enough to get them to back down.

Dealing With Creditors

In your credit repair efforts you may find yourself needing to correspond with creditors either in the form of fact finding letters and phone calls, or even direct dispute letters asking them to correct or remove information that they are illegally reporting.

The approach when writing creditors is similar to that when dealing with the credit bureaus:

1. Write them in order to dispute information. Include factual reasons and documentation.
2. Await their response. If the response is not favorable, follow up with a secondary tactic.

Sometimes you can call the creditor first for the purpose of fact finding. You might need to find out what the information the creditor has to verify the account with, or simply to make an initial call to determine whether the account is even "actually" yours.

Depending on the results of your fact finding, you would follow up with a creditor using dispute letters that do all of the following (for review):

- ✓ Your disputes should indicate which item or account is being disputed
- ✓ Your disputes should indicate <u>WHY</u> the item or account is being disputed
- ✓ Your disputes should indicate what action you want the creditor to take in response to your dispute
- ✓ Your disputes should include <u>documentation</u> to support your claim
- ✓ Last but not least, your disputes should be <u>factual</u>

You will also want to include sufficient information to verify your identity—but again—not so much that you do the creditor's job for them.

When dealing with creditors, there may be more laws working in your favor than just the FCRA.

The FCBA (Fair Credit Billing Act) gives you the right to request certain information from creditors. This is information you can request in your fact finding correspondence. If they fail to respond properly, there is a good chance they have violated the law and this may be the leverage you need to get them to **delete** the information in question from your credit report.

Dealing With Collectors

Bill collectors are notorious for abusing consumers. There is a long list of common abuses that are, in fact, so common that many of them are specifically named in the laws governing collection agencies.

Introduction to The FDCPA

FDCPA stands for "Fair Debt Collection Practices Act", which is the primary set of laws governing collection agencies. When they are reporting collection accounts on your credit report or pulling your credit report (placing "hard inquiries"), they are also subject to the laws of the FCRA (Fair Credit Reporting Act).

The FDCPA spells out a number of common violations of bill collectors and also gives you as the consumer certain rights and remedies when dealing with collectors. (For example you have a right to tell them when they can and can't call you, within reason.)

Among the prohibited acts of collectors spelled out in the FDCPA are the following common and important ones:

- Impersonating someone they are not

- Using deception as a means to collect a debt
- Abusing or harassing consumers

Again, these are three big ones... but this is far from the full list of violations. The FDCPA definitely goes into more detail, but these three are all <u>very</u> common violations that frequently come into the picture when dealing with collectors.

Here's the big thing to keep in mind about violations of the FDCPA that bill collectors commonly make:

Every single violation has the potential to give you legal leverage, and the more violations they make, the better your case will be.

If a debt is very large, a collector might not be scared off by a few violations of the law. Keep this in mind if you are dealing with collection accounts where the account has a very high balance. You could end up being sued and getting into even more problems, so use caution! (Again, this is yet another reason people sometimes opt to use a professional instead of going it alone.)

Debt Validation

One important right given to you under the Fair Debt Collection Practices Act is the right ***to request validation of the debt from the collector.*** This is called "debt validation", and it is something you can ask for whether the debt is yours or not and whether the account is accurate or not.

The reality is, with any debt that has gone to collections, that there may be details of the account that have gotten mixed or jumbled in the process of transferring debts. The amounts may not be verifiable, or the original details of the account may have been lost. The collector may even be trying to collect on a debt that they do not have a legal right to collect. For these and other reasons, debt validation is an important tool for use with debt collectors.

The process is complicated, of course, by the fact that "validation" isn't actually defined in the FDCPA. There have been court cases that have helped to spell it out more clearly.

Invalid forms of validation include affidavits that "promise" the debt is valid, and printouts that simply reflect what the debt collector has in their records. These and other insufficient forms of validation are common. In this way, dealing with collectors is much like dealing with the credit bureaus: they will often do what they can to get around (or outright ignore) the law, so you've got to be diligent and persistent.

With this in mind, the validation process generally goes something like this:

1. Send a validation request to the collector. This is often simply a letter that asks them to "validate the debt with current creditor records."
2. If they have not sent sufficient validation or failed to respond at all within 30 days, then check your credit reports to see if the account is still there.
3. If the account is still there, then proceed with secondary (follow-up) tactics as necessary to get the collector to comply with the law.

Conclusion

I've indicated several times this chapter that credit repair can sometimes get complicated. It's true, it can. It doesn't always have to be complicated though.

If you are thorough, studious, deliberate, and organized, you will be able to navigate even some of the more complicated parts of the process with relative ease.

With that said, I can understand how some of the more complicated aspects can be scary. This is one reason I've tried to stress that you ***don't*** have to go it alone necessarily. There ***are*** options out there for help with the credit repair process.

This is one step along the road to home ownership for which you can certainly enlist outside help if you need to. If you're in that boat, I encourage you to look into the options.

You might not realize it, but there are even MORE tactics available to raise your credit score than what we've covered this chapter. It's not <u>JUST</u> about removing negative items. There is more to it, the book doesn't end here.

For more simple and <u>EASY</u> steps you can take to boost your score, along with endless financial tips, check out YourHomeProgram.com.

Your dream home, awaits.

Your Home Program
Our Advisors Are Available To Answer Your Questions
Call **1-800-245-7349** for Home Ownership Made Easy!

RESOURCE DIRECTORY

This is a compilation of video resources noted in this book. You can access all videos at YourHomeProgram.com/BookResource.

Video Name	Chapter(s)
How does Bankruptcy affect your Credit?	27, 4
Cash Flow, Savings and Debt	25, 7
Spending Habits, Budget and Home Ownership	21-24
Rent-to-Own: Lease Option	11-16
Bad Credit, but looking to Buy a Home: Options	1, 4
Being a Number (credit score): Pros and Cons	2, 3
Get more Cash for Home Ownership	18-20, 9
Home Loan after Bankruptcy	27
Credit Repair Process	29, 3
Is Bankruptcy a Credit Score killer?	27, 4
Rent-to-Own: Process	11-16
What is Credit Repair?	29, 3
Function of a Budget	21-24
Income for Home Ownership	17-20
Credit Bureaus, Creditors, and Collection Agencies	2
Income versus Debt: Front-end to Back-end Ratio	6
Incorrect Balances on a Credit Report	29
Repossessions and Home Ownership	8
Credit Utilization and Home Ownership	3
Credit Bureaus, All you Need to Know	2
Income versus Saving	17-20

*Check YourHomeProgram.com for BONUS videos, blogs and more!

About the Author

After witnessing an industry collapse in on itself and nearly take the rest of the country with it, Robert Ellerman wanted to see a change. After dealing with thousands of customers who were in the dark and had no idea where to turn it was clear to him the professional world was missing the personal connection and step-by-step approach he was looking for, and that he knew hard working people deserved.

In reaction to consumers losing their confidence in the sometimes predatory lending and real estate industry, Rob sought out the best people and the best research in the industry to create a real-life, real-applicable solution ...

Your Home Program is the result of this coupled with years of customer interactions.

Enjoy!

-Rob